The Erosion of Traditional Values in American Culture

Truth Decay

STEVE HALE

RIVERSTONE GROUP
PUBLISHING

Acknowledgements

There are many to whom I would like to express gratitude for making *Truth Decay* a reality. These are not in order of importance because truthfully, this volume would not have come together without the help of each of these individuals.

To my parents who gave me a Christian upbringing, and to my Mom, in particular, who committed me to the Lord after experiencing the death of three daughters. It was Mom who recognized my writing ability and encouraged me to major in journalism. For such a rich heritage I will always be indebted.

To my wife, Debbie, who is the epitome of an evangelist's wife. Those who know her will agree. For the past 27 years, I have been on the road an average of about 40 weeks a year, and never once has Debbie complained. She is an awesome companion who embraces the same concerns I do. Admittedly, there were times in this project when I felt my brain was fried. When walking upstairs from my study, I was probably not in the best of moods, but Deb's loving disposition and sweet spirit provided me with the reality check I needed.

To my children, Melody and Josh, who through the years have been incredible beyond words. The greatest challenge of any parent is that of transferring truth to the next generation. Oftentimes, it is caught more than taught. I can only thank God for two children who have blessed my life more than I can say. Thanks, kids!

To those who made sacrificial financial investments for the express purpose of seeing this book in print, I thank you. To all of our ministry partners who, through the years, have stood beside me, I cannot thank you enough. Our ministry strives to maintain the highest standards of financial integrity. Every dime given is your way of saying, "Steve, we believe in the work to which God has called you and the Word that you preach." What an encouragement you are to me!

To my administrative assistant, Wynelle, thanks for the laborious hours of proofing and re-proofing, typing and re-typing, and maintaining an upbeat, joyful disposition in the midst of it all. While you deserve a trip to the spa, an appointment with the chiropractor is probably more appropriate. Thanks for running the race faithfully.

To my pastor, Johnny Hunt, who passionately preaches an uncompromised message and holds high the standard of righteousness. He embodies what he preaches and motivates me with his godly example. He has unashamedly preached the issues addressed in this book, and the church has still grown from 200 to more than 15,000 members. Go figure. Thanks for your friendship and partnership, Brother Johnny.

To all of the many pastors who believe in me enough to relinquish their pulpits and invite me to preach the truth with no restraints or conditions. Thanks to every dear pastor who has reached out to me and used me in a crusade. There is no greater challenge than that of being a pastor, and I thank God for each of you.

Finally, to my Lord and Savior Jesus Christ, without Whom none of this would be possible. At the age of 14 on a Saturday afternoon, He stepped out of Heaven and came into my life. His faithfulness through the years has been amazing. He promised an abundant life in the here and now, and an eternal life in the hereafter. What more can one ask? I owe Him everything, for without Him I can do nothing.

Contents

Foreword

In a day when it seems the key word has become "moderation," as preachers advocate Christian liberty to the point of crossing a moral line so clearly illustrated in Scripture, I am grateful that God has raised up Dr. Steve Hale for such a time as this to write this new must-read book, *Truth Decay.* I believe that it is an understatement to say that truth is decaying in our nation. You will see throughout the chapters of this book issues that are at the heart of holiness in the life of the believer. I believe this book has the potential to call us back to the truth that sets men free.

The book of James deals head-on with the issue of being deceived. It is true that we may attempt to deceive God, which will serve as an impossibility, but we do, seemingly, have the potential of deceiving others and even ourselves. I believe that it is a moral deception in the lives of believers when we begin to use Christian liberty to hurt our own personal testimony and create a stumbling block to weaker brothers and sisters in the body. If ever we needed the church of the Lord Jesus to stand up and begin to live for others and, most of all, for the glory of Christ, it is today! I pray that God will use this book to raise the standard in each of our lives, so that we will become more concerned with personal holiness than personal happiness. I trust that the truth of this book will begin to build the hedge of protection around your life as you seek to be the person that God has called you to be. Our nation is in dire need of revival, and I believe that revival will come when we hold high the standards of God's holiness, His righteousness, and His truth. May the lie of moral relativism forever be put to bed, and may we awake to a new morality based on the precepts of His Word—and may it happen now. Thank you, Steve Hale, for your time of study, preparation, and passion to bring us a much-needed book that we believe has the potential to raise the standard in our lives and in the context of His body.

I pray that you will read this book and pass it on to your friends. Most of all, I pray that each of us would emulate its truths, resulting in even greater passion for God's glory.

Dr. Johnny Hunt
Senior Pastor
First Baptist Church
Woodstock, Georgia

Preface

I don't know anyone who enjoys going to the dentist. Reclining in a dental chair and letting someone probe inside my mouth with pointed instruments is not my idea of relaxation. Of course, the real dread comes when a cavity is discovered. Hearing the shrill-sounding drill as it touches the tooth enamel is enough to raise anybody's blood pressure! I still remember my first root canal. Now *that* will test your Christianity. Everything was fine until the anesthetic began to wear off. That's when I think I re-dedicated my life seven times. OK, so I'm a wimp when it comes to visiting the dentist. All it takes is one tense moment in that chair and I'm promising God to floss for the rest of my life!

While I am reclining in the dental chair, sermon illustrations are not foremost in my thinking, but I do find a few parallels between tooth decay and truth decay. In talking with a couple of dentist friends, I asked how cavities develop. They began using a bunch of technical terms that were contributing factors in developing a cavity. Finally, I said, "Hold up a minute. Break it down in simplistic terms." So, here it is. For a cavity to occur, three things must be present: a tooth, sweets, and bacteria. The bacteria uses sugar to cause the acid in the mouth to drop and dissolve the enamel. In this acidic environment, the type of sweet that is used is critical. A PH level lower than seven is acid. Any PH level greater than seven is alkaline. (OK, that's as technical as I'm going to get. I didn't understand it either.)

Hang with me. The length of time the sweet is on the tooth is important, but drinking water and brushing are two of the best disciplines to prevent tooth decay. If the teeth are not brushed, flossed, or flushed by drinking water within 24 hours of eating the sweets, then bacteria colonizes and the process of decay begins. So, here's the formula for tooth decay: tooth + bacteria + sugar = acid, which produces decay. I found it interesting that everybody has bacteria, but not everybody has the kind of bacteria that produces tooth decay.

"So, what does this have to do with *truth* decay?" you ask. Let's make this analogy. The tooth is truth. To corrupt and undermine the truth, Satan uses something "sweet" that appeals to the carnal nature of man. Just as sugar is a pollutant to our teeth, lots of people have a "sweet" tooth for truth. The taste of candy, cake, pie, and soft drinks all appeal to our taste buds, but they contribute nothing nutritionally. They are empty calories. Likewise, we are being told today that for the church to be culturally relevant, we must eliminate offensive language and doctrines. That means we must refrain from preaching about hell, the blood of Christ, abortion, evolution, divorce, or homosexuality. While the Bible clearly addresses these things, it is considered by many to be out of step with the times and politically incorrect to breach such subjects. This is the "lite Gospel"; it's sweet but has little spiritual nutrition. Additionally, it helps to eliminate Sunday night services, confine Sunday morning services to an hour's time limit, and yes—try to refrain from passionate preaching or raising your voice when you speak. This is a "sweet" environment that appeals to the carnal nature of a person, but the congregant leaves nutritionally malnourished. Spiritually, this approach offers empty calories. Granted, it will draw a crowd, and some truth is being presented. However, it is not always what is being preached, but rather what is *not* being preached that raises concern.

There is a large church in the metro-Atlanta area that I am often asked about, so a few years ago my wife, Debbie, and I attended. It has a very casual and contemporary atmosphere with thousands in attendance. The greeters made us feel welcome, and the atmosphere was loud and laid-back. The sermon was good and magnified the God of Scripture. However, at the conclusion of the service, the pastor abruptly finished his sermon and gave no opportunity for a response to the Gospel. I had heard that public invitations had no place in this church's philosophy, but I fully expected to see response cards in the chair racks, or counselors to be available in an inquiry room, or a place at the resource table for a "seeker" to register his or her interest in knowing more about Christ. There was none of that. Only a simple expression of appreciation saying, "Thanks for coming, and we'll see you next week." As we walked through the parking lot, I was troubled. In fact, I sat in the car trying to

introspectively process what I was feeling. The emotion was unlike anything I had ever experienced. There was a churning in my soul and heav-
iness in my spirit. I concluded that the Holy Spirit seemed to be weeping within my soul as thousands of people walked out of the building
stirred, but having received no explanation of how to accept Christ as
their personal Savior.

That was three years ago. Realizing that every preacher and church can
have an "off" Sunday, I tried not to be critical, and kept my opinions to
myself unless pressed by someone to be blatantly honest regarding my
impression of this "successful" church. Since I was still receiving inquiries
from curious pastors across the country, Debbie and I decided recently
to return for another visit. Two services were being conducted simultaneously and both were filled to capacity. The auditorium was darkened,
like a theater. The praise band was "rockin" as the leader strummed the
guitar in magnifying our Lord. I don't get hung up on appearances. I
really don't. I've conducted too many youth crusades with gothic students sporting multi-colored spiked hairdos and pierced eyebrows, noses,
and tongues only to see those same young people be the most responsive
to the Gospel. So, the fact that the young man leading the music had
long hair with his shirttail hanging out and sporting holes in his jeans
wasn't an issue for me. Obviously, it wasn't a big deal to the thousands in
attendance either.

The pastor was out of town, so the youth pastor preached. He was an
effective communicator who really connected with the congregation.
After speaking for 20 minutes without ever referring to the Bible, he concluded his last ten minutes by declaring, "Jesus Christ is the treasure you
are seeking. It is not His blessings or what He can do for you, but it is
Jesus Himself that is life's Treasure." I'm thinking, "Right on, bro." But as
before, the service concluded with no opportunity to receive the Treasure.
I stood amazed that anyone could lead thousands to the well and then not
give them a drink. He had the congregation in the palm of his hand.
Their attention was riveted. I am confident that a simple explanation of
how to receive this Treasure, coupled with an appeal to "let us help you,"
would have resulted in perhaps hundreds receiving Christ as Savior.

How any Gospel preacher can scripturally justify such an approach is beyond me. I suppose this is an extreme example of Calvinism. I can only imagine they believe in a predestination that negates the will of man and relegates "whosoever will" to being non-existent. In my thinking, this was a "sweet" atmosphere. It was certainly non-threatening and non-confrontational. I have a friend whose son attends this church. He and his wife wanted to become members, but were perplexed as to how members were received since there was never a public invitation. Finally, the gentleman approached a staff member at the close of the service to express his interest in joining the church. The staff member informed him "we are not looking for members, but only attenders." Once again, without membership there is no demand for any level of commitment or moral accountability.

I realize this is only one of many examples of churches that offer a "sweet" atmosphere, which, in my thinking, appeals to the carnal nature of a person. To its credit, this church embraces the Bible and presents it in bite-size portions, and Jesus is being exalted. I certainly do not believe that my approach to worship is the only or even the best method. There is much room for diversity when talking about methods. However, when a church's methods eliminate the biblical doctrines of hell and other delicate but extremely important doctrines, then a line has been crossed. When truth is shared without an appeal to embrace the truth, then a line has been crossed. When we attempt to be so culturally relevant that we are fearful of offending anyone, then a line has been crossed. When we try to accommodate the mentality of an unbelieving world by excluding repentance, then a line has been crossed. Hey, I don't step into the pulpit with the intention of ever offending anyone. But let's face it, the Gospel can be offensive. Many churches have become so preoccupied with their methodology that in the process they have compromised their theology.

Once this "sweet" environment has been established, the stage is set for the bacteria to enter. The bacteria is *relativism*: the assertion that absolute truth does not exist. "What may be right for you may not be right for me. What may be wrong for you may not be wrong for me. Who am I to judge?" Relativism contends that there is no objective standard by which to judge right and wrong. Researcher George Barna says 75% of our population adheres to this viewpoint. Eighty-eight percent of our youth agree with the moral relativism way of thinking. Within the church, 62% doubt the existence of absolute truth.[1] This is the bacteria that is eroding the moral fiber of our nation and has eaten away the spiritual strength of the church. These germs must be removed by returning to our roots. What we are seeing in Christendom today is more than a fad. I fear that it is more than a temporary experimentation to see what works and what doesn't. *Truth works!* In the pages that follow, we'll observe how this dangerous bacteria has diseased the church. It's a silent plague bent on destroying our nation.

So, as you brush your teeth in the morning, remember that a tooth + sweets + bacteria = a cavity, that is, unless you brush, floss, or drink water within 24 hours after eating. Otherwise, you'll be reclining in a comfortable chair with an uncomfortable feeling staring up at a masked man holding sharp instruments and telling you to "open wide" as he places a filling in your tooth. Likewise, decay has set in for the church as a whole. We need a filling . . . *the* filling of the Holy Spirit that accompanies repentance and a return to biblical truth. May God use *Truth Decay* to that end.

CHAPTER 1

A Nation In Crisis

On April 14, 1912, the waters out in the ocean were icy and the midnight air was frigid, but inside a luxurious ocean liner 2,000 people were comfortably sound asleep and totally oblivious to any impending danger. Little did they know that their ship had charted a course that would lead to a watery grave. The ship's captain was asleep, but the man who stood at the helm could see in the distance a huge iceberg blocking their path. In fact, they had been repeatedly warned that there was ice ahead and they should turn around. Yet, those warnings were ignored. After all, this was a state-of-the-art ship and supposedly unsinkable. It was a masterpiece of technology, weighing 46,328 tons, stretching over 882 feet long, and standing 11 stories tall.

When it became apparent that a collision was inevitable, the captain sounded the alarm and began yelling at the top of his lungs that danger lay ahead. The ship that was thought to be unsinkable and took years to build required only two hours and forty minutes to sink. With a glancing blow, the *Titanic* hit the ice, causing a 300-foot gash in the ship.

But here is what's interesting. Even after being awakened from their sleep, most of the people refused to believe that this great ship was actually sinking. In fact, many would not even get in the lifeboats. Instead, they laughed and joked as the band continued to play. They simply could not, or would not, believe that the great *Titanic* was about to sink. It wasn't long before the laughter and jokes turned into screams and prayers for those who were perishing. The band stopped playing ragtime music and began playing a hymn. Suddenly, the music stopped, and within seconds the *Titanic* disappeared 13,000 feet below the ocean's surface.

There came a point when it was too late to stop, too late to turn back, too late to sound the alarm, and too late to choose another direction.

The only thing left to do was to gather the passengers on the deck for a final eulogy of one last prayer and one last hymn. What happened to the *Titanic* is now happening to America. Understandably, most people do not want to believe it. We don't want to hear it, much less think about it. So, we continue to play on the deck, oblivious to the moral freefall going on around us.

There are plenty of voices telling us that America is unsinkable. Look at our science. Look at our technology. Look at our resources. Look at our history. Look at our military. "It could never happen to us," we are told. Oh, we hear the alarm, but we choose to ignore it and continue to play games as though all is well. But all is not well. An iceberg lies ahead, and those who see the impending danger are trying to warn the nation that we are, indeed, on a collision course that is inevitable and unavoidable unless we turn the ship around. At the risk of sounding like a prophet of doom, *Truth Decay* will clearly show our ship is taking on water. The only question is how much longer can we stay afloat before it's too late to do anything about it.

FOUNDATION PRINCIPLES

In Matthew 7:24-27, Jesus describes two foundations upon which a person can build his life:

> "Therefore whoever hears these sayings of Mine, and does them, I will liken him to a wise man who built his house on the rock: and the rain descended, the floods came, and the winds blew and beat on that house; and it did not fall, for it was founded on the rock. But everyone who hears these sayings of Mine, and does not do them, will be like a foolish man who built his house on the sand: and the rain descended, the floods came, and the winds blew and beat on that house; and it fell. And great was its fall."

Storms are unavoidable. Storms hit both foundations. The difference in the two foundations was directly related to how God's Word was received. Obedience to and reverence for God's Word creates a solid foundation that withstands the storms. However, disobedience to and defiance for God's Word creates a sandy, unstable foundation that leads to a great fall. What can be said of individuals can likewise be said of nations. America was undeniably built upon the rock of Scripture. There was a time when God's Word in our land was highly esteemed, and throughout our history God's protective hedge sustained America. However, it is well documented that the centrality of the Bible has now been replaced with other ideologies. Our forefathers' commitment to absolute truth as contained in Scripture has now been substituted by moral relativism. America, as we now know it, is in a precarious position. We have strayed from our roots and are in danger of losing everything that is near and dear to our hearts. Even the average person on the street knows that something is wrong, but is unable to articulate exactly what. The typical knee-jerk reaction is to point an accusing finger at the White House or at self-serving politicians in Congress. That's a cop-out. It goes much deeper than that. We are a nation that finds itself in deep, dark, unexplored waters, groping for answers, searching for direction, and looking for some familiar landmark that will put us back on course. Jesus warned that any person or nation that disregards God's Word would experience a great fall. History proves Him right. America will not be the exception, but in our arrogance and spiritual blindness we continue to move forward toward an iceberg that is inevitable and unavoidable. In this late hour, nothing short of a massive spiritual awakening can save us.

AUTOPSY OF A DEAD NATION: ROMANS 1

America is named nowhere in Scripture, but perhaps there is not a more relevant chapter that reflects our nation than Romans 1. This chapter serves as a mirror and could appropriately be called the autopsy of a dead nation. Here, God gives us the step-by-step explanation of how and why the great Roman Empire fell. It is a lesson from history that we cannot ignore.

Verse 18 of Romans 1 says,

> "For the wrath of God is revealed from heaven against all ungodliness and unrighteousness of men, who suppress the truth in unrighteousness."

This verse depicts the wrath of God being poured out for one primary reason: His truth is being suppressed (or smothered) throughout the land. When people tamper with God's truth, God takes personal offense.

Romans 1:19 goes on to say,

> "because what may be known of God is manifest in them, for God has
> shown it to them." So, how has God shown His truth to the nation? Verse
> 20 says, "For since the creation of the world His invisible attributes are
> clearly seen, . . ."

"For since the creation". . . *(not evolution)*. The invisible is clearly seen?
How does that happen? Verse 20 explains:

> "being understood by the things that are made, even His eternal power
> and Godhead, so that they are without excuse."

This verse refutes evolution. Through creation we see a reflection of
the power and attributes of God. A casual observation of the vastness of
the oceans, the majesty of the mountains, or the beauty of a sunrise or
sunset should cause any person to conclude, "There must be a God."
This Scripture says that it is clearly seen and clearly understood. There
are no naturally born atheists. A person does not grow up with the natural tendency of denying the existence of God. There is a design to the
universe; therefore, there must be a Designer behind it.

When a nation chooses to smother the truth of God and then rejects
the God of the truth, notice what happens. In verses 24, 26, and 28 we
see three identical phrases: "God also gave them up," "God gave them
up," and "God gave them over." This is an example of God abandoning
a nation. In these verses, God is backing away and removing His protective hand from the nation. There comes a time when the collective mind-
set of the nation embraces the "Do your own thing" or "If it feels good
do it" philosophy. God responds by saying, "You want to do your own
thing? Fine. Then go ahead and do it." The result is that God gives the
nation over to its own desires, which results in corrupt leadership, corrupt education, corrupt legislation, and gradually each person begins to
do what is right in his or her own eyes.

One of the ways that God judged Israel was to simply back off, remove
His protective hand, and leave her alone for the devil to do the rest. Israel
was God's chosen nation, yet repeatedly throughout her history, God
gave Israel up.

Check out these passages:

PSALM 81:9-14

"There shall be no foreign god among you; nor shall you worship any foreign god. I am the Lord your God, Who brought you out of the land of Egypt; . . . 'But My people would not heed My voice, and Israel would have none of Me. **So, I gave them over** to their own stubborn heart, to walk in their own counsels. 'Oh, that My people would listen to Me, that Israel would walk in My ways! I would soon subdue their enemies, and turn My hand against their adversaries.'" (emphasis mine)

Israel embraced false gods from different cultures, choosing to walk in the wisdom of men and refusing to obey God's truth. What was the result? God gave them over to a stubborn heart.

PSALM 106:35-42

"But they mingled with the Gentiles and learned their works; they served their idols, which became a snare to them. They even sacrificed their sons and their daughters to demons, and shed innocent blood, the blood of their sons and daughters, whom they sacrificed to the idols of Canaan; And the land was polluted with blood. . . . Therefore, the wrath of the Lord was kindled against His people, so that He abhorred His own inheritance. And **He gave them** into the hand of the Gentiles, and those who hated them ruled over them. Their enemies also oppressed them, and they were brought into subjection under their hand." (emphasis mine)

Does this not describe infanticide and reflect the spirit of abortion? The people were sacrificing their own sons and daughters to demons and shedding innocent blood. The Bible vividly describes the entire land as being "polluted with blood." Likewise, America is built on blood. The Vietnam War Memorial contains 68,000 names and stretches 500 feet long. However, if we built a memorial for the innocent, defenseless babies whose blood we have shed since the 1973 *Roe v. Wade* decision, it would have 50 million names inscribed on it and stretch for 80 miles! It was for "this cause" that Israel was brought into subjection to her enemies. When she chose to abandon truth in pursuit of false gods, then the shedding of innocent blood, including the blood of her own children, polluted the land. Thus, God gave the people of Israel over to a foreign power.

PSALM 78:58-62

"For they provoked Him to anger with their high places, and moved
Him to jealousy with their carved images. When God heard this, He was
furious, and greatly abhorred Israel, so that He forsook the tabernacle of
Shiloh, the tent He had placed among men, and delivered His strength
into captivity, and His glory into the enemy's hand. **He also gave His
people over** to the sword, . . ." (emphasis mine)

Once again, the pursuit of false gods activated the wrath of God, even
to the extent of delivering His glory into the enemy's hand and giving
the nation over to destructive forces.

NEHEMIAH 9:29-30

"And testified against them, that You might bring them back to Your law.
Yet they acted proudly, and did not heed Your commandments, but sinned
against Your judgments, 'Which if a man does, he shall live by them.' And
they shrugged their shoulders, stiffened their necks, and would not hear.
Yet for many years You had patience with them, and testified against them
by Your Spirit in Your prophets. Yet they would not listen; therefore, **You
gave them** into the hand of the peoples of the lands." (emphasis mine)

Did you notice that in His patience God did not annihilate the nation
for pursuing false gods? It says, "for many years" He had patience with
them. One way that God expressed His patience was by raising up men
who boldly proclaimed impending judgment. With the anointing of His
Spirit, they warned the nation of what lay ahead unless they repented.
Sadly, they would not listen. Once again, the result was enslavement to
foreign powers. This seems to be where America stands today. For many
years, God has been patient with us, and He continues to lovingly warn
us of catastrophic judgment. Yet, we have turned a deaf ear to the God
who birthed this nation.

1 KINGS 14:9,16

"But you *(Jeroboam)* have done more evil than all who were before you,
for you have gone and made for yourself other gods and molded images to
provoke Me to anger, and have cast Me behind your back— . . . **And He
will give Israel up** because of the sins of Jeroboam, who sinned and who
made Israel sin." (emphasis mine)

Jeroboam was the nation's leader, and God judged the entire nation because of his sinful influence. This is a sobering reminder of the importance of electing godly leaders. However, the overriding message gleaned from all of these Old Testament passages is this: To entertain, embrace, and pursue any system of religion that opposes the true and living God as revealed in the Holy Bible is to invoke God's displeasure and experience catastrophic judgment beyond description. Yet, in our multicultural, pluralistic society, this is precisely what we are doing under the banner of political correctness, tolerance, and moral diversity.

In each of these Old Testament passages, God gave the nation over to violence. In the Romans passage, however, God gave the nation over to sexual immorality. Can you think of two things that better describe our nation today?

GOD GAVE THEM UP

Romans 1:26 says, "For this reason God gave them up . . ." To identify the reason, you have to look at the previous verse that says they "exchanged the truth of God for the lie, . . ." And how did they do that? They "served the creature rather than the Creator, . . ." This certainly reflects the New Age Movement that claims we are all little gods. You just have to realize your divinity and tap into it. Many religions today deify man as the center of the universe. In describing the last days, 2 Timothy 3:2-4 says, "For men will be lovers of themselves, . . ." and "lovers of pleasure rather than lovers of God," all of which reflects "serving the creature rather than the Creator."

What does it look like when God gives up a nation by removing His protective hand? Romans 1:26-27 gives a chilling description: "For this reason God gave them up to vile passions. For even their women exchanged the natural use for what is against nature. Likewise also the men, leaving the natural use of the woman, burned in their lust for one another, men with men committing what is shameful, and receiving in themselves the penalty of their error which was due."

I say this in tenderness and with loving concern, but this passage declares four things about the homosexual lifestyle:

1. It is unnatural (vv. 26-27).

2. It is shameful (v. 27).

3. It is in error to the truth (v. 27).

4. There is a penalty to be paid whenever a nation endorses homosexuality as a morally acceptable alternative lifestyle (v. 27).

It should be said that God loves the homosexual as much as He loves anyone, but in no uncertain terms He warns the nation against accepting homosexuality as a way of life. It undermines the nuclear family and sets destructive forces in motion. Not to be misunderstood, I want to say once again that these strong words do not come from a judgmental, uncaring heart. Admittedly, few groups in America have faced as much condemnation from the church as homosexuals. The false impression is sometimes conveyed that homosexuals are excluded from God's love and grace. Nothing is further from the truth.

A strong distinction is made in verse 26 claiming that homosexuality was not the *cause* of God's judgment, but rather the *consequence*. Note, the Bible does not say that God gave them up *because* of vile passions such as homosexuality, but rather "God gave them up *to* vile passions . . ." This is no small play on words. The apostle Paul himself seemed to marvel at the fact that God would actually give a nation over *to* homosexuality, and for that reason he repeated it three times. Homosexuality was an instrument of God's judgment. It was an expression of God's wrath upon the nation. The ever-increasing acceptance of homosexuality within our children's classrooms, its gainful favor in our judicial system, and its continued prevalence in the media outlets are not glowing evidences of a progressive civilization as some would have us believe. Instead, for those who hold a biblical worldview, it is a clear and indisputable sign of society's disintegration, degradation, and God's wrath upon the nation.

It grieves me to say such a thing. Yet, if we believe the Bible to be true and if we believe that God has not changed, then after reading the Minor and Major Prophets of the Old Testament, we cannot help but make the comparison with America. Like focusing a camera, the picture becomes all too clear. For example, in Jeremiah 5 and 6 we are told that Israel refused to repent, and she developed a stubborn and rebellious heart, even to the point that the nation did not know how to blush. (Jeremiah 6:15). After many warnings, the nation was destroyed. Again, in 2 Chronicles 36:15-16 we read that "The Lord, the God of their fathers, sent word to them again and again by His messengers, because He had compassion on His people and on His dwelling place. But they continually mocked the messengers of God, despised His words, and scoffed at His prophets, until the wrath of the Lord arose against His people, till there was no remedy."(NASB) As you carefully read those words, you can feel the compassion of God and how painful it was for Him to make the decision to destroy Judah. In mercy, He repeatedly sent messengers to warn the nation. But in defiance of such mercy, the people despised the words of His prophets by mocking and scoffing at them, until the only recourse was catastrophic judgment.

Case in point, I was recently watching the Comedy Channel. I can always use a good laugh, but to my dismay, the featured comedian was mocking Christianity and practically every moral value that we cherish. His jokes were trivializing the Bible, heaven, hell, Jesus, salvation, and on and on it went. His entire routine revolved around blasphemous religious satire. What bothered me even more than his monologue was the audience's response. There was backslapping, sidesplitting laughter over the most vulgar and irreverent jokes. Don't get me wrong. I like a good joke as much as the next person. I am not a killjoy who walks around with a sanctimonious frown. However, there is a line to be drawn somewhere, and many of the comedians and television sitcoms today are stepping across it. You can discern the spiritual barometer and the moral standards of a culture by what makes them laugh.

THE GREAT EXCHANGE

One of the pivotal verses in Romans 1 is verse 25 that states, "who exchanged the truth of God for the lie, . . ." It is actually possible for a nation collectively to exchange God's truth for the lie. In the next chapter, we'll talk more about "the lie," but the question for now is, "When did this great exchange of God's truth occur?"

While in Florida several years ago, I came across a full-page, color article in *USA Today* with a huge headline that read, "1987: The Year America Changed." Richard Whitmire wrote the article, and at the top of the page, in bold print, he raised three questions:

"What if it turned out there was a clue behind what triggered our social chaos?"

"What if there was a plausible explanation why so many families collapsed?"

"What if there was a reason behind drug-addicted babies and increased violence in the streets?"

Then, in response to those questions, the opening paragraph said, "'That's silly,' say the social experts. 'There's no one single reason behind it all.' However, there seems to be a single point in time when America's social cauldron began bubbling out of control: 1987."

"That's the year the number of kids in foster care began rising and kept rising. The teen birth rate began climbing and kept climbing. Out-of-wedlock births and premature deliveries among African-Americans shot up. The rate of juveniles committing violent crimes skyrocketed and the national drug surveillance network showed the number of cocaine-related hospital emergency room visits exploding off the chart. There was also a big jump in the number of AIDS cases."[1]

Here is where it gets interesting. These social experts wanted to know what made 1987 so significant to cause this kind of massive change. So, they went back into the archives and chronicled the news for 1987. They searched out every major news story for that year and the article gave this review of the top four: "The big news was TV evangelists Jim Bakker and Jessica Hahn with their sex and money scandal; Jimmy Swaggart charged with plotting hostile takeovers; Oral Roberts holing up in his university's prayer tower vowing never to emerge unless he raised $8 million. The other big story featured Iran-Contra, with Oliver North charged with trading weapons-for-hostages." All four of the major news stories in '87 involved Christian leaders engaged in unethical behavior.

Surprised by their findings, these social experts thought, "Surely the Christian community has nothing to do with the moral decay of American culture," so they dismissed their findings and searched for another explanation.[2]

First, it is important to note that these secular social experts would actually acknowledge that America has changed, and it has changed for the worse. That is a huge admission and is actually a refutation of evolution, which claims that man is getting better, and society is moving toward some kind of utopia. So, both sides of the sociological and political spectrums can agree that America has changed for the worse. From that point on, however, we part company. In a strained effort to find some explanation that would not involve the Christian church, these secular social experts concluded that the reason America changed in 1987 was because of an important development in the drug trade. That's when smokeable cocaine, better known as "crack," became available to the public. Thus, the explanation for America's moral freefall can be traced back to drugs. As simplistic as it sounds, that was the conclusion drawn by these "experts."[3]

While it is true that America has morally changed for the worse, this change was not due to drugs. Drugs are merely symptomatic of the change. Better stated, America has changed because of the great exchange that has occurred. Like Rome, we have exchanged God's truth for the lie. And what is the lie? I believe the lie, for us, is the assertion that there is no such thing as absolute truth. Truth and morality are relative. The thinking is, "What's right for you may not necessarily be right for me, and what's wrong for you may not necessarily be wrong for me." In other words, there is no objective standard by which right and wrong are to be judged. After all, "Who am I to judge?" The result is that each person begins to do what is right in his or her own eyes. When a culture eliminates absolutes, it becomes increasingly difficult to enforce the laws of the land. This lays the foundation for moral anarchy. A denial of absolute truth is an attempt to do away with sin and in essence, give a person the license to sin. It is this great exchange that has accelerated the downward spiral in America's morality.

ENTER JUDICIAL ACTIVISM

When did such an exchange occur? It was not 1987. That just happened to be the year when the social experts noticed that our social cauldron was bubbling out of control. It was in 1987 when we became more keenly aware of the harvest that was being reaped from the seeds of an ungodly value system that had been sown decades earlier. Perhaps it is impossible to identify the specific date when such an exchange occurred. Some would say it began with the 1925 Scopes trial. Others would point to 1947 when evolution was first being taught in our public schools. Any discussion of America's moral freefall cannot ignore the turbulent decade of the 1960s, the beginning of judicial activism. In 1962 the U.S. Supreme Court ruled that leading in prayer in our public schools was now illegal and unconstitutional. Incidentally, the prayer that was ruled illegal was about as spiritually generic as it could be. The name of Jesus was not even mentioned. It contained only 22 words: "Almighty God, we acknowledge our dependence upon Thee, and we beg Thy blessings upon us, our parents, our teachers, and our Country. Amen."[3]

The next year, the same court outlawed the reading of the Bible in our schools.[4] Then, in 1965, the Supreme Court ruled it was against the law to verbally pray over your meal in a school cafeteria.[5] In 1973, these same nine Supreme Court justices ruled in favor of abortion on demand.[6] In 1980, it became unconstitutional for the Ten Commandments to hang in the hallways or classrooms of our educational institutions.[7] In the early '90s, it was ruled unconstitutional to pray at high school graduation exercises.[8] It has even become unconstitutional for a board of education to use or refer to the word "God" in any of its official writings.[9] Some states have gone even further. For example, public schools were barred from showing a film about the settlement of Jamestown because the film depicted the historical fact that a cross was erected at the Jamestown settlement.[10]

In retrospect, as you look at the 1960s, the supreme symbol for this decade of decadence was Woodstock, New York, where hundreds of thousands of young people traveled hundreds, and often thousands of miles, dressed up with beads, long hair, faded jeans, and bottles, pills and guitars for the express purpose to fornicate, hallucinate, and intoxicate. Regarding the liberal left, I once heard the late Adrian Rogers make the statement, "These same young people have now put on some shoes, taken off the beads, cut their hair, and gone to Washington. It's the same crowd, only dressed up."

Since 1962 (and practically every year thereafter), it seems that our nation has formally telegraphed a message to Almighty God that He is no longer welcome in the minds and classrooms of our children. When it comes to anything that even resembles Christian values we have posted a "No Trespassing" sign above the doors of our schools. Many school systems suffer from paranoia of teaching sexual abstinence in health classes for fear that it reflects a biblical morality and would be in violation of separation of church and state. Even saying the word "Christmas" on school property is now prohibited in many cities. For example, in the Alaska public schools, students were told they could not use the word "Christmas" in school because it had the word "Christ" in it, nor could they have the word in their notebooks, nor exchange Christmas cards or presents, nor display anything with the word "Christmas" on it.[11] How dare a teacher e-mail another teacher wishing him or her "Merry Christmas." Such radical behavior could lead to a reprimand or even the confiscation of his or her computer. Will somebody please restore moral sanity to this nation?

The American Civil Liberties Union (ACLU) and other liberal organizations would say, "You cannot legislate morality, so you Christians need to stay out of the political process. Hibernate in your little cell groups and musty sanctuaries, but don't get involved in politics because morality is not something that can be legislated." Hey, morality is the only thing that can be legislated. The only question is whose morality it will be.

We have so bought into the myth of separation of church and state that Christians are paralyzed with fear and school administrators are paranoid that lawsuits will be filed. Here's a little quiz for you. Where does this statement appear in the U.S. Constitution? "The Church in the

U.S. shall be separate from the state and the school from the Church."
If you are thinking, "I don't remember reading that in our Constitution,"
then you are right. I intentionally omitted two letters. The statement
should read: "The Church in the U.S.S.R. shall be separate from the state
and the school from the Church." While appearing nowhere in our
Constitution, it is article 52 in the Constitution of the former Soviet
Union.[12] Unbelievably, we have now embraced those very words as if they
held a prominent place in the philosophy of our founding fathers. Nothing
could be further from the truth. It seems we are rapidly moving to freedom
from religion rather than freedom *of* religion in America.

The prophet Hosea recorded a strong word of judgment to the nation
of Israel when he said, "My people are destroyed for lack of knowledge.
Because you have rejected knowledge, . . . Because you have forgotten
the law of your God, I also will forget your children" (Hosea 4:6). Can
this not be applied to America? Would anyone challenge the fact that we
have forgotten the law of God? No doubt, you have seen Jay Leno's man-
on-the-street interviews. During one show he cornered a group of young
college students to test their biblical IQ by asking some basic questions.
He said, "Can you name one of the Ten Commandments?" A young lady
replied, "Freedom of speech." Then, Jay instructed a guy to complete the
following sentence: "Let he who is without sin..." The response was,
"Have a good time." Finally, he turned to a young woman and asked,
"Who, according to the Bible, was eaten by a whale?" The confident
answer was "Pinocchio."[13] Yes, we have become a biblically illiterate
nation.

It was because of this rejection of God and spiritual amnesia that God
said, "I also will forget your children" (Hosea 4:6). And so it seems that
we have a nation of God-forgotten children. Not forgotten in the sense
that God no longer loves them, but forgotten in that today's generation
of kids seem far from God's intention, God's character, and God's plan
for their lives. But then God, through His prophet, lowers the gavel by
proclaiming in verse 7 of Hosea 4, "I will change their glory into shame."
How is it possible for God to change the glory of a nation into shame?

AMERICA: FROM GLORY TO SHAME

Until the 1960's, America was still respected as a God-fearing and law-abiding nation. Interestingly enough, from 1927 to 1962 there were never more than two consecutive years in which SAT scores declined. But then something happened. Since those Supreme Court rulings in 1962 and thereafter, SAT scores declined for 18 consecutive years. It can be shown on a graph that the only reason they leveled off was because of the home school and Christian school movements. Since the judicial rulings cited earlier, America has become the world leader in crime, juvenile homicides, pornography, divorce, abortion, teenage pregnancies, and illegal drug use. We're talking world leader! To top it off, we are among the world leaders in illiteracy. Can we deny that our glory has been changed to shame? I recall former Secretary of Education Bill Bennett addressing the Southern Baptist Convention several years ago, saying, "The simple fact is that we cannot expect to maintain our civilization with 12-year-olds having babies, 15-year-olds killing each other, 17-year-olds dying of AIDS, and 18-year-olds ending up with diplomas they can't even read." Our glory has been changed to shame and we don't even know how to blush. And do you know the irony of it all? In international testing, America scored the highest in self-esteem. What message does this send? That we are illiterate and immoral and proud of it?

On 19 academic tests, American students were *never* first or second and, in comparison with other industrialized nations, were *last* seven times.[14] (emphasis mine) In a test comparing average American public school sixth-graders with their counterparts in seven other Western industrialized countries, American public school students ranked *last* in mathematics and not much better in science and geography[15] (emphasis mine) Our 14-year-old science students placed 14th out of 17 competing countries. Advanced American science students were 9th out of 13 countries in physics, 11th out of 13 in chemistry and *last* in biology.[16] (emphasis mine) In a testing of 12th grade students among 11 nations, the United States placed *last* in algebra and was ahead of only Hungary in calculus. When considering only the brightest students—the top five percent in each category—the United States was *last* in both algebra and calculus.[17] (emphasis mine) In an international assessment of math and science among six developed countries, American students ranked *last* in mathematics and next to last overall in science.[18] (emphasis mine) A University of Illinois at Chicago study found that the average American high school student would rank 99th in math when compared with 100 average Japanese students.[19] A 1989 international comparison of mathematics and science skills showed American students scoring at the bottom and South Korean students scoring at the top. South Korean students performed at high levels in math at four times the rate of U.S. students. Ironically, when asked if they are good at math, 68% of American students thought they were. That was the highest percentage of any nation.[20]

When our Supreme Court declares it is unconstitutional to read the Declaration of Independence in school because it refers to God, then our glory has been changed to shame. When little children are instructed in school to read and learn about the use of condoms, but are forbidden to see the Ten Commandments hanging on the classroom wall, then our glory has been changed to shame. When a public school teacher can describe anal intercourse to a nine-year-old child in crude detail, then our glory has been changed to shame. When a rap song calling for the murder of policemen actually reaches the top of the charts, then our glory has been changed to shame. When an elementary student is forbidden from praying over his or her meal in the school cafeteria, then our glory has been changed to shame. On and on it goes.

Romans 1:28 reflects America when it says, "they did not like to retain God in their knowledge, . . ." Not unlike today's culture, the Romans preferred to take God out of their vocabulary. This Scripture has found its place in mainstream America with an attitude that says, "Let's just take God out of the classroom. Let's remove God from our history books. Let's take prayer out of the schools. Let's take the Bible out of the courtroom. Let's take the Ten Commandments off government property and away from school premises. Let's take Christmas out of the public arena. Let's remove any semblance of the God of Christianity from the life of this nation." That, my friend, is Romans 1. The result is detailed in verses 29-31: The nation was "filled with all unrighteousness, sexual immorality, wickedness, covetousness, maliciousness; full of envy, murder, strife, deceit, evil-mindedness; they are whisperers, backbiters, haters of God, violent, proud, boasters, inventors of evil things, disobedient to parents, undiscerning, untrustworthy, unloving, unforgiving, unmerciful." Vivid and relevant examples could be shown for each of these character flaws, but the clincher is in how the chapter concludes. The final verse (v. 32) says, "who, knowing the righteous judgment of God, that those who practice such things are deserving of death, not only do the same but also approve of those who practice them." Multitudes sit at home watching the immorality, irreverence, wickedness, and blatant defiance of God on the big screen and wink with approval even though they know such things are deserving of judgment.

HOW DID WE GET HERE?

The natural tendency is to point an accusing finger at Washington and say, "There's the problem." But no, the problem is not in the White House. It is in God's House. Jesus clearly handed the church the responsibility of upholding the nation's morality when He declared us to be the salt of the earth. Salt is a preservative. It keeps things from decaying. America has more churches, more Bibles, and more Christian bookstores than anywhere else in the world and yet we lead the world in practically every immoral category. Something is wrong with that picture.

Here is what I believe happened. In the 1960s, the "God is Dead" movement swept through our nation. While many assume they were unaffected by this radical agenda, it is interesting to note that the movement began, not with atheists, but professing theologians. As liberal theology infiltrated our Bible colleges and seminaries, professors were standing before thousands of students denying the virgin birth, the blood atonement of Christ, the inspiration of Scripture, and declaring miracles to be myths, all while contending that hell is a state of mind and the devil is a figment of one's imagination. The consequences of liberal theology are incalculable. As the cardinal tenets of traditional Christianity were denied, these young preachers graduated from our theological institutions with a shipwrecked faith. There was no clear sounding of the trumpet or "thus saith the Lord" from the pulpits of America. Consequently, major protestant denominations began to decline and lose their moral influence within their respective communities.

However, something equally as alarming was occurring on the other end of the theological continuum. The opposite of liberal theology was dead orthodoxy. 2 Corinthians 3:6 says, that "the letter kills, but the Spirit gives life." Indeed, many of our churches are doctrinally correct, but spiritually dead. From Hebrews 3:7 to Hebrews 4:7, the Lord repeatedly issues this warning: "Today, if you will hear His voice, do not harden your hearts . . ." It is important to note that He is speaking to Christians. We, as Christians, have the capacity of hardening our hearts and the spiritual equation is: to hear God's voice without heeding God's voice produces a hard heart.

Likewise, we have the capacity of deceiving ourselves. James 1:22 says, "But be doers of the word, and not hearers only, deceiving yourselves." Once again, this admonition is directed to Christians. Both deception of mind and hardness of heart are related to a lack of obedience to the Word of God. The pressing question is, "What is the manifestation of a hard heart and deceived mind?" May I suggest that it is not necessarily open defiance against God, but rather an imbedded indifference toward God and the things of His kingdom.

In practical terms, this explains why there is such lethargy and complacency found within today's church. For example, let's take pastors who have been faithful to preach the truth of God's Word. It is not uncommon for the congregation to file out the back door, shake the pastor's hand, and comment "Good sermon, pastor. You sure stepped on my toes today." Yet, the majority of those same people never really intend to put the sermon into practice. They have adopted a spectator mentality of cheering the preacher on, but never get out of the grandstands and onto the playing field. They have a form of godliness, but deny the power that comes from being godly. This phenomenon is the source of most pastors' frustration. They diligently study and prepare for Sunday's sermons only to be confronted with blank stares and glazed-over looks that say, "So what?" They are an adult version of how today's teenagers respond to their parents' words of instruction with an indifferent, "Whatever." The pastor, however, is bleeding inside and feels responsible for the church's lack of growth. Some in the congregation will only reinforce that by pointing an accusing finger at the pulpit, blaming the pastor for why statistics are down. It never occurs to them to first take the log out of their own eye before giving attention to the splinter in someone else's eye. After traveling the nation for 27 years and being in hundreds of churches, what concerns me most is to see these "once passionate" men of God lose their zeal, become cynical, and settle into the same complacency as their congregants. The bottom line is that an anemic church is largely responsible for the moral dilemma now facing America.

RAISING THE STANDARD

Isaiah 59:19 says, "When the enemy comes in like a flood, the Spirit of the Lord will lift up a standard against him." Do you know what a standard is? Great armies are always organized into companies, regiments, and battalions. Each unit has its own flag and banner, which are called "standards." Historically, one of the most important and honored duties a soldier could perform was to be a standard-bearer, one who carried the flag. You see, sometimes in battle, troops were scattered and cut off from their units. The only way to keep from being disoriented was to follow the standard-bearer. So, these banners and flags served a far greater purpose than decoration or just trying to be patriotic.

The enemy's strategy was to actually target and capture the standard-bearer, because by destroying the standard the entire army would be thrown into confusion. In fact, the standard was so important that if the standard-bearer fell, it became the responsibility of the soldier standing beside him to pick up the flag and continue to advance the assault against the enemy. So, in many ways, raising the standard became more important than even carrying a weapon. Without the standard, the troops were confused. The flag or the standard became the rallying point for the army.

In recent years, highly visible standard-bearers have been attacked and prestigious ministries and prominent preachers have fallen. It is no time to call a retreat. It is time to pick up the flag and raise the standard higher than ever. Because when Christianity falls, the enemies of right-eousness come out of their dark closets and begin to assert themselves. The stakes are too high to throw in the towel. Our nation's destiny hangs in the balance.

CHAPTER 2

Moral Relativism

Christian philosopher Francis Schaeffer predicted that someday we would wake up and discover that the America we once knew was gone. Those prophetic words have now been fulfilled. Many older adults are perplexed about what has and is happening to our beloved nation. Others cynically declare, "We've gone to the dogs," or "We're going to hell in a handbasket." Frankly, I don't think the average citizen steps away from the frenzied pace of life long enough to introspectively or analytically consider the erosion of our moral fiber. If so, it is but a passing, whimsical concern that says, "It's sad, but oh well, it's out of my control. Besides, it doesn't affect me anyway." Oh really? Perhaps you will come to think otherwise as we bring into focus a snapshot picture of the America that our children will inherit. You see the problem is not "out there" somewhere. It is as close as your own neighborhood or your own living room.

In the previous chapter, we noticed that the defining moment for Rome was when she "exchanged the truth of God for the lie, . ." (Romans 1:25). We, likewise, have made the same great exchange and are paying dearly for it in a shift of values so great that its destructive forces are wreaking havoc on the moral fiber of our nation. The lie we have fully embraced is the idea that there is no such thing as absolute truth. No objective standard of right and wrong exists. We cannot say that one standard of morality is better than another. Each person decides for himself what is right and wrong. After all, what is right for me may not be right for you, and what is wrong for me today may not be wrong for me tomorrow. No single value system is superior over another. Once the biblical standard for right and wrong is discarded, then truth is abandoned, and the nation's foundation shifts from the time-tested rock of Scripture to the sands of moral relativism. The annals of history scream for us to make a U-turn. To proceed forward is to face inevitable destruction. Historically, most great nations have not been destroyed by outside invading forces, but by an erosion of morality from within.

Relativism says that everything is right some of the time, but nothing is right all of the time. It's up to you to decide. Without a moral consensus, social chaos becomes increasingly prevalent. The signs of decay are all around us. Church-growth expert Thom Rainer brings into focus the clear decline of Christianity's influence throughout the past four generations:

• Builders (born 1927-1945): 65% Bible-based believers

• Boomers (born 1946-1964): 35% Bible-based believers

• Busters (born 1965-1983): 6% Bible-based believers

• Millennials (born 1984 or later): 4% Bible-based believers[1]

Scary, isn't it? It gets worse. Pollster George Barna reports that only one in ten of our Christian teens believe in moral absolutes.[2] Overall, only 32% of Christians embrace moral absolutes, while another survey found the figure to be less than twenty-two percent.[3]

The Rev. Barbara Cawthorne is a liberal Episcopalian who claims that the Bible is not the source for absolute truth. She obviously does not see the self-defeating absurdity of such a position. According to Rev. Cawthorne, "To a great degree, we are on our own in making ethical decisions, in evaluating our histories, in comprehending the meaning of them. We will not find easy-to-follow recipes for our behavior in Scripture. Our primary tool is our own intelligence . . . What we do not have is certainty. *(Are you certain of that, Mrs. Cawthorne?)* Is there a way I can know beyond a doubt that my actions are in accordance with the will of God? . . . Can I fully understand what the truth is and know beyond doubt that I am not in error? No. All I can do is try . . ."[4]

She is not alone. The Barna Research Group cites the following survey regarding Christian beliefs:

• 51% of "born-again" Christians reject the existence of the Holy Spirit.

• 35% of "born-again" Christians deny the resurrection of Jesus Christ.

- 45% of "born-again" Christians deny the existence of Satan.

- 68% of "born-again" Christians do not believe in moral absolutes.

- 26% of adult "born-again" Christians make their decisions based on biblical principles.[5]

You are probably thinking, "These people may call themselves 'born again,' but they are only 'religious.'" I agree. There is no way that Christians can be consistent in their thinking and remain relativists. Absolutism is inherent to being a Christian. We believe that what God has revealed in Scripture is absolute truth that transcends time. To abdicate truth is to abdicate Christianity.

Who among us could have predicted the political, economic, cultural, social, and moral changes that have re-shaped our nation? Dr. D. James Kennedy says, "America's physical resources and current level of wealth are unprecedented in history, but the soul of the nation is being challenged as never before. We are in a state of national emergency and cannot afford to look the other way any longer. The deterioration of our moral perspective and the willful destruction of our religious heritage are threats that we cannot afford to ignore or else we will not survive. We are standing on the brink of national disaster."[6]

Indeed, America's citizens have compromised their souls at the altar of materialism. Having too much to live with and too little to live for, we are spiritually bankrupt. Everything is permitted, but nothing is important. I think an uneasiness lurks deep within the soul of the American public that something has gone wrong. We just don't know what it is. Fundamentally, America has forgotten God. Laws are based upon morality, and morality is based upon theology. To systematically remove the basis for theology, the Bible, from the public arena is to invite moral anarchy. It is a fact that a morally bankrupt nation will not be competitive in the world economy. A nation unable to discern right from wrong will certainly be unable to solve its economic woes. Our politicians still don't understand that a prosperous economy and a strong moral fiber are inseparably linked.

It should be a no-brainer. We've robbed our kids of any connection with God in their schools. We got rid of the Bible. We eliminated our Christian heritage from their textbooks. We removed the Ten Commandments from the walls of their schools. We prohibited prayer in their classrooms and are now scratching our heads wondering why there is so much crime, violence, and disrespect for authority. Well, duh? We're in a spiritual vacuum. If that vacuum is not filled with the true and living God, it will be filled with false gods.

How sad to think that today's students know all about political correctness, the environment, the dangers of nuclear weapons, and how to have "safe" sex, but they don't know right from wrong. Each year, I speak to thousands of students in school assemblies and I'm still amazed at the number of young people who sincerely have no moral compass. Josh McDowell says, "There have always been wild and rebellious kids who would go off the track and do something wrong. But they knew where the track was and what was wrong. Many of today's youth do not know right from wrong."[7]

The nations abroad observe us from a distance. They see that we possess the greatest wealth on earth, yet we cannot control our streets. They see that we have the greatest military power in history, but we cannot control inner-city gangs, the plague of drugs, or the epidemic of moral impurity. Since 9/11, they see that we are unable to protect ourselves from foreign attacks. Statistically, travelers from third world nations are at a greater risk in the streets of America than in their own underdeveloped homelands.[8] Such vulnerability does not go unnoticed by our enemies. We must bring back the moral anchor of biblical absolutes. Psalm 9:17 still stands: "The wicked shall be turned into hell, and all the nations that forget God."

Researchers James Patterson and Peter Kim conclude that the loss of moral values is the number one problem facing our country.[9] Likewise, Bill Bennett, in his book *The De-Valuing of America: The Fight for Our Culture and Our Children*, also believes that the future of the next generation is at stake. He boldly declares, "If we lose this culture battle, we have lost the war for civilization."[10] At a symposium in Dallas, Texas, 42 Christian youth leaders were asked to identify what they saw as the dominant problem of youth today. One hundred percent of them—every single one—said that the number one issue was the loss of a biblically based value system.[11]

We could cite one authority after another to document the fact that the pressing need of the hour is a return to the biblical base of moral absolutes. My own Baby Boomer generation still controls the corporate, political, and religious landscape of America. On our watch we have witnessed an increase in morally corrupt films and television programs, an increase in perverted music, an invasion of Internet pornography, the onslaught of gay marriages, the removal of the Ten Commandments from public buildings, and on it goes. It is bad enough that only 35% of my generation affirms a belief in Scripture. But with only four percent of today's teens claiming to be Bible-believing Christians, can you imagine what America will look like when these young people become the next generation to dominate the population? Seventy-one million Millennials (33 million now in their teens) hold our future in their hands. Our national destiny is linked to their generation. Youth specialist Ron Luce is right on when he says, "We have a short window of five to seven years before most of them will be into their 20s and set the pace for American culture. Our nation is truly at a crossroad. What we do in the next five years could affect the next 50 to 100 years of American history. Every year in America, 4.5 million teenagers turn 20 years old. Research shows that once a child reaches that milestone, the odds of winning that individual to Christ are nearly 10-1."[12]

Researcher George Barna claims that if a child does not receive Christ as his personal Savior by the age of 18, there is a 75% chance that he never will. It is a haunting thought to know that beyond the age of 18, the probability of someone accepting Christ as Savior is only twenty-five percent.[13] The mandate is clear, both for the church and for the culture. It is not an overstatement to say that no other generation has ever had the opportunity to effect change of this magnitude. We must seize the moment.

Statistically, research confirms that responsibility for the moral demise of our culture lies primarily at the feet of today's Boomer generation. This was never seen more clearly than when Patterson and Kim came out with their groundbreaking work entitled, *The Day America Told the Truth: What People Really Believe About Everything That Really Matters.* After sifting through 200,000 questions from nearly 100 survey instruments, a written version was administered to 5,577 people throughout every region of the United States. People were urged to be totally honest in exchange for anonymity. Here is a summation of what Baby Boomers believe based on their actual behavior:

- Only 13% believe in *all* of the Ten Commandments.

- 77% see no point in observing the Sabbath.

- 74% see no problem in stealing from those who won't really miss it.

- 64% lie when it benefits them.

- 56% drink and drive if they feel that they can handle it.

- 53% will cheat on their spouse if given the chance.

- 50% do absolutely nothing at work about one full day in every five.

- 41% use recreational drugs.

- 30% cheat on their taxes—to a point.

- 31% put their lover at risk of disease through their own promiscuity.

- 20% say, "I may have committed date rape, but I know that she wanted it."[14]

Ninety-three percent say they alone decide what is right and wrong for them. Eighty-four percent say they have violated the established rules of their religion. Eighty-one percent say they have violated the law of the land because, in their opinion, those rules or laws were wrong. Authors Patterson and Kim concluded, "We are a law unto ourselves. We have made ourselves the authority over church, God, laws, and police."[15] Ninety-one percent lie regularly, and 66% of all Americans see nothing wrong with it.[16]

Ninety-two percent of sexually active people in America have had ten or more lovers, with a lifetime average of seventeen.[17] Thirty percent were not sure if they still loved their spouse, and only 33% listed love as the primary reason for getting married in the first place.[18] Sixty-two percent think nothing is morally wrong with the affair they are having. Yet, only 17% of the men and ten percent of the women plan to leave their mates to be with their lover. In other words, they are cheating for the mere excitement of it.[19] However, it is probably not with their neighbor's spouse because 72% do not even know their next-door neighbors.[20]

Fifty percent steal hotel and health club towels, while 29% are shoplifters.[21] As if this is not bad enough, it is believed that our crime statistics may be underestimated by as much as 600% due to unreported crimes.[22] The United States is the most violent nation in the industrialized world. The homicide rate among teenage males is 20 times higher in America than in Western Europe and 40 times higher than in Japan.[23]

The majority of workers surveyed said they spent 20% of their time at work doing absolutely nothing. Half of those surveyed regularly call in sick when they are not sick. One in six drink alcohol or use illegal drugs on the job. Only one in four say they give work their best effort.[24] Keep in mind, these are the parents of today's teens.

The picture is equally dismal regarding the church and religion. Most of those surveyed do not follow what the church says because they are not even aware of the church's positions on social issues. Only one in five ever consults a minister, priest, or rabbi on moral issues.[25] Fewer than two in five believe sin is "going against God's will," "going against the Bible," or "violating the Ten Commandments." That's right. Most people define sin as "breaking your own conscience. I am the ultimate authority on morality. If I make up my own rules and set my own standards, then nothing is sin if I don't want it to be."[26]

This, my friend, is the America in which we now live. These are your next-door neighbors. These are the parents of your child's classmates. These are the people sitting in the pew beside you on Sunday morning. This stuff does not occur in a bubble. Our kids are watching, and the trickle-down affect has impacted them in a major way.

For example, every day in America:

- 1,000 unwed teenage girls become mothers

- 1,106 teenage girls have abortions

- 4,219 teenagers contact sexually transmitted diseases

- 500 adolescents begin using illegal drugs

- 1,000 adolescents begin drinking alcohol

- 135,000 kids bring guns or other weapons to school

- 3,610 teens are assaulted

- 80 teens are raped

- 630 teens are robbed

- 16 teens are murdered

- 13 teens commit suicide[27]

This is what the Bible calls reaping what you've sown. It is called sowing the wind and reaping the whirlwind. Unless the church awakens from its slumber, the worst is yet to come once the Boomer baton is passed on to this Millennial generation.

THE TRUTH ABOUT TRUTH

Today's generation of students is being indoctrinated and inundated with the message that absolute truth is non-existent. If all truth is relative, then no belief is worth dying for. Today's Christian student must determine to swim upstream against the current of relativism if he or she hopes to make any impact whatsoever for Christ. Truth is the compass that gives our lives direction and purpose. For example, F-14 fighter pilots often experience vertigo. That's when pilots become disoriented as to how fast and high they are going. When this happens at night, pilots may be flying at ground level while thinking that they are actually thousands of feet in the air. Apparently, this is what happened in the death of John Kennedy, Jr., one night several years ago when he was flying just off the East Coast. Somewhat inexperienced as a pilot, he relied on his emotions, sensations, and memory. But the one thing that will not lie to a pilot is the plane's instrument panel. Likewise, many today have spiritual vertigo in which their decision-making is determined by human logic, emotional reasoning, and other environmental factors that allow their conscience to be their guide. Without consulting truth's compass, many end up flying by the seat of their pants, disoriented, without any real direction in life. They're making good time; they just don't know where they're going.

The great majority of students and young adults deny the very existence of absolute truth. In other words, they do not believe in an objective standard by which to judge right and wrong. They are convinced that no such standard exists. However, to embrace this belief is contrary to everything else we know about life. Our entire existence relies on standards. We have standards that measure the size of our shoes, the distance to another city, the temperature of water, and the score in a sports competition. The watch on your wrist provides a standard of time. The price tag on any item that you purchase provides a standard that allows the transaction to be completed. The lanes on an interstate highway and speed limit signs all provide a standard that dictate safety and a degree of orderliness. You get the point. If there are no standards for conduct and measurement, society cannot survive. There will be utter chaos.

Yet, these conditional standards only point to a higher absolute standard that is unchangeable and beyond our control. For example, the length of a day, the rotation of the earth, the distance from the earth to the moon, the temperature at which water freezes or boils, and many other irreversible standards only serve as reminders that there are absolute standards that demand our consideration. In every area of mathematics, medicine, geology, geography, and science, there are areas of precision that cannot be compromised because there are absolute truths. Yet, when applied to morals and spirituality, we try to deny the undeniable.

Absolute truth is that which is true for all people, for all times, and for all places whether a person believes it or not, follows it or not, and agrees with it or not. Even those who deny absolute truth will have to admit that certain things are right and certain things are wrong. If a gang of boys decides to rape an innocent young girl, everyone knows that is wrong. Torturing a baby for mere amusement is wrong. Honesty is right. Stealing is wrong. These common moral truths cannot be separated from the Ultimate Truth Giver, Jesus Christ Himself who is Truth (John 14:6). One's disregard for truth does not change the truth. We don't create truth; we merely discover it. For instance, we don't invent the law of gravity; we discover it. Oh, a person may deny it and jump off a building believing that he or she can fly. Soon, however, they will discover the law of gravity. Likewise, people are free to obey or disobey moral laws, but consequences await them.

In the world of relativism the most common question asked is, "Who are you to judge?" We've been taught to be tolerant and to keep our criticisms to ourselves. It is interesting to see this ideology being played out on the world's stage as America deals with terrorism. Those on the left side of politics want America to be perceived as compassionate and tolerant. After the 9/11 terrorist attacks in 2001, President Bush told the world that you are either for us or against us, and any nation harboring terrorists is against us. Such language was seen by many as too harsh. Even the treatment of terrorist prisoners must be seen by the world as compassionate. The point is this: when we lose the ability to make moral judgments, we can no longer make a distinction between the actions of a terrorist and that of Billy Graham or Mother Teresa. Without absolute truth, how can we distinguish between good and evil? If all values are relative to individual cultures, then the world court had no right to judge the Nazis as wrong. But the world court ruled that there was something beyond and above culture that determines right and wrong.

MORAL RELATIVISM IS UNLIVABLE

In his book *Being Bold In a Whatever World*, Sean McDowell tells the story of Professor Peter Kreeft who had an entire college class that believed morality was relative. They claimed he had no right to impose his values of absolutism on them. So he replied, "All right. Let's run the class by your values, not mine. There are no absolutes. Moral values are subjective and relative. And my particular set of subjective values includes this one: All women in my class flunk!" Immediately, the students protested: "That's unfair!" "Yes," the professor replied, "It is unfair. But what do you mean by 'fair'? If fairness or justice is only my value or your value, then it has no universal authority over both of us. I have no right to impose my values on you, and you have no right to impose yours on me. But if there is a universal, objective, absolute value called justice, or fairness, then it holds for both of us, and it judges me as wrong when I say all women flunk. And you can appeal to that justice in judging my rule as unfair. But if there is no such thing as absolute objective justice, then all you can mean when you protest my rule is that you don't like it, that your subjective values are different from mine. But that's not what you said. You didn't say merely that you don't like my rules, but that it was unfair. So you do believe in moral absolutes after all, when it comes down to practice? Why do you believe that silly theory, then? Why are you hypocrites? Why don't you practice what you preach and stop appealing to justice, or else preach what you practice, and stop denying it?"[28] The students were willing to be moral relativists until it involved their own grades. Then, they quickly cried out for an objective standard!

Proponents of moral relativism actually share more in common with absolutists than they may want to admit. For example, every society believes in some version of the Golden Rule. All societies have laws protecting human life. All societies condemn stealing. Even pro-choice and pro-life advocates share the belief that all people have certain rights granted to them by the Declaration of Independence. Pro-choice advocates simply deny that a fetus is a full human being. There still remains disagreement on moral issues, but there is more common ground than we realize.

The relativist claims that there is no such thing as absolute truth. Thus, he or she is declaring relativism as absolutely true. His or her statement in itself is self-defeating and inconsistent with his or her position as a relativist. It is impossible to deny the existence of absolutes without appealing to an absolute.

If there is no God, then all is permissible. As Romans 1:25 states, society begins to worship the creature rather than the Creator. If there is no greater source for morality than ourselves, then we're all living an illusion. Everybody has a point of view they think is right, and everybody makes moral judgments on a daily basis. Unfortunately, it seems Christians are the ones who get labeled as judgmental. The truth is, everyone else judges as well. It's an inescapable consequence of standing for morality. Anyone who says you should not judge has already made a moral judgment about you, namely, that you are wrong for judging others. The next time someone says, "Who are you to judge?" you might reply by asking, "Who are you to ask the question, 'who are you to judge'?"

Because Americans have exchanged the truth of God for the lie, we are staggering in a drunken stupor and walking in darkness. God is light. To exchange His truth for the lie of relativism is to turn out the light and commit moral, spiritual, and national suicide.

WHAT SEEMS TO BE THE PROBLEM?

What seems to be, and what actually is are two different things. The basic problem with America is we have turned away from God. Experts say, "That's being too simplistic. Our problems are much more complicated." We have government programs galore, committees and subcommittees, and multi-billion dollar budgets for every conceivable problem in the world. But instead of going away, the problems just seem to escalate. The reason is simple. Government and education are not the answer.

We have complex problems today, but those problems are the result of one basic root cause. For example, an atom of enriched plutonium splits, releasing particles that collide with many other plutonium atoms causing them to split, releasing particles that collide with many other plutonium atoms, and on and on. This chain reaction is the principle behind the atomic bomb. The massive destruction of Hiroshima was the result of a simple plutonium atom split. Simplistically speaking, that single split set into motion a complexity of problems that had catastrophic results. Likewise, when you identify the enormity and complexity of America's problems, they can all be traced back to the simple root cause . . . the exclusion and rejection of Jesus Christ and biblical principles from our nation's most fundamental institutions. We need God in America again!

CHAPTER 3

Truth Matters

Every generation of teenagers has its own jargon, musical tastes, and clothing styles that give it a unique identity. The one word that has found prominence in the vocabulary of today's youth and seems to reflect an "attitude" toward life in general is: "whatever." Express concern about their grades, work ethic, appearance, friends, or time spent on the computer, and you may very well get an indifferent "whatever." Instead of engaging in conversation or offering an explanation, "whatever" seems to cover it all. The student can then walk back into his or her own world without having their space invaded, their life inconvenienced, or their actions held accountable to anyone. With the shrug of the shoulders, "whatever" is intended to say, "I heard you, but I don't care. Now get off my case." This "whatever" attitude in moral relativism finds expression in such statements as:

- "You're into Christ. I'm into yoga and meditation. We all have to choose what works best for us, but you know, whatever."

- "Hey man, I believe in a loving God as much as you do. I just don't think He would send anybody to hell for not believing in Jesus. I mean, what about all those who haven't even heard of Jesus. That's not the God I believe in, but hey, whatever."

- "I believe parts of the Bible, but I think many of the miracles were just myths and accommodated the cultural superstitions at that time. Dude, it's all a matter of interpretation, but you can believe whatever."

- "I'm not into religion anymore. I'm still a spiritual person, but I just feel that if I do the best I can and try to live right, then someday I'll go to heaven when I die, if there really is such a place. But hey, you have yours, and I have mine. You know, whatever."

Other than catastrophes like Hurricane Katrina, or the terrorist attacks on the World Trade Center, or a school shooting like Columbine, there is very little that can produce more than a "whatever" response until it personally impacts their own lives. Then, and only then, do most students ask the deeper, soul-searching questions like, "How could this have happened?" and "What would cause anyone to do such a thing?"

I am probably being a little too hard on our youth. Many of them are volunteers for disaster relief and lead the charge for spiritual resurgence throughout the nation. In fact, I am convinced that our youth are the key to turning America back to God and to reviving the church out of its slumber. In no way do I minimize what God desires to do through this generation of teenagers. I strongly believe in them. However, the concern regarding this "whatever" attitude extends beyond a personal indifference toward life to an underlying mind-set that says, "If that's what you think, believe, or do, then fine. If it works for you, cool. You have your value system. I have mine. Whatever."

But wait a minute. Does truth matter or not? This is not some deep, philosophical question requiring hours of solitude in a monastery before arriving at an answer. Yet, moral relativism's answer is that "we have no objective standard by which to determine right from wrong. One person's opinion is just as valid as another's. Morality is simply a matter of personal preference, which results from one's cultural, ethnic, or sexual orientation. There is no such thing as absolute truth." Oh really? We demand truth in other areas of life, don't we? We want physicians to tell us the truth about prescribing the right medication or doing the right kind of surgery. We want stockbrokers to tell us the truth when it comes to investments. We want the courts to tell us the truth as it relates to convicting the guilty and vindicating the innocent. We want employers to be honest when it relates to salaries. We want airlines to be truthful as it applies to safe planes and sober pilots. We want the news media to be truthful in their reporting. We want road signs, medicine bottles, and food labels to be truthful. So, here's the question. Why do we demand truth in every other area of life except as it pertains to morality and religion? Our culture has blindly embraced the claim that truth does not exist. The prevailing attitude is that it's all a matter of opinion, and who are you to judge anyway? If truth is relative, then no one is ever really wrong.

THE TRUTH ABOUT TRUTH

In their book, *I Don't Have Enough Faith To Be An Atheist*, Norm Geisler and Frank Turek give the following criteria for truth:

• Truth is transcultural: if something is true, it is true for all people, in all places, at all times. ($2+2=4$ for everyone, everywhere at every time.)

• Truth is unchanging even though our beliefs about truth change. (When we began to believe the earth was round instead of flat, the truth about the earth didn't change, only our belief about the earth changed.)

• Truth is not affected by the attitude of the one professing it. (An arrogant person does not make the truth he professes false. A humble person does not make the error he professes true.)

• All truths are absolute truths.

• Beliefs cannot change the truth, no matter how sincerely they believe something to be true. (Someone can sincerely believe the world is flat, but that only makes him or her sincerely mistaken.)

• Truth is discovered, not invented. It exists independent of anyone's knowledge of it. (Gravity existed prior to Newton.)[1]

Truth is not a subjective matter of taste, but an objective matter of fact. Truth is truth no matter where you live on the planet. Those who claim that truth in morality doesn't really matter certainly don't embrace that position when someone treats them immorally. For example, they might claim that lying isn't wrong, until someone lies to them. Moral relativists don't want their spouses to live like relativists. A wife doesn't want her husband to be relatively faithful. Most male relativists expect their wives to live as if adultery were absolutely wrong. Do you think the moral relativist would accept the morality of a murderer or a rapist if someone wanted to kill or rape them? As Geisler and Turek point out, "Moral law is not always the standard by which we treat others, but it is nearly always the standard by which we expect others to treat us."[2] When people are the victims of bad behavior, they have no trouble understanding that the behavior is absolutely wrong. Yes, truth in morality does matter. It undergirds everything we do. It affects us financially, socially, psychologically, spiritually, and physically. False ideas about morality lead to immorality. In fact, one's success in life often depends upon moral choices in areas such as sex, marriage, children, drugs, money, and business dealings.

We often hear the mantra that you cannot legislate morality, but the reality is that virtually every law declares one behavior to be right and another to be wrong. The only question is, "Whose morality are you going to legislate?" If it is morally wrong to kill innocent people, shouldn't that truth be legislated? Issues of public policy that affect your health and finances will be legislated. Surely you are concerned about whose morality determines such legislation.

But what about religious truth? Some think that religion and morality should be isolated in their own separate categories as if there is no connection between the two. The fact is, they are inseparable. Morality comes from religion. Therefore, religious truth is of supreme importance, so we had better get it right. If it involves teaching kids to be suicide bombers and fly planes into buildings, then it matters. If it involves training kids to believe that everyone who is a non-Muslim should be terrorized and killed, then truth in religion matters. If the Bible is true, then everyone's eternal destiny is at stake. You owe it to yourself to find the truth and act on it. Truth matters.

MORAL RELATIVISM IS SELF-DEFEATING

Most relativists believe that relativism is true not only for himself or herself, but also for everyone else. However, if they are true relativists, then believing that relativism is true for everyone is the one thing they cannot believe because in doing so, they are declaring it to be an absolute truth. And absolute truth is what relativists say does not exist. So, their absolute claim that there is no absolute truth cannot be true since it affirms the very thing they are trying to deny. Even still, the relativist remains absolutely sure that there are no absolutes. The relativist wants everyone to value him or her as a person even while denying that there are values for all people.

WHO ARE YOU TO JUDGE?

How many times have we all heard that statement? Yet, the prohibition against judging fails to meet its own standard because the underlying question of "Who are you to judge?" is in itself a judgment. Non-Christians often complain that Christians are narrow-minded because of the claim that Jesus Christ is the only way to heaven, making all other non-Christian systems false. They seldom stop to consider the fact that their claims are equally as narrow. If Christianity is true, then all non-Christian systems are false, but if a non-Christian system is true, then Christianity is false. Both views are equally narrow. That's the nature of truth. Whenever anyone makes a claim of truth, all other claims opposing it are false. Whenever the relativist claims that relativism is true, it is he or she who is being dogmatic, judgmental, and narrow-minded. Truth, by its very nature, is exclusive and narrow.

When I fly on an airplane, I prefer a narrow-minded pilot. I don't want some voice coming over the intercom saying, "Ladies and gentlemen, this is your pilot speaking. We're going to be broad-minded today and land in this cow pasture." No, I want the pilot to sit the plane down on that narrow landing strip. Two plus two equals four. It does not equal five and it does not equal three. A child can raise his or her hand all day and say, "But teacher, that's being too narrow minded." Yet, if they answer any other way, they will flunk. At 212°, water boils. At 32°, water freezes. It is not 211° or 33°. When I am sick and go to the doctor, I prefer a narrow-minded physician. I don't want some doctor saying, "I don't know. It might be this, or it might be that. Let's try these pills and hope they work." No, I want a doctor to properly diagnose my condition and prescribe the right medication so I can get well. In every area of mathematics, medicine, science, geography, or geology, there are areas of precision that cannot be compromised. Yet, when it comes to religion and morality, we are told that the rules don't apply. Doesn't it seem strange to have universal truth in these other areas of study, but not in morality and religion?

TOLERANCE: OUR NATIONAL ICON

Unless you have been living in a cave in some third-world country, you know that "tolerance" is the en vogue word for our culture. However, the word goes beyond the traditional idea of respecting the viewpoints of those with whom you disagree. Today, there is a "new tolerance" which insists that we have no right to disagree with the liberal social agenda. This "new tolerance" claims that all beliefs and religions are equal. Erwin Lutzer says, "This word, which at one time meant that people should be free to believe whatever they wished, now means that they can do whatever they wish, and it is improper to judge their conduct."[3] While respecting all sorts of weird religious ideas and esteeming the most bizarre views of a "new" morality, this tolerance seethes with anger toward those who claim to embrace truth as absolute. The supreme virtue today is to be open-minded and non-judgmental toward those who are different from us. Christians have no problem with that, but when we voice our convictions regarding biblical morality, then those who preach the tolerance message are regarded as intolerant. It's an intolerant kind of tolerance.

If I go into the public square and say, "I believe in Jesus Christ," most likely no one would have a problem with that. But to go into the same arena and say, "Jesus Christ is the only way to heaven," I would probably be heckled off the platform. Sadly, Christianity is perceived as the religion of intolerance. The question to ponder is, "Where did these protesters get their idea of intolerance and their perception of what is right and wrong if they sincerely do not believe in absolutes?" When you ponder such a question, you begin to see that moral relativism is a self-defeating belief system.

Interestingly, the relativist does not see his or her intolerance as hypocritical. They boldly proclaim that there is no standard of right and wrong—except when you violate what they say is right. While proclaiming there is no such thing as absolute truth, he or she is in essence declaring an absolute truth. It's as if they are saying, "It is an absolute truth that there is no such thing as absolute truth."[4] Such inconsistencies are also observed in the area of tolerance. They only "tolerate" those who agree with them, which violates the definition of tolerance.

BUSH V. CLINTON

Consider, for example, the different worldviews of President George W. Bush and his predecessor, President Bill Clinton. Bush is an absolutist, and when he took a strong stance against Iraq, many opposed him by saying, "What gives the United States the right to impose its values on others by being the world's policeman?" In an interview with Bob Woodward, Bush said, "There is a value system that cannot be compromised—God-given values. These aren't United States-created values. What's very important as we articulate foreign policy through our diplomacy and military action, is that it never look like we are creating these values. It leads to a larger question of your view about God."[5]

Contrast Bush with his predecessor, Clinton. After the terrorist attacks of September 11, 2001, Clinton addressed the students at Georgetown University and partly blamed the attacks on America's "arrogant self-righteousness." He said, "Nobody's got the truth . . . You're at a university which basically believes that no one ever has the whole truth, ever . . . We are incapable of ever having the whole truth."[6]

By the way, Georgetown University is not the exception, but the rule. In his influential work, *The Closing of the American Mind*, the late philosopher Allan Bloom made the observation that "there is one thing a college professor can be absolutely certain of: Almost every student entering the university believes, or says he believes, that truth is relative."[7] Yet, parents all over the world are paying thousands of dollars in college tuition so their sons and daughters can be taught that there is no truth, there are no absolutes.

Zogby International took a poll of American college seniors in which 97% said they believed their professors had given them a good education in ethics. When asked what those professors had taught them, 73% responded, "What is right and wrong depends on differences in individual values and cultural diversity."[8]

Similarly, a reporter for *Forbes Magazine* observed an ethics class at Harvard Business School in which the professor and students discussed case studies, but avoided coming to any moral conclusions. Of course, this is the game plan: to indoctrinate our youth with a radical ideology that rejects any semblance of absolutes so that all values are of equal importance. The reporter wrote that students in this kind of class, rather than develop moral principles, merely "develop skills enabling them to rationalize anything short of cannibalism."[9]

Speaking of cannibalism, did you hear about a guy named Armin Meiwes who placed an ad on the Internet seeking "a young, well-built man who wants to be eaten"? Believe it or not, Bernard Brandes responded to the ad and allowed himself to be killed and eaten. Meiwes was given $8^1/_2$ years in prison. Although this took place in Germany, killing on request is also legal in Oregon. If he or she is consistent, the relativist will not dare condemn such action, however repulsive it may be to his or her senses. After all, they did not hurt anyone else. They were two consenting adults, so what right do we have to interfere? Brandes apparently believed that it was in his best interest to be eaten, and who are we to judge otherwise? By what standard can we judge such behavior as inappropriate?[10] This, my friend, is the slippery slope we are going down, and there seems to be no end in sight.

Is this what Romans 1:26 alludes to when it says they "exchanged the natural use for what is against nature"? Does this have any resemblance to verse 24 that says, "God also gave them up to uncleanness, in the lusts of their hearts, to dishonor their bodies among themselves"? Does verse 28 have a familiar ring? "God gave them over to a debased mind, to do those things which are not fitting." And let's not omit verse 22, "Professing themselves to be wise, they became fools." (KJV)

The question that comes to mind is, "If there is no truth, why should any student listen to his or her professor? What's the point of going to school, much less paying for it? What's the point of obeying the professor's moral prohibitions against cheating if there are no moral absolutes?" If we teach students that there is no right and wrong, why are we surprised when there is a school shooting? Why should our youth act "right" when we teach them there is no such thing as "wrong"? Without question, today's Christian student must determine to swim upstream against the current of relativism if he or she hopes to make any impact whatsoever for Christ.

As I was writing this chapter, the *Dr. Phil Show* featured a couple whose marriage was on the rocks because they each shared opposite worldviews. The husband was having an affair with a very attractive friend whom he had known for 13 years. He invited his mistress to move in with him and his wife, provided that the wife would agree. This husband naively thought that his wife could become a good friend to his mistress, and that they would make a great threesome. Boy, did he ever underestimate his wife's reaction! It was obvious that she held a biblical worldview when she said, "I believe in traditional values and was always taught that being intimate with my husband is sacred and not something to be shared with another woman." He expressed his viewpoint by saying, "The Bible mentions having multiple partners, and other cultures have used it successfully for thousands of years. Why should I be victimized just because I live in America?" When the guy called this threesome arrangement "poly-fidelity," Dr. Phil wittily replied, "Charlie, when I look up poly-fidelity in my dictionary it's called 'cheating.'"[11] Forget about the fact that Charlie still had four boys at home, ages 18, 16, 11, and six. He was simply doing what felt right for him.

Connect the dots. There is a direct correlation between abdicating biblical absolutes in lieu of relativism and the subsequent increase in immorality, crime, violence, and all other socially unacceptable behavior.

A MODERN DAY PARABLE

In order to drive a point home, Jesus often spoke in parables. His disciples often had difficulty comprehending what He was saying, so Jesus would simplify it in easy-to-understand terms. I realize that the subject of moral relativism can be confusing and not as palatable as we would like. The premise of *Truth Decay* is that America has made a seismic shift from a biblical worldview to one of humanism expressed as moral relativism. All of our social and moral problems can be traced to this change in our core beliefs. Author Frank Peretti has done us all a favor by providing a modern-day parable to help us understand the cultural shift from moral absolutes to relativism. Read it and weep.

> "It was the Daddy of all playgrounds, stretching out acre upon acre with boys and girls running, laughing, chasing, and screaming playfully. The playground was a happy place and usually a safe environment for kids to enjoy. The playground rules were clearly posted on a big wooden sign beside the entrance. They helped provide peace and order and were enough for any eight or nine-year old to understand. No hitting. No pushing or shoving. No fighting. Share the equipment. Take turns. No spitting on the girls. No chasing the boys.
>
> You see, the playground rules were sacred and inscribed on every heart and mind. For example, when Jordan Smith first arrived on the playground, he assumed that once the baseball was in his hand, he had sovereign control over it. When his teammates tried to reason with him, he still wouldn't change his mind, but appealing to the playground rules he finally did.
>
> Clyde Saunders always seemed to have extra saliva in his mouth and apparently felt compelled to put it somewhere else. Rachel Parks was the nearest available depository, and he was happy to share with her out of his abundance . . . until she appealed to the playground rules, and he was required to swallow.
>
> Yes, the playground rules were a shelter for the oppressed, the defender of the weak, the guarantor of social stability. Of course, we cannot over-look the importance of Mrs. Kravitz, the teacher on playground duty. Mrs. Kravitz represented the

authority that put up those rules in the first place. Without her presence, the playground rules would be nothing more than words painted on a board. She was sharp-eyed, always ready to help in time of trouble, but also ready to deal with troublemakers. She had a stern expression for that purpose, as well as a whistle, a clipboard, and a stack of pink slips, which could mean a visit to the principal.

Some kids appreciated her presence on the playground and naturally, some of the kids preferred she not be there. The former felt secure and the latter felt imposed upon. But like it or not, the playground was reasonably safe and orderly, because Mrs. Kravitz and the playground rules kept it that way.

Then, one day something was different on the playground. It took a while for the kids to notice, but eventually they realized that Mrs. Kravitz was nowhere to be found. Some were glad, of course, but some were concerned and asked the other teachers where Mrs. Kravitz had gone.

'Well,' said the teachers, 'We've decided there is no authority, and you kids are inherently good and able to decide for yourselves the right thing to do. You have the capacity within yourselves to solve all your own problems and make this a better playground. You don't need Mrs. Kravitz.'

'But what about the playground rules?' they asked. The teachers said, 'You can decide for yourselves if the playground rules are right for you. It's really not our place to say that one set of rules is better than another.'

And so the kids were left to their own wills to do what seemed right and felt right in their own hearts. For a time, the playground rules still held sway in their minds. The rules worked well in the past, so they continued to bring stability in the days that followed.

But then one day, Clyde Saunders stopped to consider the excess saliva in his mouth and whether or not he should swallow. 'It is my mouth and my spit,' he reasoned. 'Nobody else has any business telling me how I should get rid of it.' So, he fired off a huge glob and hit Rachel right in the eye. She felt violated, betrayed, and insulted.

'Clyde, you're not supposed to do that,' she said. 'Oh yeah? Who says?' Clyde responded. Rachel promptly took him over to the old sign displaying the playground rules. 'See here? The rules say, 'No Spitting On The Girls.' 'Well, those rules are out-dated, irrelevant, and no longer in effect,' Clyde said. 'So, I can choose to live by those rules or not.'

Not long after this, the baseball game came to a screeching halt when Jordan Smith caught a pop fly and abruptly walked off with the baseball. 'Hey, that's our ball.' 'It's mine now,' he replied. 'But you have to share.' 'Oh yeah? Who says?' They pointed to the rules. It says, 'Share Equipment.' 'Do you really believe that old sign?' Jordan responded. Although they tried reasoning with him, they discovered that with the absence of authority, Mrs. Kravitz, and the playground rules, reason alone would not suffice. The rules just didn't apply anymore.

This new way of thinking eventually caught on. They began to reason, 'We've evolved beyond the rules and have no need of authority.' Each child became his own authority and the children finally tore down the sign and threatened to kick or punch any kid who tried to put it back up. So, the playground was theirs and the kids lived and behaved according to what felt right to them.

When the first incidence of violence broke out, the kids debated what may have caused it, but none of them could say that it was anybody's fault or that it was even wrong. Since there were no rules, every kid soon felt entitled to have his own way or do anything by any means. The playground fell into chaos. The equipment would always go to the strongest kid or the biggest gang. The unwritten rule was, 'Might Makes Right. Survival

Of The Fittest. Natural Selection.' Now it was forbidden to
even speak of the old authority the children had once known,
and the memory of Mrs. Kravitz quickly faded. The playground rules were gone, not only from the old wooden sign,
but now also from the minds and hearts of the children."[12]

Author Frank Moore shares another similar illustration out of his
childhood experience, which brings the absence of moral authority into
sharper focus. He says, "Our teacher, who had to be out of the classroom
for a while, left us with an assignment to be completed in her absence.
To that point in my young life I had no awareness of any personal hostility toward authority. However, the minute our teacher left the room
and closed the door behind her, the entire classroom was transformed
almost magically into a world of chaos. Students exploded in frenzied
activity; I was positioned in the big middle of it. I knew there was a time
and a place for free expression, and this was it!

"One of the girls in the class interrupted the festivities with 'You guys
had better get quiet and work on your assignment!' Our quick and clever
response was, 'Oh yeah? What are you going to do about it?' Her reply
stopped us dead in our tracks, like hitting the pause button on a VCR:
'The teacher appointed me to take names, and when she gets back, I'm
going to show her this.' She held up a piece of paper with all our names
on it. She had our attention!"

The lesson is this: when the authority figure is absent and can't see our
actions, and when chances are favorable that we won't be held accountable, then we are prone to do just about anything we want to do.
Lawlessness lurks just below the surface.[13]

If we need further verification of this fact, consider the aftermath of
hurricanes in which there is rampant looting. During the Los Angeles
riots several years ago, people were caught on camera toting televisions,
VCRs, clothes, and anything else they could steal while police were preoccupied trying to bring order out of chaos.

Both of these stories clearly portray what has happened to America.
Through the teaching of evolution and the emergence of moral rela-

tivism in the classrooms of America, we have managed to indoctrinate our children with secular humanism, which claims there is no God to whom we must answer. There is no objective standard for right and wrong. Do whatever feels right to you—no rules, no authority, no consequences. It cannot be stated loudly enough. The moral chaos in our nation is the direct result of our rejection of moral absolutes. The fact that America leads the world in abortions, teenage pregnancies, illegal drugs, pornography, divorce, crime, and juvenile homicides can be traced to the rejection of a biblical worldview.

WHOSE STANDARDS PREVAIL?

If there is no absolute standard for right and wrong that transcends the local culture, what happens when different cultures with conflicting views and values come together? America has become a melting pot of multiple subcultures. For example, let's talk about the challenge of communication. I check into motels, and I encounter front desk clerks who I can hardly understand, and who can barely understand me. I drop clothes off at the cleaners, and I encounter employees who speak sporadic English. I call for technical support regarding computer repair, and I get some guy on the other side of the world who has absolutely no idea what I'm talking about. When I hire manual laborers to do painting, landscaping, or concrete repair, I inevitably get immigrant day laborers who have no clue what I am saying and vice versa. So, here is the question: when you have different cultures living within one nation, whose standards ought to prevail? Somebody has to make an ethical choice, but who will it be? Without a common biblical worldview, laws become unenforceable because no one can legitimately force his or her idea of right and wrong on me. Today, we are seeing Judges 21:25 re-enacted where "each man did what was right in his own eyes."

It is apparent that what we are now doing is not working. We can determine what will work in the future by observing what has worked in the past. The definition of insanity is to keep doing what we've been doing and expecting different results. We are in a state of moral insanity.

Dr. D. James Kennedy observes that every great nation in history has been built upon some sort of religious foundation. Consider the Hinduism of India, the Islam of Saudi Arabia, the Confucianism of China, the Shintoism of Japan, or the Judaism of Israel. These, and others, have had some form of religious commitment that contributed to their greatness. Did you know that as recent as the eighteenth century, 99.8% of Americans were committed to the moral values contained in Scripture?[14] Yet, we have abandoned our heritage.

Humanists, liberals, and other like-minded individuals contend that America is not a Christian nation. To be sure, we are living in a post-Christian era, but America is still considered to be a Christian nation. For example, less than 20% of Israel's population claim to be Jewish (70% claim no religious belief), and yet no one denies that Israel is a Jewish state. In India, just over 80% claim to be Hindus, and yet no one questions that India is a Hindu nation. Interestingly enough, even in the midst of our moral freefall, many studies indicate that 85% of Americans still identify themselves as Christians (at least nominally).[15] But there is a small group of activist judges, militant homosexuals, liberal educators, revisionist historians, and left-wing politicians who are determined to dismantle and overthrow the core beliefs upon which America was founded. The greatness of America cannot be separated from the foundation upon which that greatness was built. Without the God of the Bible on our side, we all fail. Only a return to Christian values and virtues can save us. The path we are now on leads to anarchy and self-destruction.

CHAPTER 4

The Way We Were

Stephen Williams is a conscientious fifth grade history teacher at Stevens Creek School in Cupertino, California. Assuming that any course in American history would be incomplete without studying the Declaration of Independence, Williams decided to hand out excerpts of the document to his students. To his utter amazement, the school district prohibited such action on the basis that its religious nature would be a violation of separation of church and state.[1] On another occasion, Williams was teaching about Christopher Columbus' explorations and mentioned that Columbus was a missionary who spread Christianity to the new world. One of the students raised his hand and asked, "What's a Christian?" When Williams explained that a Christian is one who follows the teachings of Jesus Christ, he was immediately reprimanded by the principal.[2]

Then, in May of 2004, Williams taught a unit on presidential powers and the president's ability to issue proclamations, such as the National Day of Prayer. Once again, this ignited serious concerns within the administration, which prompted them to issue Williams a memo that said, "I am directing you to provide me with an advance copy of materials you will be sending home at least two days prior to their being sent out so I can make sure that the materials will not be of concern to the parents or violate the separation of religion and public education."[3] In short, Williams was being told to revise his curriculum and not teach history accurately. Williams has filed a lawsuit saying, "I'm not doing my job as a teacher if the kids are not getting a correct picture of history because of the policy enacted over me. The Founders had a just cause in breaking ties with Great Britain and forming a new nation. My cause is much less than theirs, but I can relate to what they went through."[4]

Rest assured, this is not an isolated case. It looks like a conscientious effort is being made to hide God from the minds of our children and to distort historical facts so that all references to Christianity are removed. I challenge you to find a public school history book written in the 1950s and compare it with one being used in today's classroom. In fact, try comparing an American history textbook used in the *Abeka* home school curriculum with one used in public schools. Take a look at "historical facts" our kids are studying. One current history textbook has 30 pages on the Pilgrims, but there is not a single reference to religion, even as part of the Pilgrim's lives. Another textbook describes the Pilgrims simply as "people who make long trips." Many public schools now portray Thanksgiving as a multicultural feast in which American colonists gave thanks to the Indians.[5] One high school American history textbook devoted six lines to George Washington and more than six *pages* to Marilyn Monroe.[6] Recently, the New Jersey Department of Education omitted America's founding fathers, including George Washington, Thomas Jefferson, and Benjamin Franklin, from the revised version of the state's history standards until an outpouring of public objections caused it to reverse its decision.[7]

Yes, if you put them side by side, it's as if the books are talking about two different nations. The history textbooks of public schools and those used in other Christian curricula are poles apart in their descriptions of America because they are approaching history from two different world-views. There is an all-out effort being made to reinvent our values and redefine what it means to be an American. The game plan of political elit-ists is to indoctrinate the youth of our nation with a radical ideology that says there are no absolutes. Their agenda is to guide our nation toward a new world order of cultural and moral diversity that says there is no ulti-mate source of truth. To go down this road much further will lead to national disaster. These historical revisionists are lying to our children.

As a child, I can remember reading my history book and listening to my teachers without ever questioning their integrity. However, a large percentage of today's parents are oblivious to this subtle moral shift and academic defiance of America's Christian heritage. Without knowing where we came from and without understanding the biblical principles that our founding fathers stood upon and fought for, kids today are deprived of an accurate view of our history. In fact, by omitting all references to God from the curriculum, our children are being deceived into believing something about America that is not true. They are being told that our forefathers came to America from diverse religious backgrounds, and that while some were Christians, most were secularists who believed that religion was fine as long it was confined to the church and home. Wrong! This misconception came to light when political science professors Donald Lutz and Charles Hyneman from the University of Houston carefully researched 15,000 documents written by our founding fathers, which they felt impacted the birth of our nation. To their surprise, they discovered that 94% of the content came either directly or indirectly from the Bible.[8]

In order to even attend the Constitutional Convention, each delegate was required to meet certain religious qualifications. For example, Article 22 of Delaware's Constitution says, "Every person who shall be chosen a member of either house, or appointed to any office or place of trust . . . shall . . . make and subscribe to the following declaration, to wit: 'I…do profess faith in God the Father, and in Jesus Christ His only Son, and in the Holy Ghost, one God, blessed for evermore; and I do acknowledge the holy Scriptures to the Old and New Testament to be given by divine inspiration.'"[9] This hardly sounds like something that a secularist would write, does it? It is no wonder that Ken Woodward, writing for *Newsweek* magazine said, "Now historians are discovering that the Bible, perhaps even more than the Constitution, is our founding document."[10]

Every nation that has ever existed has been built upon some sort of religious foundation. A survey of schoolbooks published prior to the American Revolution indicated 92% of their content focused on the religious themes of Christianity. In fact, America's first 100 colleges were church-related and were established for the purpose of training preachers. Yet, today we make every effort to hide God from the minds of our students. Andrew Jackson, our first log-cabin president, pointed to the Bible and said, "That book is the Rock on which our republic rests."[11] Sadly, today we are no longer resting upon the Rock, but upon the shifting sands of moral relativism.

But then again, the lie that is filtering through the left-wing National Education Association (NEA) and is propagated by the ACLU and other liberal organizations is the contention that secularists founded America. The idea that this nation was founded by God-fearing Christians is considered a myth and greatly overstated. So, in order to support such a view, a concerted effort is being made to rewrite the history books to conform to this more modern, politically correct view. You can see the clashing of these two worldviews even while watching the U.S. Supreme Court confirmation hearings of Chief Justice John Roberts and Justice Samuel Alito. One side wants a justice who views the Constitution as a living document capable of changing with the times. The other side wants a strict constructionist who interprets the Constitution according the intent of our founding fathers and respects the legal precedents of the past. John Adams, one of the founders, said, "Our Constitution was made only for a moral and religious people. It is wholly inadequate for the government of any other."[12] This is why we need like-minded justices on the bench.

Again, it can easily be proven that 53 of the 56 signers of the Declaration of Independence were unashamed followers of Jesus Christ.[13] No doubt, it would surprise many to know that the same men who signed the Declaration of Independence were also responsible for founding the American Bible Society (an organization dedicated to the printing and distribution of the Bible), the American Tract Society (an organization devoted to distributing Christian pamphlets), and the Philadelphia Bible Society.[14] Of the 55 delegates who participated in writing the Constitution, all but three were members of a Christian denomination and most were deeply religious.[15] In fact, our Constitution was actually born out of a prayer meeting, and to this day Congress continues to open its sessions with prayer.[16]

Were you aware that in 1892 the Supreme Court actually declared America to be a Christian nation? As you might imagine, this was not a hasty, irrational decision. Quite the contrary. It was one of the most exhaustive studies of the historical and philosophical foundations of American law ever made. They spent ten years on the study before reaching this momentous decision. The only logical conclusion that could be drawn was the fact that the principles of Christianity were the very core and fiber of our nation. Interestingly enough, that ruling was reaffirmed in 1931 and 1952 by the highest court in the land.[17] So, what has changed? How can historians go back and reverse what is so well established? How can they get away with it?

Just listen to some of these state charters:

- The charter of Virginia reads, "We live to propagate the Christian religion to such people as yet live in ignorance of the true knowledge and worship of God."

- The Plymouth Charter reads, "The colony is established to advance the enlargement of the Christian religion to the glory of God Almighty."

- Delaware's Charter succinctly defines the purpose of its existence as "the further propagation of the holy Gospel."

- Maryland's Charter explains the motivation of its settlers as having "a pious zeal for extending the Christian religion." Rhode Island's charter of statehood declares, "We submit our persons, lives, and fortunes unto our Lord Jesus Christ, the King of Kings, and Lord of Lords."[18]

Not many children will read those words in their history books. To show how far removed we are from those early colonial days, imagine a person being required to first make a public profession of faith in Jesus Christ before being allowed to hold a public office.[19] That is how strongly the American public wanted God and Christian principles to be incorporated into our government. This alone should tell us that separation of church and state was never intended to be separation of God from government.

Early Pilgrims built their churches before building their own homes. The first textbook in our schools was the Bible, with the first teachers being pastors. Where do you suppose our founding fathers came up with the idea for three branches of government? It came from Isaiah 33:22. Where do you suppose the idea of separation of power came from? It is found in Jeremiah 17. What about the idea of tax-exempt status for churches and charitable organizations? It came from Ezra 7:24. Yes, we have been the beneficiaries of the blessings and freedoms that our founding fathers set into motion. However, bit by bit, the biblical foundation that built this nation is being removed from our educational system, our government, and the public life of this nation. The initial result will be chastisement from God, but the ultimate consequence will be bondage—economically, morally, and politically. John Adams, one of our founding fathers, said, "Statesmen may plan and speculate for liberty, but it is religion and morality alone which can establish the principles upon which freedom can securely stand."[20] National disaster is staring America in the face unless there is a return to the very foundation that made us great. Are we so blinded that we cannot see that educators who talk about freedom, but deny the right to talk about God are actually educating us for slavery? Don't we remember the Constitution states we are endowed by our Creator with certain inalienable rights? Are we oblivious to the hypocrisy of those who demand freedom of expression, but then attempt to silence the voice of Christians or deny any expression of the Christian faith in the public arena? Those who scream the loudest for tolerance and diversity are often the first ones to protest with vehement intolerance the public singing of Christmas carols or the display of a nativity scene. The Bible is a book of freedom. Our only right to freedom is granted by God. Thus, to deny the historical preeminence of God and His Word from the minds of our children, especially in the academic context of America's founding, is to be a traitor to our own national heritage.

Sound a little extreme? Perhaps. But not compared to what happened in 1811. A man made a derogatory remark about Jesus Christ in a public school. Somebody filed suit against the man, and believe it or not, it reached the Supreme Court. Here is the ruling handed down by the highest court in the land: "If you attack Jesus Christ, you attack Christianity, and if you attack Christianity, then you attack the government upon which this nation was built. Therefore, an attack on Jesus Christ is equivalent to an attack on the United States." That man was given a prison term and fined $500 for verbally attacking Jesus Christ.[21]

If we sent people to prison today for such behavior, we couldn't build prisons fast enough to accommodate the need. Today, it's no longer those who profane the name of Jesus Christ, but those who proclaim and promote His name who are the ones viewed as breaking the law. Cursing Jesus is no big deal in most schools. But, you let a student quote from the Bible, pass out a religious tract, or wear a Christian T-shirt, and he or she is the one who is reprimanded and penalized for expressing their faith. It's just another example of how we have changed foundations by exchanging the truth of God for the lie.

Patrick Henry perhaps said it the strongest when he proclaimed, "It cannot be emphasized too much or repeated too strongly that America was not founded by religionists, but by Christians; not upon religions, but upon the Gospel of Jesus Christ."[22] Well, Mr. Henry, I am afraid that to make such a statement today is to be out of step with the times.

James Madison, known as the father of the Constitution, said, "We have staked the whole future of American civilization, not upon the power of government, far from it. We have staked the future of all of our political institutions upon the capacity of each and all of us to govern ourselves, to control ourselves, to sustain ourselves according to the Ten Commandments of God."[23] Now, keep in mind, this is not some random religious fanatic who is making this claim. This is the father of our Constitution. Yet, today we have removed the Ten Commandments from public schools and government property, all under the banner of separation of church and state.

It is ironic that liberal courts and activist judges have robbed our children of any connection with God. They have taken prayer out of the schools, removed the Bible from our classrooms, omitted any references to the Christian foundation of America in school textbooks, and gotten rid of the Ten Commandments. Then these "wise guys" scratch their heads in dismay at America's moral freefall. It is really not that complicated. Everything the liberal courts stand for is diametrically opposed to the principles upon which this nation was built. Proverbs 23:10 says, "Do not remove the ancient landmark, . . ." Proverbs 16:12 says, "A throne is established by righteousness." Psalm 9:17 warns, "The wicked shall be turned into hell, and all the nations that forget God." Yes, history teaches that great nations are seldom, if ever, destroyed by outside forces or invasions. Nations fall because they compromise their own foundational beliefs and abandon the moral and spiritual values that made them great. The result is violence and internal chaos.

One of the great documents in our nation's history is the Northwest Ordinance of 1787. The same men who wrote our Constitution also wrote the ordinance, in which Article 3 states that religion is essential to good government.[24] If that is true, then why are many trying to remove it from government? Regarding political prosperity, George Washington, the father of our nation, claimed, "Religion and morality are indispensable supports."[25]

SO, WHAT'S THE BIG FUSS?

It's called "separation of church and state," a term that you won't find in the Constitution. Let's take a brief history refresher course. Keep in mind that the framers of the Constitution had just separated from England because King George was trying to force the English state church on its citizens. The men who wrote the Constitution wanted to make sure that a state church could never again be forced upon the people, thus, the reason for the First Amendment. The states wanted to prevent the establishment of a national religion or the elevation of a particular religious sect to preferred status. James Madison drafted the wording of the First Amendment, which went through a few revisions before it became, "Congress shall make no law establishing religion, or prohibiting the free exercise thereof."[26] The founders not only wanted Americans to be as religious as they wanted to be, but they also wanted to insure that Congress would stay out of the church's business. Anytime you hear the concept of separation of church and state it is seldom in regard to maintaining the restraints on government. Instead, it is always talking about what Christians can or cannot do. In other words, the First Amendment is perceived as protecting the government from religious people, which was just the opposite of our founders' intentions. And how do we know that? For one thing, in 1789, the same year that

Congress approved the First Amendment, James Madison, the writer of the First Amendment, served on a committee that approved congressional chaplains. Madison was the one who recommended on four separate occasions that days be set aside for giving thanks to God. During this time, Congress approved printing Bibles to give to the American Indians and even funded missionaries to be sent to the American Indians. They called the nation to prayer and fasting. What is even more astonishing is that federal buildings in Washington, D.C., were actually used as churches on Sundays.[27] Now, keep in mind that no one thought these actions were in conflict with the First Amendment. Yet, when Attorney General John Ashcroft conducted a Bible study in his office during lunch or before work, the secularists came unglued, yelling about separation of church and state.

I daresay if you were to randomly ask the average person on the street to explain what the Constitution says about religion and government, he or she would immediately claim that it requires separation of church and state. However, the Constitution says *nothing* about separation of church and state. That's right. Those words are never mentioned . . . anywhere . . . zilch . . . nada . . . zippo. So, if that's the case, then where in the world did the idea come from, and who came up with it?

It all started back in 1801 with a group of Baptists from Danbury, Connecticut. They were concerned that the Congregational denomination was about to be declared the national denomination of the United States. Having heard horror stories about the state-established religion in England, they contacted President Thomas Jefferson. On January 1, 1802, Jefferson penned these words that eased their fears: "I contemplate with sovereign reverence that act of the whole American people which declared that their legislature should 'make no law respecting an establishment of religion, or prohibiting the free exercise thereof,' thus building a wall of separation between Church and State."[28]

Where did Jefferson come up with this terminology? Trying to connect with these Baptists, Jefferson was quoting one of their prominent preachers, Roger Williams, who had said: "When they have opened a gap in the hedge or wall of Separation between the Garden of the Church and the Wilderness of the world, God hath ever broke down the wall it selfe *[sic]* . . . and that therefore if he will ever please to restore his Garden and Paradice *[sic]* again, it must of necessitie *[sic]* be walled in peculiarly unto himselfe *[sic]* from the world."[29]

Obviously, the wall that Williams had in mind was a wall to protect the church from the world, not the world from the church. Jefferson certainly understood this and used Williams' words to assure those Connecticut Baptists that the church would be protected from the government. It cannot be said loudly enough that understanding Jefferson's purpose in using the phrase "separation between Church and State" is the key to understanding its meaning. As author Robert Jeffress says, "Never in their wildest imaginations did Jefferson or the framers of the Constitution envision that the First Amendment would be used as a rationale for separating our nation from its Christian foundation."[30] Can we be sure about that? Well, you tell me. One year after writing that infamous letter, Jefferson recommended that the United States Congress provide government financial support for missionaries to the Kaskaskia Indians and for certain parcels of land be reserved for "Christian Indians." On three separate occasions during his administration, Jefferson reaffirmed this arrangement with the American Indians. He understood the importance of integrating government and Christianity.[31]

It is interesting to note that 50 years after Jefferson's letter to the Danbury Baptists, a group came before Congress requesting a separation of Christian principles from government, not unlike what has happened in recent decades. The petition was referred to the House and Senate Judiciary Committees, both of which investigated it for one year to see if it was proper to separate Christian principles from government. Here is what the report concluded: "At the time of the adoption of the Constitution, the universal sentiment was that Christianity should be encouraged and not any one denomination. Christianity was the religion of the founders of this republic, and they expected it to be to their descendents. The thing that holds our system together is the clear doctrines and truths of the Gospel of Jesus Christ."[32] In other words, Christianity is the foundational cement that holds this nation together.

Such was the case until the 1947 *Everson v. Board of Education* case in which the courts ruled for the first time that the First Amendment was written to protect the government from the church instead of the church from the government.[33] It was only 15 years later when the unthinkable occurred. For the first time, Christian principles were judicially removed from our educational institutions when the Supreme Court made it unconstitutional for our children to be led in prayer while at school.[34] As attorney David Barton observes, "The removal of school prayer was the first visible manifestation of a war on all public religious expression; it provided the judicial 'toehold' needed to accomplish the subsequent extraction of other beliefs and practices rooted in religious teachings which has long been held as fundamental to national behavior and thus national policy. Where school prayer is found, it is not surprising also to find the Bible, the Ten Commandments, traditional moral teaching, etc. Conversely, where there is an absence of prayer, it is not surprising that there is also an absence of Biblical principles or traditional values."[35] From that time on, the snowball has continued to gain momentum, and we now find ourselves in the midst of a moral avalanche.

When President George W. Bush was elected in 2002, he immediately tried to implement faith-based initiatives, not unlike those that Jefferson lobbied for more than 200 years earlier. He saw the benefit of bringing together all faiths to join the government in fighting the moral and social problems facing our nation. It was a lightning rod that soon faded on the political horizon like a darting meteorite.

In 1811, the Supreme Court affirmed in *The People v. Ruggles* that "We are a Christian people, and the morality of the country is deeply engrafted upon Christianity, and not upon the doctrines of worship of those imposters."[36] In today's politically correct environment, can you imagine calling other religions "imposters"?

In 1844, the case of *Vidal v. Girard's Executors* reached the Supreme Court when Stephen Girard left his estate to the city of Philadelphia for the establishment of a college. In his will, Girard made it clear that the professors of this newly founded college were to instill principles of morality in the students, but with no references to the Bible or

Christianity. The unanimous decision handed down by our Supreme Court reads as follows: "It is unnecessary for us, to consider the establishment of a school or college, for the propagation of . . . Deism or any other form of infidelity. Such a case is not to be presumed to exist in a Christian country."[37] Once again, the court affirmed that all other religions are infidelities compared to Christianity. Keep in mind, these are not right-wing extremists or religious fanatics. These are rational, highly educated, thinking men sitting on the judicial bench and ruling according to the foundational principles of our nation and in accordance with the Constitution. Are you still wondering, "How did we get from where we were then to where we are now?" Good question. For about 160 years, it was not even an issue. In fact, in 1782 the United States Congress said, "The Congress of the United States approves and recommends to the people the Holy Bible for use in the schools."[38] But, that was then and this is now.

A DEFINING MOMENT

While many might point to the Supreme Court's removal of prayer from the schools as being the watershed decision for political correctness, it actually happened 15 years earlier. In 1947, *Everson v. Board of Education* proved to be the landmark case in which the Court prohibited the state of New Jersey from expending tax dollars for religious education. It had been well over a century and a half since the term "separation of church and state" had been invoked in a judicial setting. Yet, Justice Hugo Black not only reinstated the term, but also reinterpreted the term by saying, "A wall of separation between church and state must be kept high and impregnable." This, according to Justice Black, was intended "not only to keep the states' hands out of religion, but to keep religion's hands off the state, and above all, to keep bitter religious controversy out of public life by denying to every denomination any advantage from getting control of public policy or the public purse."[39]

To give further insight into this man's thinking, he wrote, "The 'establishment of religion' clause of the First Amendment means at least this: Neither a state nor the Federal Government can set up a church. Neither can pass laws, which aid one religion, aid all religion, or prefer one religion over another. Neither can force nor influence a person to go to or to remain away from church against his will or force him to profess a belief or disbelief in any religion. No person can be punished for entertaining or professing religious beliefs or disbeliefs, for church attendance or non-attendance. No tax in any amount large or small, can be levied to support any religious activities or institutions, whatever they may be called, or whatever form they may adopt to teach or practice religion. Neither a state nor the Federal Government can, openly or secretly, participate in the affairs of any religious organization or groups and vice versa. In the words of Jefferson, the clause against establishment of religion by law was intended to erect 'a wall of separation between church and state.'"[40]

How could Justice Black ignore 160 years of history? According to this ruling, religion is to be sequestered from public life. Faith is private and should not influence our laws. From this one pivotal moment in our history came the removal of the Ten Commandments from state buildings, the removal of prayer from public schools, and the challenge to anything that smells or looks like religious overtones on school campuses. Had this law been in place during the 1770s, most of our founding fathers would have been in violation of it. At least, this was a travesty and misuse of the judicial system and, at most, a gross misrepresentation of historical facts. University of Chicago law professor Philip Hamburger gives an insightful look into the mind of Hugo Black. He says, "You can't understand the period when Justice Black was on the court without understanding the fear American elites had of Catholic influence and power."[41] It is Professor Hamburger's claim that Justice Black's anti-Catholic bias was due to his former membership in the Ku Klux Klan, which was known for its anti-Catholic stand. Hamburger's conclusion is that Justice Black was not so much interested in building a wall between church and state, as he desired to build a wall between the Catholic Church and the rest of society.[42]

In refutation of Justice Black's biased ruling, Supreme Court Chief Justice William Rehnquist said, "There is simply no historical foundation for the proposition that the framers intended to build a wall of separation. The wall of separation between church and state is a metaphor based on bad history, a metaphor which has proved useless as a guide to judging. It should be frankly and explicitly abandoned."[43]

If Chief Justice Rehnquist is too conservative for your taste, then try Chief Justice Earl Warren, who was not particularly known for his right-wing stance. Indeed, he was regarded as a liberal and often called a "Communist pinko." Yet, in 1954 he gave this assessment of our nation's Christian heritage: "I believe no one can read the history of our country without realizing the Good Book and the Spirit of the Savior have from the beginning been our guiding geniuses . . . whether we look to the First Charter of Virginia, or to the Charter of New England, or to the Charter of Massachusetts Bay, or the Fundamental Orders of Connecticut. The same object is present; a Christian land governed by Christian principles. I believe the entire Bill of Rights came into being because of the knowledge our forefathers had of the Bible, and their belief in it; freedom of belief, of expression, of assembly, of petition, the dignity of the individual, the sanctity of the home, equal justice under the law, and the reservation of powers to the people. I like to believe we are living today in the spirit of the Christian religion. I like also to believe that as long as we do so, no great harm can come to our country."[44]

Wow, those are strong words coming from the former chief justice. Sadly, the damage has already been done, and the political correctness snowball continues to gain momentum. President George W. Bush said, "America is a nation that values our relationship with the Almighty. We need common-sense judges who understand that our rights were derived from God."[45] Well said, Mr. President. Only time will tell if the Bush appointments of Chief Justice John Roberts and Justice Samuel Alito will help turn the tide. Take heart. It is possible to overturn this ruling just as slavery was eventually outlawed. In the meantime, the cultural war rages out of control.

POLITICAL CORRECTNESS OVER THE TOP

America's cultural war is never more intense or more in focus than at Christmastime. This was especially true during the Christmas of 2005 when the traditional greeting of "Merry Christmas" became a huge issue. To avoid offending patrons, retailers enforced a "Happy Holidays" substitute that employees were required to embrace. Wal-Mart caught a lot of heat for yielding to these secularists. In fact, they reversed their policy in the following year so that patrons in 2006 were greeted with "Merry Christmas." The city of New York banned all nativity scenes in its public schools during the Christmas season. Macy's department stores banned the word "Christmas" from their ads and store displays. A fourth grader in Ephrata, Pennsylvania, was prohibited from handing out religious Christmas cards to classmates. Two middle-school students in Rochester, Minnesota, were disciplined for wearing red and green scarves in a Christmas skit.[46]

In December 2001, Thomas Elementary School in Plano, Texas, was getting ready to hold its annual winter party for students. Parents were asked to bring supplies and food, but they should only bring white napkins, white paper plates and cups. Even the cupcakes were to only be frosted in white. Red and green, the colors of Christmas, were not allowed lest someone be offended.[47] Give me a break! You've got to be kidding! Are there actually people in this country who would be offended by the red frosting on a cupcake? Get a life! It only gets better. Check out a few of these examples:

• The public display of Christmas trees was prohibited in Eugene, Oregon because to city officials "Christmas" meant "Christianity."[48] They failed to recognize that hostility to religion is just as unconstitutional as the official establishment of religion.

• The Christmas tree in the atrium of the Indiana Law School had to come down because "The law school is committed to diversity and the tree was divisive and inappropriate. There were individuals who believed that the tree sent the wrong message to the law school community and would make some people feel excluded."[49] Ironically, a few blocks away a huge Christmas tree stood inside the state capital building in Indianapolis . . . where the state Supreme Court is located.[50]

- In December 2002, an order from the school district offices canceled a grade-school field trip to see the Dickens classic *A Christmas Carol,* stating that the religious content was inappropriate. Humbug! I don't recall Ebenezer Scrooge or the ghosts of Christmas being all that religious. In December of 2004 in the same school district, instrumental versions of Christmas music were banned in the schools.[51] God forbid that someone might be softly singing the words to "Away In A Manger."

- In December 2003 in Baldwin City, Kansas, Santa Claus was banned from the city schools. You see, the man who played Santa happened to be an assistant pastor at Grace Community Church. The ACLU claimed that he used his access to kids to proselytize Christianity. Here is what happened. Santa would make his round of "ho-hos," and then he would ask, "Who can tell me why we celebrate Christmas?" Somebody would say, "It's Jesus' birthday." Santa would reply, "That's exactly right. It's traditionally been the reason we celebrated Christmas. You know if we didn't celebrate Jesus' birthday, you and your teachers would probably be in school the next two weeks instead of getting ready to go out on holiday."[52] The "J" word was the death knell.

- Ah yes, the "J" word. There is something about that name. In May of 1995, Judge Samuel B. Kent of the U.S. District Court for the Southern District of Texas decreed that any student uttering the word "Jesus" would be arrested and incarcerated for six months. His ruling stated, "And make no mistake, the court is going to have a United States marshal in attendance at the graduation. If any student offends this court, that student will be summarily arrested and will face up to six months incarceration in the Galveston County Jail for contempt of court. Anyone who thinks I'm kidding about this order better think again . . . Anyone who violates these orders, no kidding, is going to wish that he or she had died as a child when this court gets through with it."[53]

- Connecticut law enforcement officials threatened to arrest a man for corrupting the morals of a minor if they could prove that he passed out religious tracts to a student.[54] Since when has the Gospel corrupted the morals of a teenager?

- A teacher in Denver, Colorado was forced by the principal to remove his personal Bible from his desk where he kept it to read during silent time. School officials didn't want that book in the students' sight, so the teacher had to hide it during the day. The same principal proceeded to remove the Bible from the school library.[55]

- Following Columbine's massacre in 1999, my family and I walked through the halls of the school where the shootings took place. As a memorial to the 13 who were slain, 2,100 painted tiles decorated the halls. Unfortunately, 90 had to be removed because they contained "offensive" messages such as "God is Love" and "4/20/99 Jesus Wept."[56]

All of these decisions were made in good faith, believing that to do otherwise would be unconstitutional.

WHAT DOES "UNCONSTITUTIONAL" MEAN?

For anything to be ruled unconstitutional, it simply means that the founding fathers would have opposed it. That's why it is important to study past cases where similar precedents have been established. For example, in a case prior to 1962, the courts cited 87 precedents to confirm the necessity of biblical principles in government and schools. Yet, when prayer was removed from our schools in 1962, the court cited zero legal precedents. It referenced previous legal cases but zero historical evidence.[57] Think about it. The highest court in our land, which is charged with upholding the Constitution, was itself acting unconstitutionally. Without any legal or historical base, a new direction was taken, and America has never been the same.

Since then, our public schools have become spiritual war zones. The primary problems with students back in the 1950s were chewing gum in class, running in the halls, and littering. Today, the top problems are suicide, teenage pregnancy, alcohol, drugs, rape, and vandalism. Listen to this. In 1946, the Board of Education in Dallas, Texas, printed a textbook that was a required credit for graduation. Some of the questions in the book included:

- "Who was Christ before He was born on earth?"

- "What titles did John apply to Christ?"

- "For what purpose was John sent by God?"

- "Name five things the angel told Mary concerning her son, Jesus."

- "What does the word 'Jesus' mean?"

- "How did the angel explain the miraculous birth of Jesus?"

- "Memorize the pre-existence of Christ, John 1:1-14."[58]

In fact, the earlier courts said that a community could not have a school if it did not teach the Bible. Yet, when the court kicked the Bible out of public schools in 1963, here was its rationale: "If parts of the New Testament were read to the students without explanation, they could be psychologically harmful to the child."[59]

Ironically, in 1892, the NEA issued this statement in response to religion and education: "If the study of the Bible is to be excluded from all state schools, if the principles of Christianity are to have no place in the daily program, if the worship of God is to form no part of the general exercises of these public elementary schools, then the good of the state would be better served by restoring all schools to church control."[60] The NEA was basically saying, "If we ever get to the place where we fail to teach the Bible to our young children and fail to worship the God of the Bible in our daily classrooms, we had better allow the churches to have control of the education of our children."

When a nation exchanges the truth for the lie, right becomes wrong, and wrong becomes right. We live in an upside-down, topsy-turvy culture. This means that when you stand for biblical principles, you will sound like a voice crying in the wilderness. Be prepared to be misunderstood, reviled, slandered, and persecuted. Light repels darkness. It's like a huge rock in your front yard. If it is pushed aside, the little insects underneath scurry for cover. They feel uncomfortable when the sunlight shines upon them. The bugs feel more comfortable living in darkness than in the light.

Similarly, the air in a room can appear to be clean until the rays from the sun shine through the window. That is when you see particles of dust floating in the air. The sun did not produce the dust. It merely exposed it. Likewise, when Christians allow the light of Christ to shine through them, it can sometimes make an ungodly culture feel uncomfortable. The light of God's Word rebukes those who are comfortable in their sin and think they are clean. Restoring His truth is what our culture needs, but it is the very thing that is met with resistance. His truth unsettles and causes discomfort as it confronts the reality of our wickedness. And above all, we don't want to be inconvenienced with feelings of discomfort. So, we continue to anesthetize ourselves with busy schedules, glitzy cars, fancy houses, manicured lawns, luxurious vacations, and chemical substances. We would rather deaden the pain than face the reality that the wages of sin is death.

Much more could be said, but when Noah Webster wrote his *History of the United States,* he summed it up by stating, "Almost all the civil liberty now enjoyed in the world owes its origin to the principles of the Christian religion . . . the religion which has introduced civil liberty is the religion of Christ, and His Apostles, which enjoins humility, piety, and benevolence; which acknowledges in every person a brother or sister and a citizen with equal rights. This is genuine Christianity, and to this we owe our free constitutions of government."[61]

French philosopher Alexis de Tocqueville came to the United States decades ago searching for the explanation as to why America was the greatest nation on earth. He said, "I sought for the greatness and strength of America in her commodious harbors and ample rivers, but I didn't find it there. In her rich mines and worldwide commerce, but I didn't find it there. In her boundless prairies and fertile fields, but I didn't find it there. Not until I stepped inside her churches and found her pulpits aflame with righteousness did I discover the source of America's strength." He concluded, "America is good. And as long as America is good, America will be great. But when America ceases to be good, then she will cease to be great."[62] One can only wonder what Tocqueville's assessment of America would be today.

CHAPTER 5

America's Favorite Pastime

Any discussion of the erosion of America's moral fiber would not be complete without considering the influence of the media. The purpose of this book is not to explore all the contributing factors for why we are in a moral freefall. *Truth Decay's* intent is to expose *the one* big factor: the abdication of absolutes in lieu of moral relativism and the positive spin that relativism deceptively puts on the hot-button moral issues of our day. The disregard for absolute truth has been America's defining moment in exchanging the truth of God for the lie. The "big lie," the exchange of God's truth for moral relativism, is the hub from which all other lies proceed.

One of the major instruments in the assault on moral absolutes is the media. I am not oblivious to the fact that many will not agree with my assessment. Some will defend the media by saying that the demise of moral absolutes has had a negative effect on the media instead of the media contributing to the demise of moral absolutes. No doubt, a strong case can be made for both sides of the argument. Nevertheless, it is difficult to deny the correlation between the media and the ensuing decline in national morality. The statistics speak for themselves.

Television is the singly most-shared experience in our society. We are TV addicts. It is our drug of choice. More than 98% of all households have at least one television set.[1] In fact, more American households have televisions than have indoor plumbing.[2] Unbelievably, more families own a television than own a telephone.[3] The average household in America has the television turned on 49 hours a week. If children are around, it climbs to 59 hours a week.[4] The average teenager watches 22 hours per week, and (depending on age and gender) the average adult watches between 27 and 42 hours per week.[5] Research also shows that the average MTV viewer consumes five hours of music videos a day.[6]

A Detroit newspaper made an offer to 120 families in the city. Each family was promised $500 if they would agree to not watch TV for one month. Ninety-three families turned down the offer. Of the 27 families that agreed, five were studied and reported on in a magazine article. Each family had been watching television between 40 and 70 hours a week. That's between 5.7 and 10 hours a day. You can imagine this was a huge adjustment for them. After the month concluded, the families admitted the experience brought them closer together. More communication took place. Creativity was enhanced, and there was an observable increase in the level of patience family members displayed toward each other. This experiment introduced an intriguing consideration. We should not only be concerned about the behavior watching hours upon hours of television produces, but also in the behavior it prevents.[7]

A guest speaker for a youth group was trying to illustrate how powerful the media's influence has been upon the Christian community, so he asked the group, "Who's the character in *Seinfeld* with the funny hair?" Everybody's hand went up and a chorus of voices resounded, "Kramer!" Next question, "What time does *Friends* come on?" Again, the youth group shouted "Eight! Thursday night. NBC." "Complete this line from the movie, *Spiderman*: 'With great power comes . . .'" "Great responsibility!" came the unison reply of 70 students. "Now, someone tell me the difference between rap and hip-hop." After a brief pause, several students began to enthusiastically give the distinctions and identified their favorite artists in the process.

"OK," the speaker said, "Let's change gears a bit. Who was the prophet in the Old Testament who had no hair?" Silence. "What hour of the day did Jesus die on the cross?" Again, silence. "Complete this line from Proverbs 3: 'Trust in the Lord with all your heart and . . .'" "Obey Him?" came the reply. By now, the silence of this college youth group was deafening.[7] No doubt, this scenario could be repeated many times over in your own community. Media saturation is an epidemic and big business. Advertisers paid $75,000 *per second* in the 2005 Super Bowl for the privilege of putting their products before the eyes of 130 million viewers in the United States and five times that many viewers throughout the world.[9]

To put the problem in perspective, consider the fact that on school nights teenagers spend three hours per night watching the tube.[10] That may not seem like a big deal until you consider that the same teenagers spend only 54 minutes on homework, less then 16 minutes reading, 14 minutes with their mothers, and five minutes with their fathers.[11] Something is wrong with that picture. So, what do you think our kids are watching during those three hours? Nearly 61% of all television programming contains violence, with children's programming being the most violent.[12] By the end of grade school, the average child will have seen 8,000 murders and 100,000 acts of violence.[13] By the time he or she graduates from high school that number will have doubled.[14]

Prime-time family hour on television contains more than eight sexual incidents per hour. In fact, each year teens are inundated with 15,000 sexual references, with less than 170 of them referring to abstinence, birth control, or sexually transmitted diseases (STDs). Seventy percent of all primetime programming contains alcohol and drugs. For every anti-drug commercial on television, there are between 25 and 50 slick beer commercials that portray alcohol favorably. Advertising executives are paid big bucks and will spend $2 billion to produce the most eye-catching commercials on TV for the purpose of luring our kids to "drink up and live it up."[15]

Who are these "behind-the-scenes" people who pump this sewage into our homes? Let's face facts: everybody has a worldview. It is the lens through which we see our world. It causes us to integrate all of the information that comes into our lives and put it into a unified picture of reality. A worldview is a philosophy of life by which the facts of life are interpreted. For example, Christians have a biblical worldview by affirming that the Bible is our ultimate authority on how we should conduct our lives. As Christians, we believe the Bible is the inerrant record of God's revelation to man and is the source of all truth. We believe that the holy Scriptures contain specific guidelines for living that are timeless and transcend all cultures. The Bible is the filter through which Christians are to see the world.

Sociologists surveyed more than 100 of Hollywood's most influential writers to determine their worldview. The ideological beliefs of Hollywood's most elite writers revealed that:

- 93% seldom or never go to worship services.

- 97% believe in abortion.

- 95% support homosexuality.

- 84% see nothing wrong with adultery.

- 99% believe that television should be more critical of Judeo-Christian values.[16]

Believe it or not, Hollywood has not always been such a cesspool of filth. During its early days, Hollywood's self-imposed standards of moral restraint were designed to uphold the biblical values the nation embraced. The industry actually created a committee called the Hays Association that checked every film for blasphemy, filthy language, explicit eroticism, violence, ethnic slurs, and anti-American sentiment.[17]

Here is a summation of the Hays Code:

- Brutal killings are not to be presented in detail.[18]

- Theft, robbery, safe cracking, and dynamiting of trains, mines, buildings, etc. should not be detailed in method. The use of firearms should be restricted to essentials; methods of smuggling should not be presented.[19]

- Illegal drug trafficking must never be presented.[20]

- The sanctity of the institution of marriage and the home shall be upheld.[21]

- Adultery, sometimes necessary plot material, must not be explicitly treated or justified, or presented attractively.[22]

- Scenes of passion should not be introduced when not essential to the plot.[23]

- Seduction or rape should never be more than suggested, and only when essential for the plot, and even then never shown by explicit method.[24]

- Sexual perversion or inference of it is forbidden.[25]

- Obscenity in words, gesture, reference, song, joke, or by suggestion is forbidden.[26]

- Pointed vulgarity or vulgar expressions, however used, are forbidden.[27]

- Complete nudity is never permitted. This includes nudity in fact, or in silhouette, or any licentious notice by other characters in the picture.[28]

- No film or episode may throw ridicule on any religious faith.[29]

- Ministers of religion, in their character as such, should not be used as comic characters or as villains.[30]

Consider these classics that were produced under the Hays Code: *It's a Wonderful Life, Sergeant York, The Grapes of Wrath, Mr. Smith Goes to Washington, Mutiny on the Bounty, Moby Dick, Gone with the Wind, Citizen Kane, Watch on the Rhine, For Whom the Bell Tolls, Casablanca, A Tree Grows in Brooklyn, Miracle on 34th Street, Key Largo, All the King's Men, East of Eden, High Noon,* and on the list goes. Indeed, this was Hollywood's "Golden Age." Contrast the Hays Code with this comment from a recent Oscar-winning writer and director: "The more realistic the violence and the steamier the sex, the more likely you will be to forget you are watching a film."[31]

Do you know what is really sad? During the 2004-2005 TV season, Nielson Media Research claimed that one of the highest-rated television shows among 12- to 17-year-old girls was *Will and Grace,* whose main characters engaged in homosexual, bi-sexual, and/or lesbian sexual relationships. For boys in the same age group it was *The Simpsons,* a cartoon whose characters often undermine parental authority.[32]

Keep in mind, television is just one small slice of the media pie. Every year there are more than 4 billion video rentals, and almost 2 billion subscribers watched a pay-per-view program last year.[33] Teens in grades seven through twelve, listen to 10,500 hours of rock music per year.[34] That is less than the total number of hours spent in the classroom from kindergarten to graduation. Thirty-nine percent of teens own personal computers and more than 68% have access to the Internet.[35] The average time spent on the Internet is three hours per day.[36]

Through the Internet, pornography is readily available with just a click of a button. Porn is now a $12 billion business in the United States. That is more than the National Football League (NFL), the National Basketball Association (NBA), and Major League Baseball combined.[37] Richard Land, president of the Christian Life Commission, believes porn is now destroying more lives than the 4,000 babies that are being aborted each day. Contrary to what he believed in the past, he is now persuaded that porn is the number one social concern facing America. There are 4.2 million pornographic Web sites and 372 million pornographic pages generating 68 million search engine requests each day.[38]

In over 1,000 studies, it has been shown there is a connection between media violence and aggressive behavior in kids.[39] Likewise, in a study of 1,792 teenagers ages 12 through 17, it was shown that watching sexual behavior on television influences teens to actually engage in sexual activity.[40] A 2004 study by the RAND Corporation, published in *Pediatrics*, shows the clear connection between what is viewed by the teen and what is practiced: "Teens who watch a lot of sexualized programming are twice as likely to engage in sexual intercourse themselves. The impact of television viewing is so large that even a moderate shift in the sexual content of adolescent TV watching could have a substantial affect on their sexual behavior."[41]

The media defends itself by saying they are only creating what people want to buy. They are merely reflecting the morals embraced by society. That's like arguing, "Which came first, the chicken or the egg?" The reality is we have become immune to the effects. A steady diet of this stuff will impact anybody's life. When you add the violent and perverse content of many video games into the mix, the combined result is a recipe for cultural disaster. Some may consider this viewpoint as "out of step" with the times. We have been so brainwashed and hypnotized by this powerful medium that it has become a way of life. We're addicted.

In his book, *Dismantling The Myths,* Frank Moore lists some of the dangers of the media. He says:

1. It offers a false view of reality by teaching that truth is relative; true meaning in life comes from materialism; and we are entitled to immediate gratification.

2. It presents celebrities as heroes.

3. It tends to destroy self-esteem and self-worth by presenting beauty as a requirement for personal worth and ownership of possessions as a requirement for self-importance.

4. It makes life boring and results in reduced attention spans.

5. It portrays Christians in a negative light and often defames ministers. Rock music especially incorporates religious language in its lyrics with an unholy message.[42]

THE AMERICAN FAMILY

See if this describes anyone you know. Dad is trying to provide the "good life" for the family, so he is driven to work overtime and is preoccupied with his work even when he is home. Like any conscientious family, the parents want their kids to be well rounded which, by most definitions means being involved in three year-round sports programs, clubs, church, piano lessons, cheerleading, dance, and a part-time job. Mom becomes the chauffeur who shuttles the family tribe to all their activities while also maintaining her responsibilities of cooking, cleaning, washing clothes, and grocery shopping. This is not to mention the fact that approximately half of all mothers work outside the home, so eating a meal as a family unit is the exception rather than the norm in many households. Home has become a place to eat, sleep, and get ready for the next day. Home has become a hotel for family members who are, in reality, strangers to one another.

Consider the fact that teenagers are the most depressed group in America with one million of them wounded each year from the divorce of their parents.[43] The average marriage in America lasts seven years, and the typical father only gives 35 seconds of his undivided attention to the children each day.[44] Enter the make-believe world of television, the electronic anesthetic designed to deaden the pain of loneliness and isolation. Given the above scenario, it is understandable that 72% of families watch television every day, and of those families, 35% keep their TVs turned on *all* day . . . morning, noon, and night.[45] Interestingly, psychologists have found that the very thing intended to alleviate the depression is the very thing that actually intensifies the loneliness and depression.

As a kid growing up, I can remember coming home and playing sandlot baseball, football, or spending countless hours in the driveway or at the gym shooting hoops. My world revolved around sports. I always had an eye out for a pick-up basketball game or someone wanting to shag fly balls. Today, I continue to be amazed at the vacant basketball courts and how seldom I see youth playing outside. It's a different world than when I grew up. Today's teens retreat to their rooms, put on the headsets, and become absorbed in a world of high-tech toys and isolation. An unbelievable 47% of teens have a television in their room, and 80% of sixth- to ninth-graders rate their top afternoon activity as watching television.[46]

The fragmentation of the home, busyness of schedules, isolation, peer pressure, and blended families containing a new step-parent and step-siblings, have all combined to create an emotional upheaval within the lives of millions of teens. Many do not feel their parents care. Millions do not find a listening ear or even a hint of concern from their parents. It is no wonder teens are more likely to seek advice from a peer than from a parent.[47] Television becomes a temporary escape into a fantasy world that allows a person to forget his or her problems.

HEALTHY DIVERSION OR SUBTLE DESTRUCTION?

Given the emotional challenges of today's youth, it seems that television would be a God-sent blessing. It keeps children preoccupied and entertained while parents get on with their busy agendas. However, there is little censoring of what is watched by the children. Graphic violence, vulgar language, and explicit sex scenes dominate much of the airwaves.

Where religion is concerned, it seems that the media goes out of its way to express its own hostilities by portraying Christians as fanatics, psycho killers, or just plain idiots.

The average viewer will see about 14,000 references to sex every year, the vast majority of which occur between unmarried people.[48] Let's do the math. Between the ages of 10 and 20, a child will view 140,000 sex scenes on TV alone. The average soap opera includes two intimate sex acts per hour, 94% of which are between unmarried people.[49]

Remember when cartoons were clean and innocent? Today, they average 41 violent acts per hour. In fact, by 18 years of age, the average viewer has witnessed 250,000 violent acts, including 40,000 murders.[50]

Look, I am not advocating the life of a hermit or suggesting that Christians should retreat to monasteries in total isolation from the real world. My concern is this. If a 30-second commercial or a 20-second vignette of some movie star can influence the buying habits of millions, what kind of cumulative effect does watching 40,000 murders and 140,000 sex scenes have on a teenager's brain that is still developing and on his or her worldview that is still formulating? One 20-year study, conducted by Drs. L. Rowell Huesman and Leonard Eron at the University of Illinois, found that eight-year-olds who watched significant amounts of television violence were consistently more likely to commit violent crimes or engage in child or spousal abuse by the age of 30.[51] Dr. Nuchapart Venbrux of Pennsylvania State University College of Medicine studied the effects of television on 1,100 elementary school children. She found a direct correlation between the amount of television children watched and their violent behavior. The heavier the viewing time, the more aggressive and impulsive the children became.[52]

WHAT DOES THE BIBLE SAY?

Well, you won't find a *TV Guide* within the pages of the Bible, but you will find a guide for life. In the days of Noah, there was a preoccupation with violence, sex, and the abuse of chemical substances. The thoughts of man were continually evil, and God was compelled to destroy the world. It is more than a little disconcerting that the same three trends that once brought about the destruction of the earth now dominate the entertainment industry. Consider the following passages:

Ephesians 5:3-5 states, "But fornication and all uncleanness or covetousness, let it not even be named among you, as is fitting for saints; neither filthiness, nor foolish talking, nor coarse jesting, which are not fitting, but rather giving of thanks. For this you know, that no fornicator, unclean person, nor covetous man, who is an idolater, has any inheritance in the kingdom of Christ and God."

The root word for "foolish talk" is "moros," which refers to gutter talk. Need we say any more? From the cursing on television to the repulsive f-word in the movies to the blasphemous lyrics of many contemporary musicians, this biblical principal is violated most. "Coarse jesting" in its original Greek usage refers to sexual innuendos.[53] Movies and music aren't the only ones propagating sexual innuendos. Advertisers use sex to sell everything from toothpaste to automobiles.

The blood and gore of violence is also a blockbuster attraction at theaters. Violence seems to have a numbing effect upon the conscience causing the viewer to tolerate scenes today that would have been prohibitive and repulsive ten years ago. Proverbs 13:2 says, "But the soul of the unfaithful feeds on violence." Proverbs 4:14–17 says, "Do not enter the path of the wicked, and do not walk in the way of evil. Avoid it, do not travel on it; . . . For they eat the bread of wickedness, and drink the wine of violence." The simple observation here is that those who promote violence are described as evil and wicked. Psalm 11:5 declares, "The Lord tests the righteous, but the wicked and the one who loves violence His soul hates." The person who claims to love God and loves graphic violence as well has a problem with the God he or she claims to love.

AN ASSAULT ON THE MIND

As Christians, we are admonished to cultivate the mind of Christ (Philippians 2:5), and the fruit of the Spirit listed in Galatians 5:22-24 is an outgrowth of His mind. This includes love, joy, peace, longsuffering, kindness, goodness, faithfulness, gentleness, and self-control. These are the character qualities resulting from walking with God. Seldom do we see these portrayed on television or in the movies. However, Galatians 5:19-21 mentions the results of not walking with God: adultery, fornication, uncleanness, lewdness, idolatry, sorcery (drugs), hatred, contentions, jealousies, outbursts of wrath, selfish ambitions, dissensions, heresies, envy, murders, drunkenness, revelries, and the like. Many of these are the very things that dominate television and popular movies today.

To expose oneself to a secular worldview for hours at a time, day after day, will inevitably impact the Christian in a negative way. He or she will inevitably compromise their standards, justify their watered-down morality, and rationalize their behavior by pointing to other Christian examples. However, the Bible is the standard by which to judge right and wrong. Ephesians 2:3 describes the Christian's B.C. (Before Christ) days by saying that "we all once conducted ourselves in the lusts of the flesh, fulfilling the desires of the flesh and of the mind, . . ." He goes on to say that once we have received Christ into our lives, we are to put off those former things.

The issue for Christians is who will control your mind. Here lies the battlefield. It is an internal war that is constant. But here's the deal. Romans 12:2 says, "And do not be conformed to this world, but be transformed by the renewing of your mind, that you may prove what is that good and acceptable and perfect will of God." God has a plan for every person. His plan is good, acceptable, and perfect. Jeremiah 29:11 says, "For I know the thoughts that I think toward you, says the Lord, thoughts of peace and not of evil, to give you a future and a hope." God's future for each of His children is awesome and filled with optimistic hope. However, to see His plan unfold requires a renewing of the mind, which also requires a commitment *not* to be conformed to this world's value system. Let me be quick to say that Christianity is not about obeying a bunch of rules, and God is not a celestial killjoy who has come to rain on your parade. He loves you and wants only the best for you. However, to allow our minds to be assaulted daily by a value system that we know is diabolically opposed to Jesus Christ is to set ourselves up for a great fall. Balance seems to be the key. A daily study of His Word, coming into His presence in prayer, hanging out with friends who reinforce God's standards, worshipping the Lord regularly, listening to godly music, and developing a mentoring relationship with a mature Christian are some of the safeguards that a conscientious Christian needs in his or her life. Apart from these spiritual disciplines, any Christian is vulnerable to the criticism of being a hypocrite.

SOMETHING TO DIE FOR

A steady diet of the wrong kind of media will deplete one's passion for the things of God. Consequently, we have a generation of young people who all too often lack the passion to pour their lives into anything. Keep in mind, this is the first generation of latchkey youth to emerge into adulthood, 50% of whom are the products of divorce. They have been virtually reared by an electronic babysitter. They have been called Generation X because they have no distinctive style, sports, or activities. Even their music does not really distinguish them from other generations; it is often remakes of tunes from previous decades. In contrast to their parents pre-occupation with image, Generation X-ers embrace the grunge look of oversized flannel shirts, sloppy hair, and worn, tattered jeans. They lack a purpose for living. Many are disillusioned by the hypocrisy they see in the church. Many of them still come to church, but they sit in the back and roll their eyes at the youth leader who is trying too hard to be cool. What seems to be the problem? I fear we are oblivious to the fact that our kids have been kidnapped by the media. We don't need to simply give them something to live for, but something to die for. The life that Jesus offers is greater than anything we could ever create on our own. We have been assigned the task of transferring it to this generation. Moral relativism does not hold the answer to their soul-searching questions.

THE CHRISTIAN'S RESPONSE TO HOLLYWOOD

It is all too easy for Christians to blast Hollywood as being a modern day Sodom and Gomorrah that is beyond saving. Christians who are Hollywood insiders tell us that such an attitude has only created a greater rift between the entertainment industry and the evangelical community.

Certainly, it is important that we understand the depravity and the negative influence the entertainment industry is having upon our culture. The statistics we have seen bear this out. However, we cannot have such a narrow, judgmental mind-set that causes us to appear hateful. Hollywood is a mission field. It's the world's most influential mission field. If we minister to Hollywood, we will be impacting the entire world.

Karen Covell is a television producer in Hollywood and an evangelical Christian who is the director of the Hollywood Prayer Network. She makes a persuasive case for sending our children to Hollywood as missionaries. She correctly observes that "the church lifts up and celebrates young people who feel called to go to Africa, China, and the far reaches of India. Are these places any safer or more blessed by God than Hollywood? The Los Angeles Film Studies Center offers a semester program to students through the Council for Christian Colleges and Universities. Young people have the opportunity to intern with companies like Miramax, Universal, and Sony while living in a supportive Christian community. Is this any less valuable or holy than learning how to farm with a family in China?"[54]

While all of us within the Christian ranks would like for Hollywood to produce cleaner and more family-oriented entertainment, we must understand the only way that is going to happen is by changing the hearts of the producers. It will not happen through protests or boycotts. God did not send His Son to condemn Hollywood, but that Hollywood—through Him—might be saved.

The media has managed to rob kids of their innocence. More importantly, adults have allowed themselves to be duped into believing a false message and a value system that is morally bankrupt. All too often parents send their children to their rooms to watch television, surf the Internet, or listen to their music. By failing to censor their child's viewing and listening habits, they are partially to blame for the moral outcome of that child. I understand that we parents catch enough heat and shoulder more than our share of "guilt trips" whenever our kids step out of line. However, we shouldn't be surprised when arrogant attitudes surface, bad language spews out, or defiance toward authority is expressed, when the majority of their time is spent sitting in front of the television, blocking the world out with music blasting through headphones, surfing the Internet, or playing video games. This is the generation that will soon be parenting our grandchildren.

Let's look at some of the lies we are being fed by the culture, and the positive spin that moral relativism places on these six hot-button issues.

CHAPTER 6

The Danger of "Safe" Sex

Moral Relativism's Spin:
Safe Sex, Affairs, and Significant Others

A radio talk show host was addressing the subject of adultery and said, "We would like for any of you out there who have committed adultery to call in to the show. Let's discuss that experience on our show today." Fifteen minutes passed. Thirty minutes passed. The phone lines were dead, and the host was getting nervous. Finally, the host said, "If any of you out there have had an affair, call in, and let's discuss it." Immediately, the phones started ringing and a lively discussion ensued. Coincidence? No, it is one more example of how moral relativism has impacted our society. We are too sophisticated and too tolerant to call sexual sin "adultery." "An affair" sounds so much more in step with the times than old-fashioned "adultery." We don't call people who steal "thieves." It sounds better to call them "embezzlers." A person who is addicted to alcohol is no longer a "drunkard" but is instead classified as an "alcoholic." These euphemisms put a positive spin on sin, but the consequences remain as negative as ever.

Everyone has a different opinion on what is right and wrong. "My truth" is different from "your truth." "Truth, for me, is whatever I decide it to be," declares the post-modern thinker. The attitude is, "If you think that sex outside of marriage is wrong, that's fine. I have no problem with that. Just don't say it's wrong for everyone." It seems the greatest sin today is to claim to be right about anything. We tolerate everything. In *The Closing of The American Mind,* Alan Bloom describes the effect relativism has had on this generation of students. In one of his courses at the University of Chicago, he asked the class to identify an evil person. No one could do so. Not one! They didn't even know what he meant by the term "evil."[1] I suppose we shouldn't be shocked by such a lack of response, but I cannot help but feel burdened knowing that today's youth do not recognize the existence of absolute moral principles which transcend time. Society proceeds to substitute its own standards for God's standards. Anybody with an IQ above plant life ought to be able to see that this insane experiment of tampering with God's truth is not working. For example, when teachers in the 1940s were asked to identify their top problems with students in public schools, the top three were: "talking out of turn, chewing gum, and making noise." Today's teachers tell us that the top concerns are: "drug and alcohol abuse, pregnancy, suicide, rape, robbery, and assault."[2] It is difficult to deny the correlation between the Judeo-Christian worldview of the 1940s and the cultural shift to moral relativism since the 1960s.

This shift in attitude is perhaps seen more clearly in the sexual mores of our society than in any other single area. Unlike the past, anything sexual is morally permissible as long as it involves consenting adults. In order to accommodate teenagers with this lenient standard, society bends the rules by saying, "These kids are going to have sex anyway, so we might as well teach them how to do it responsibly by giving them the resources, information, and contraceptives to eliminate the consequences. And by the way, if you accidentally do get pregnant, we can solve that by giving you an abortion."

Can you imagine what would happen if we adopted that same philosophy in dealing with America's drug problems? It would sound like this: "Well, our kids are going to take drugs anyway so we might as well make it safe for them. Let's establish drug clinics at our schools, pass out clean needles, and give our children safe places where they can get high." As ridiculous as that sounds, we've managed to do just that with the unsafe practice of premarital sex. If it is possible to "Just Say No" to illicit drugs, then it is also possible to say no to illicit sex. When the epidemic of lung cancer hit our nation, did we encourage people to practice safe smoking? Of course not. The government conveyed a strong message to the nation by intervening and banning cigarette commercials from television. Yet, when it comes to premarital sex our approach has been to throw contraceptives at the problem and teach sex education in our schools.

Practicing "safe sex" has become the justified terminology for engaging in fornication and adultery, two archaic terms by today's standards. Every day 8,000 teenagers in the United States become infected by a sexually transmitted disease (STD), accounting for one-quarter of the nation's sexually active teens. Think about it. This year alone, three million teenagers will become infected with a disease resulting from their sexual activity, and most STDs are incurable.[3] In the United States, more than 65 million people are currently living with an incurable STD. An additional 15 million people become infected with one or more STDs each year.[4] What we don't often hear is the fact that sexually active teens are less happy, more depressed, and more likely to attempt suicide than teens who are not sexually active.[5] It is no wonder that 67% of sexually experienced teens wish they had waited longer before becoming sexually active.[6]

The average age for first-time sex is less than 16 and the relationship will typically last less than four months. In fact, one-fourth of all adolescents who had their first sexual relationship did so in the first month of the relationship. Thirty-seven percent had sex in the first three months and 40% after four months.[7] Today's teens think the message of safe sex makes it all right.

COUNT THE COST

I dislike credit cards, but I carry one for gasoline, one for ministry purchases, and a MasterCard for family needs. They seem harmless enough, but during my 30 years of marriage there has been more than one occasion when I was surprised when the bill arrived. In today's world, it seems that everywhere you turn advertisers encourage you to buy now and pay later. It seems like more and more gas stations are implementing a "pay at the pump" policy . . . using a credit card. TV offers and radio programs all encourage instant purchase power by simply picking up the phone and rattling off the 15 or 16-digit number that appears on the plastic. What a great country! Using credit gives the illusion of saving time and money without adversely affecting your cash flow . . . until the bill comes. You see, you never really own anything until it's paid for. By that time, you're probably no longer enjoying it.

To add pain to the purchase, you are required to pay interest each month unless you pay your bill in full, which the majority of Americans do not. By the end of 12 or 24 month's worth of bills, the item you initially purchased may be broken, or at best, has lost its appeal. Yet, the bill still has to be paid. This is how millions of people get into financial trouble each year. They accumulate things without paying for them up front. The same is true with illicit sexual activity.

It is human nature to want to get rather than give, to want to have rather than go without. We hate paying the price and calculating the cost. I try not to be impulsive with my spending habits. However, there have been times when I went against my better judgment and made an expenditure I thought I couldn't live without. Weeks passed, and then the moment of truth arrived in the mail. I had completely forgotten about the purchase. I had managed to ignore it and felt ambushed when opening the bill. I had no one to blame but myself.

Sex is like a credit card. You can play now (the present payoff being sexual activity) and pay later (the adverse consequences discussed in this chapter) or you can pay now (sexual abstinence) and play later (sexual relationship in marriage). Abstaining from sex prior to marriage means you may be ridiculed, rejected, or put down. My daughter was a cheerleader in high school. One day the cheerleaders were taking a break from practice. Their coach was absent, so while sitting in a circle one of the girls asked, "How many of you have had sex?" With the exception of three girls, everyone's hand went up. The follow-up question was, "How many of you have had sex with more than one guy?" Again, the same hands went up. Melody was surprised and felt a little awkward by being in such an obvious minority. Yet, throughout her high school career she maintained a high standard of purity, endured some rejection from peers, but earned the respect of the entire school by being voted homecoming queen and Miss Etowah High. During lunch one day, she was sitting in the cafeteria and was approached by a guy with a notebook and pen. He said, "Melody, I am here representing the football team. We want to know what's up with you." "What do you mean?" she replied. "Well, we think you're one of the hottest girls in school, but you never date. We just want to know why. I'm supposed to take notes and report back to the team." My sweet daughter proceeded to give him a list of moral standards she had adopted and refused to compromise. The point is, there is a price to be paid for abstinence. Maintaining moral purity alleviates the fear of pregnancy, the danger of disease, the worry of what a future spouse may think, and the pain and guilt that so often accompanies immorality. It is liberating! God's boundaries are not about denying you the freedom to live but giving you the freedom to experience life in all of its fullness.

I like how Pam Stenzel describes it. She says, "It's always better to save your money and pay cash than to put off payments until later. It's always better to spend the extra money required to get the genuine, top-of-the-line authentic article. In sexual terms, that translates into saving yourself sexually for marriage. Be willing to invest yourself in the genuine, top-of-the-line authentic article. Yes, it means giving up any and all sexual activity right now, but the return you'll get on your investment will be greater than you ever imagined."[8] Pay now and play later.

In each moral topic addressed in this book, the lie is disguised with a positive spin that makes it more acceptable and attractive to the culture. For example, abortion is "pro-choice." Alcohol's mantra is "drink responsibly." Homosexuals march under the banner of "alternative lifestyle." For the adulterer and fornicator it is "safe sex."

The argument for safe sex sounds like this: "What two consenting adults do in the privacy of their bedroom is nobody else's business." Now that sounds logical. Hey, if a couple wants to get pregnant or contract a disease, then they're the ones to suffer the consequences, right? Wrong! It costs the federal and state governments an average of $100,000 in medical and welfare expenditures for every teenager who has a child.[9] Multiply that by one million each year. Twenty years ago the government spent $16.5 billion in welfare costs to support the families started by teenage mothers.[10] We are now spending in excess of $100 billion to pay for the private bedroom behavior of teenagers.[11]

The healthcare costs for AIDS patients are over $19 billion a year. When combined with other STDs, you are talking about paying $30 billion a year for the private acts of two consenting adults.[12] AIDS alone is costing insurance companies over $100 billion in claims each year.[13] Who do you think is paying for this? We are. Every year taxpayers are paying billions of dollars to underwrite the expenses of abortions, pregnancy counseling, welfare for unwed teenage mothers, and astronomical health insurance premiums. We, the taxpayers, are covering the costs incurred by those who are sexually promiscuous and morally irresponsible. Then, these "consenting adults" have the audacity to say that it is none of our business what they do. If I am footing the bill, then they have made it my business. We hear the same arguments coming from the abortionists. "It is the woman's right to choose," they indignantly scream. Listen up—loud and clear: *no one* has the right to choose to kill an innocent baby. It is the height of arrogance and injustice to murder a little baby because of self-centered, immoral choices and then turn around and ask us to pay for it.

HAS THE CONDOM SOLVED OUR PROBLEMS?

In an attempt to cover our sin and eliminate the consequences, we have created a latex savior designed to perpetuate society's immorality without paying the price of guilt and inconvenience. When the infamous condom came onto the scene, it was assumed that all worries about disease and pregnancy that stemmed from illicit sexual activity were now behind us. What an ingenious invention! Sexual sin without consequences, commonly known as "safe sex," was now made possible by the condom. Yet, to the dismay of safe sex advocates, 43% of the 3.3 million unplanned pregnancies each year happen to people using some method of birth control.[14] In fact, a 14-year-old girl faithfully using the pill has a 44% chance of getting pregnant at least once before she finishes high school. While on the pill, she has a 69% chance of getting pregnant at least once before she finishes college. But if using condoms, the likelihood of an unwanted pregnancy rises to nearly 87 percent.[15]

The Department of Health and Human Services reports, "One of

every five batches of condoms tested in a government inspection program over the last four months failed to meet minimum standards for
leaks."[16] Food and Drug Administration inspectors checked more than
150,000 samples from lots representing 120 million condoms. The
agents had to reject about one lot in ten because too many leaked. For
imported condoms, the rejection rate due to leakage was one in five
lots.[17]

As risky as condoms may sound for protecting against pregnancy, the
stakes are considerably higher when trying to prevent AIDS, because the
AIDS virus is 450 times smaller than a sperm. Most people are unaware
of the fact that condoms have microscopic holes of about .5 microns in
size. That's not a problem in preventing sperm from passing through, but
the HIV virus is only .1 micron in size. It is 50 times smaller than the
holes in latex condoms, and yet we are bombarded with the illusion that
condoms are synonymous with safe sex. Somebody is lying. Don't just
take my word for it. The Department of Education says, "A condom
must work ten times better. A woman is fertile roughly 36 days a year,
but someone with AIDS can transmit it 365 days a year."[18] Dr. Theresa
Crenshaw, past president of the American Association of Sex Educators,
Counselors, and Therapists, and a member of the Presidential AIDS
Commission says, "To say that use of condoms is 'safe sex' is in fact playing Russian roulette. A lot of people will die in this dangerous game."[19]
Dr. Malcolm Potts, president of Family Health International and one of
the inventors of condoms lubricated with spermicides, gives this analogy: "Telling a person who engages in high-risk behavior to use a condom
is like telling someone who is driving drunk to use a seat belt."[20]
Infectious disease specialist Robert Noble warns that using a condom is
about as effective as shooting a squirt gun at a four-alarm blaze. The
point these authorities are driving home is that "safe sex" is a lie designed
to create a false sense of security. When our youth are influenced by
teachers and other outside educators, not to mention parents, government officials, and youth workers who promote the "safe sex" message,
then we can expect nothing less than for them to trust these voices of
authority. Add to this the bombardment of television programming,
movies, and the cult heroes of teen idols in the world of music, most of

whom promote this lifestyle, and you have the recipe for this epidemic that we have been witnessing for the past 45 years.

IT GETS EVEN SCARIER

While the average person may have a few sex partners prior to marriage, that same individual would never think of having sex with hundreds of partners. Yet, to his or her uninformed mind, that is often what is happening when he or she slips under the covers with the lover who seems so fine and feels so right at the time. True story: a 16-year-old girl had sex with 16 guys, and as a result, she was responsible for 218 cases of gonorrhea and more than 300 cases of syphilis. How is that possible? The math works like this: those guys had sex with other people who also had sex with other people. The number of indirect contacts added up to 1,660. One can only shudder at the thought of that girl having AIDS instead of gonorrhea or syphilis.[21]

Are you still having difficulty with this? It's hard to grasp the enormous impact that one act of sex may have upon another unsuspecting partner. Former Surgeon General C. Everett Koop explained it like this: "It is a very frightening thing. Today if you have sexual intercourse with a woman, you are not only having sexual intercourse with her but with every person that woman might have had intercourse with for the last ten years and all of the people they had intercourse with."[22] It is a medical fact that you are bringing every sexual partner you've ever had, along with all their previous partners into the same bed when having sex with a person. Stop and think about the high price a person is paying for a brief few moments of sexual pleasure. Untold thousands of men and women get married without discussing each other's sexual history only to later experience the heartbreak of infertility, which comes with many of today's STDs. Think, for example, about the man who's had a one-time experience with a prostitute. The average prostitute in the United States has had sex with 2,000 men. While that man may unknowingly assume that he is having sex with that one prostitute, he could not be more misguided. He has just had sex with her, plus all of her partners for the past ten years—up to 12,000 people! What's so sad is that this same man will go home and eventually have sex with his precious wife, who is faithful to her husband and doesn't have a clue that he has been cheating. In total innocence, she makes love to her husband but is unaware that she is also having sex with the prostitute, plus her 2,000 partners, plus all their partners for the last ten years.[23] Or take the wife whose husband has been engaged in an ongoing affair. He repents, asks his wife's forgiveness, and comes back home to his family. However, from now on, when he has sex with his wife, he is subjecting her to the other woman's sexual history as well.

Or what about the wife who thinks flirting with her male co-worker is harmless fun? Then come long "business" lunches, late night "business" dinners, and "business" meetings at all hours of the day or night until one day the full-fledged affair comes to light, decimating the immoral woman's unsuspecting godly husband and kids.

While writing this chapter, I came across a bit of information on some entertainment show that said Charlie Sheen was boasting about having sex with 5,000 women! Using the above stats, that means whoever gets intimate with Sheen is also potentially having sex with 30,000 others at the same time.

Dr. Lawrence Laycob rightly observes, "When you're casual about sex, chances are the person you're casual with has been casual with someone else. So, there's a third, fourth, or twenty-fifth party out there that you have no knowledge of."[24] Is it just me or is there a strange silence regarding this information? Somebody is lying to us. Our kids' futures, their families, and the destiny of our nation are at stake.

This is no small issue, but it's another by-product of a politically correct agenda that exalts tolerance as the crowning virtue of the day. In a culture of moral relativism, everyone possesses his or her own truth and does whatever feels right to him or her. It is the perfect equation for moral anarchy and the collapse of a nation.

When you watch the track and field events in the Olympics, the thing that gives the competition meaning is the fact that there are lanes to run in and rules to follow. Otherwise, everybody would be running in different directions doing their own thing. It would be mass confusion. Without these parameters, no one can win. Likewise, God has given us rules to follow. His rules are not given to cramp our style, but because He wants us to win. Our nation is in a moral freefall and state of confusion because we have thrown out God's rulebook, the Bible, and substituted our own rules. The insanity of it all is that no one can say whose standard is right. So, we have a nation running in different lanes and different directions. We are out of control and searching for a moral compass, but we're not willing to look outside ourselves. It is no wonder that America leads the world in crime, juvenile violence, teenage pregnancies, abortion, divorce, illegal drugs, and pornography. We are reaping what we have sown.

Every day 33,000 people in America contract an STD.[25] In a typical year, more babies will be born with birth defects caused by STDs than all the children affected by polio during the entire ten-year epidemic in the 1950s.[26] In the United States, more than 65 million people are currently living with an incurable STD. An additional 15 million people become infected with one or more STDs each year, roughly half of whom contract lifelong infections.[27]

In the state of Virginia, statistics show that in every school district that taught comprehensive sex education in 1988, with one exception, the number of teen pregnancies increased. At the same time, there was 15.8% average *decrease* in pregnancies in all but one of the school districts that were not teaching comprehensive sex education.[28] Today, more than 75% of the nation's school districts teach sex education, and there are more than 300 school-based birth control clinics in operation. Yet, the percentage of illegitimate births has increased from 15% to an astonishing 51% over the past three decades.[29] Go figure. Furthermore, we are told that three of five married couples using contraceptives will have unplanned pregnancies over a five-year period. Adolescents will have four to five times that failure rate.[30]

Even Planned Parenthood admits that teenagers using contraceptives are not stemming the increasing number of pregnancies. In their own words, "More teenagers are using contraceptives and using them more consistently than ever before. Yet the number and rate of premarital pregnancies continues to rise."[31] The Human Life Center bluntly says, "It is perhaps one of the cruelest myths to lead children to believe that pregnancy cannot occur if contraception is used."[32] It is interesting to note that in the decade of the 1970s the states with the highest rate of government expenditures on birth control also had the greatest increases in abortion and illegitimate births.[33]

California has consistently spent twice as much as the national average on government-funded birth control. However, in one year the teenage pregnancy rate jumped 30% above the national level, and the teenage abortion rate more than tripled.[34]

Former Secretary of Education William Bennett observes "there is no evidence that making contraceptive methods more available is the surest strategy for preventing pregnancy—to say nothing of preventing sexual activity. . .Seventy percent of all high school seniors have taken sex education courses. Yet when we look at what is happening in the sexual lives of American students, we can only conclude it is doubtful that much sex education is doing any good at all."[35] Bennett also said, "Instead of teaching them about birth control we should be teaching them about self-control. Instead of telling kids, 'Play it safe,' we should be telling them, 'Don't play!'"[36] Think about it. The very problems that sex education was supposed to solve have only become worse.

More than 3,000 teen girls get pregnant every day. If a teen couple has sex without birth control, there is a 90% chance the girl will get pregnant within one year. Pregnant teen girls are seven times more likely to commit suicide as other girls their age. One-third of these teen moms will drop out of school. Teenage pregnancy is, in fact, the leading cause of suicide among girls and the leading reason for girls quitting school. Half of these young moms will live below the poverty level.[37] While nine out of ten guys abandon their pregnant girlfriends, that one guy will end up paying between $50,000 and $250,000 in child support over the next 18 years.[38] That's a high price to pay for a few moments of fleeting pleasure.

WHAT CAN WE DO?

A Lou Harris poll concluded only two things will effectively impact the teen pregnancy problem: church attendance and parental oversight—the very things that sex education courses are designed to circumvent.[39]

In short, we are ending up with the wrong results because we are starting with the wrong premise. Sex education does not reduce pregnancies. Strong morals derived from God's Word must be the basis of a society's moral fiber. Isn't it ironic that at a time in our kid's lives when they need adult guidance more than ever, we have abdicated our moral responsibility? Schools take a value-neutral stance. With no one saying not to do it, we are condoning it by default. Right has become whatever they decide.

It is talking out of both sides of our mouths to declare in the name of political correctness that we cannot legislate or teach morality. For example, in the classroom, sexual activity is either presented as having parameters or not having parameters. Either way, both are moral statements. The only question is: "Whose morality will it be?" While priding themselves in not making moral judgments, these liberal educators have indiscreetly imposed their own brand of morality upon our kids. I do not doubt that some of these teachers have good intentions when they say, "It's okay to say no to sex, and it's okay to say yes to sex. Whichever one that you feel is right at that time, then that's okay." A thousand times *no*! What a wimpy statement. This teacher has just told the entire class that ultimately everything is okay. Such garbage is anything but morally neutral.

Maybe I am just dense and slow to process this stuff, but we don't take a morally neutral position when it comes to cheating, stealing, lying, or violence. In fact, some schools have a zero tolerance policy on many of these issues. Yet, we are trying to take a morally neutral position in the area of sexual activity. Is it just me, or is something is wrong with this picture? Apart from drug addiction, there may not be any other single activity that has the potential of devastating the lives of our children more completely than premarital sexual activity, and we are telling them to do whatever feels right at the time. God help us! Former teacher Anne Marie Morgan gives this assessment: "Our laws recognize the immaturity of teenagers in restricting minor's access to alcohol and tobacco products, as well as other areas, such as marriage-licensing, consenting for medical care, and entering into contracts. Yet, sexuality educators expect adolescents to make adult-level decisions in areas of sex, family planning, and abortion, when frankly, even adults don't always make the most appropriate choices at times."[40]

How would you like for your daughter to enroll in college and be given a safe-sex kit during orientation week? That's what happened at Dartmouth College, according to Gregory Fossedal, a former editorial writer for the *Wall Street Journal.* He writes, "Students arriving at Dartmouth College this winter received . . . free of charge what Dartmouth is pleased to call the 'safe sex kit.' One enclosure is the brochure . . . which describes options for 'enjoying sex to the fullest without giving or getting sexual diseases.' Similar kits, health experts say, are available at many colleges around the country. Dartmouth's sex kit included two free condoms, plus a lubricant and 'rubber dam' recommended for love acts between two men. . . . Women students . . . may receive the controversial morning–after pill."[41] Does that make you a little nauseated? Is it any wonder that 50% of all women over the age of 18 have herpes, not to mention any of the other 29 STDs they may have unknowingly contracted?[42]

After experimenting with a generation of students, the Department of Education finally concluded that "the most important determinant of children's actions is their understanding of right and wrong."[43] Finally, somebody had a light-bulb moment in Washington, D.C. I don't mean to sound too facetious, but for crying out loud, it should not take billions of dollars experimenting with our children's future to figure out some of this stuff. Do you remember the values clarification experiment of the '80s? It marked a departure from teaching the academics of education courses by introducing hypothetical situations that were intended to give our children clarity on real-life moral issues. Values clarification was a psycho-therapeutic mode to manipulate students away

from their parents and their own religious beliefs. The programs imple-
mented by values clarification did not deal in reality. The student was
taught to make his or her own reality in a false world without absolute
rights or wrongs. Values clarification renounced the traditional concepts
of family, community, and authority, and replaced them with a vague,
gray world of situational ethics.[44] Professor Alan L. Lockwood, Assistant
Professor of Education, University of Wisconsin, says: "Values
Clarification embodies ethical relativism as its moral point of view and
Values Clarification is a form of client-centered therapy."[45] Educators
now agree that values clarification failed miserably to clarify anything. It
only produced confusion over right and wrong and reinforced the
impression that all behavior is relative depending on the situation. The
Washington Post reported a consensus that "schools should take clear
positions on right and wrong behavior and personal morality—teaching,
for example, that students should not engage in sex."[46]

The Centers for Disease Control reported in a 2001 study that 45.6%
of high school students in the United States stated they had engaged in
sexual intercourse, 60.5% of high school seniors admitted to past sexual
intercourse, and 21.6% had been with more than four sexual partners.
In 1997, teenagers accounted for 2,445 pregnancies every day.[47] While
we have seen some decrease in these numbers, there has been nothing to
declassify its epidemic status.

Unfortunately, there is little difference in the morality of those inside
the church and those outside the church. It hurts to report such a thing,
but study after study documents this fact. Not long ago a researcher sent
shockwaves through the evangelical community when he reported a few
years ago that the divorce rate within the church was higher than in the
world at large. A.W. Sipe, a former Benedictine monk, studied the sexuality of Catholic priests. Over a 25-year period, he interviewed 1,500
priests and laypersons. Based upon his years of extensive research, he estimated that at least half of the 53,000 Roman Catholic priests in the U.S.
have broken their vows of celibacy.[48] So, it can easily be seen that the
anemia of today's church crosses all denominational lines. Truly, it is a
sad commentary and huge indictment upon the one institution that

represents the King of Kings, the only begotten Son of God. We are giving the world very little incentive to want to know the Jesus whom we claim to know, love, and serve. It is little wonder that there is so much cynicism and so many accusations of hypocrisy from the unbelieving community. However, let's remember that a hypocrite is a counterfeit. The very nature of a counterfeit demands the authenticity of the real thing from which it is counterfeited. Otherwise, you cannot have a counterfeit. So yes, there are hypocrites in the church. But their lives do not discount the authenticity of the Bible, the claims of Christ, nor the fact that millions of Christians are living exemplary lives that do, indeed, reflect the character of Jesus Christ. When we come to the end of life's journey and stand before Almighty God, we are going to give an account for our lives, not theirs.

Sociologists have completed studies that reveal an indisputable fact: there is a much higher incidence of divorce among people who live together before marriage than among people who do not. Furthermore, among those who lived together before marriage, there is a much higher incidence of infidelity during marriage.[49] There is also a much lower incidence of infidelity in marriage among couples who respect and obey God's commandments regarding sexual morality.[50]

Years ago, the most authoritative survey ever done on sex became the cover story for *U.S. News and World Report* as well as *TIME* magazine. The survey was designed by academics at the University of Chicago's National Opinion Research Center. It said, "According to the study, married couples have the most sex and are most likely to have orgasms."[51] Thus, sexual satisfaction isn't found in one-night stands, but in the stability of marriage.

Under scientific conditions, a psychologist and her colleagues were curious about how sexual experimentation affects the personality. They decided to administer the well-known Minnesota Multiphasic Personality Inventory (MMPI). This standardized test is used in mental health centers across the nation. Psychologists gave the test to a group of people who were highly "sexually active." Here's what they found. Half of these people demonstrated abnormal depression, introversion, nervous activity, and even delusional thinking. They also scored low on telling the truth. The conclusion was this: as a whole, the group was not well-adjusted; they were emotionally unhealthy and immature.[52]

THE MEDIA'S INFLUENCE

The Journal of Communication reported that "television portrays six times more extramarital sex than sex between spouses and 94% of the sexual encounters on soap operas are between people not married to each other."[53] When Madonna, America's sex goddess of the '80s, starts censoring this stuff from her kids, that should be a clue to the rest of the nation. Former Surgeon General Koop gave this report: "In Michigan, in four cities that studied junior high and high school girls, it was found that the girls watch an average of two-and-a-half to three hours of soap operas per day, and that there is one episode of sexual intercourse per hour on those films—almost always between unmarried people. But more surprising to us was that the movies these youngsters wanted to see most were R-rated movies, and we found that 66% to 77% of the girls in these four cities had seen the six top R-rated films that year. The fascinating thing to me is that not one of these girls was ever challenged at the box office although all of them were under age, and the movies contained eight instances of sexual intercourse among unmarried people per film. Two of those films had even more than that. One had fourteen. That film was so popular with young people that it has now been made into a television series."[54]

Even the American Academy of Pediatrics, which represents more than 40,000 physicians, has urged parents to keep their children from watching MTV because of the heavy content of sex and violence. Their official reasoning was, "Too many music videos promote sexism, violence, substance abuse, suicides and sexual behavior."[55]

EMOTIONAL STARVATION

The problem with STDs and the epidemic of sexual activity outside the confines of marriage is not about thrill seeking or a lack of information. The enormity of this social problem brings to light a much deeper problem. It raises the question, "Why? What is the motivation?" The problem can be reduced to one simple answer: unmet emotional and spiritual needs. With illicit sex, there it is an escape from loneliness, an attempt to find acceptance and security through love, and a temporary fix that serves as an emotional Band-Aid temporarily covering the pain. Sadly, those who enter into the experiment come away with their needs still unmet, only to find the pain intensifying. Coleen Mast made this apt comparison with junk food: "There are enough calories in a can of pop and a bag of potato chips to satisfy one's hunger. But these foods do not meet the individual's nutritional needs. Usually, the result is that one eats more and more junk food to satisfy these needs. While a person may certainly feel full after eating junk food, such a diet will, in fact, leave him undernourished. In the same way, the deep human need for love cannot be met by sex alone—even by 'protected' sex. Too often people seek to fill their need for love with 'junk food,' more partners and a greater variety of sexual experiences, only to find frustration, emptiness, and self-destruction. Contraception contributes to the confusion between a perceived need for sex and the true need for love and acceptance."[56]

Pollster George Barna reports that 83% of America's 33 million teenagers believe that moral truth depends on their circumstances. He also found that only six percent of them believe that moral truth is absolute, and even more disturbing is the fact that only nine percent of born-again teens believe in moral absolutes.[57] That is less than one in ten of our Christian kids.[58] These kids are discovering that there is not a condom for the heart and mind. Our national destiny is linked to this generation.

WHAT DOES THE BIBLE SAY?

A lot! There is a wealth of biblical material addressing the subject of sexual sin. Yet, in a morally relativistic world, massive numbers of people are uninformed and unaware that sex outside marriage is always wrong. It is amazing how the human mind rationalizes adulterous behavior. When reading the Bible, it is helpful to know that fornication is a broad term referring to sexual sin outside the bonds of marriage. Adultery is sexual unfaithfulness within the marriage relationship. Fornication encompasses premarital sex, homosexuality, bestiality, pornography, incest, and so forth. In fact, we get our word "pornography" from "porneia," which is translated "fornication." Here are just a few passages that directly address the fornicator or adulterer:

"You shall not commit adultery."   —Exodus 20:14

"Moreover you shall not lie carnally with your neighbor's wife, to defile yourself with her."   —Leviticus 18:20

"But that we write to them to abstain from things polluted by idols, from sexual immorality, . . ."   —Acts 15:20

"But now I have written to you not to keep company with anyone named a brother, who is sexually immoral, . . ."   —1 Corinthians 5:11

"Now the body is not for sexual immorality but for the Lord, . . ."
                                                   —1 Corinthians 6:13

"Flee sexual immorality . . . he who commits sexual immorality sins against his own body."   —1 Corinthians 6:18

"Nor let us commit sexual immorality, as some of them did, and in one day twenty-three thousand fell."   —1 Corinthians 10:8

"But fornication . . . let it not even be named among you, as is fitting for saints."   —Ephesians 5:3

"For this is the will of God, . . . that you should abstain from sexual immorality; that each of you should know how to possess his own vessel in sanctification and honor, not in passion of lust, like the Gentiles who do not know God; . . . Therefore he who rejects this does not reject man, but God, who has also given us His Holy Spirit."
                                                   —1 Thessalonians 4:3-5, 8

"Do not be deceived. Neither fornicators, nor idolaters, nor adulterers, nor homosexuals, nor sodomites, nor thieves, nor covetous, nor drunkards, nor revilers, nor extortioners will inherit the kingdom of God."
                                                   —1 Corinthians 6:9-10

The above is only a sampling of what God has to say about this all-important subject. There are heartbreaking examples in Scripture that bring to life the real consequences of this sin. From King David to mighty Samson to wise Solomon, the Bible is replete with the warnings to avoid, abstain, and flee this all-too common sin. There is not a more vivid and direct warning than what is contained in Proverbs 5, 6, and 7. Ponder these words: "For the lips of an immoral woman drip honey, and her mouth is smoother than oil; but in the end she is bitter as wormwood, sharp as a two-edged sword. Her feet go down to death, her steps lay hold of hell. Remove your way far from her, and do not go near the door of her house" (Proverbs 5:3-5,8).

Or listen to this stern warning: "For the commandment is a lamp, and the law a light; reproofs of instruction are the way of life, to keep you from the evil woman, from the flattering tongue of a seductress. Do not lust after her beauty in your heart, nor let her allure you with her eyelids. For by means of a harlot a man is reduced to a crust of bread; and an adulteress will prey upon his precious life. Whoever commits adultery with a woman lacks understanding; he who does so destroys his own soul. Wounds and dishonor he will get, and his reproach will not be wiped away" (Proverbs 6:23-26,32-33).

Finally, God gets in our ear with a megaphone and shouts, "My son, keep my words and treasure my commands within you. That they may keep you from the immoral woman, from the seductress who flatters with her words. With her enticing speech she caused him to yield, with her flattering lips she seduced him. He did not know it would cost his life. Do not let your heart turn aside to her ways, do not stray into her paths; for she has cast down many wounded, and all who were slain by her were strong men. Her house is the way to hell, descending to the chambers of death" (Proverbs 7:1,5,21,23,25-27).

WHERE ARE WE HEADED?

Apart from divine intervention, history screams to us that we are moving toward inevitable destruction. Anthropologist J.D. Unwin conducted an extensive study of the 86 civilizations in world history and discovered that the common denominator leading to their destruction was sexual immorality.[59] There was a time in America's history when we had criminal laws prohibiting adultery, fornication, and sodomy. In fact, until the last 40 years the homosexual act was called "a crime against nature" in our law books. A FOX News channel commentator recently reported on the epidemic of out-of-wedlock births among teenagers. He reported that 25% of babies born to white teens and 70% of those born to black teens are illegitimate. The billions of dollars being spent on disease control, welfare, abortion clinics, and mental illnesses resulting from illicit sexual activity is staggering . . . all because of violating God's law. It may sound puritanical, like a voice crying in the wilderness, but most of our problems are of our own making. We have sinned against God and continue to engage in sinful sexual practices with no accountability from society, while at the same time, we arrogantly claim that it is "our right" to do so. Mark it down. Unchecked perversion in sexual relations will bring harm to the society that tolerates it. The Bible is replete with warnings. History verifies it. With love and forbearance, God is compassionately calling America to return to the faith of our forefathers. He is our only hope . . . and our greatest threat. His mercy will not strive forever. Judgment awaits. The clock is ticking.

CHAPTER 7

Abortion:
The American Holocaust

Moral Relativism's Spin: "Pro-Choice"

Suppose that you are the mother of four children and pregnant with your fifth child. Your husband has syphilis, and you are dying of tuberculosis. Your first child was born blind. Your second child died. Your third child was born deaf, and your fourth child, like yourself, is dying of tuberculosis. So, given this kind of history, rather than bringing a fifth child into the world, you are considering an abortion.[1] What would you do?

Consider this scenario: you are a teenage girl who is unmarried and pregnant. You live in abject poverty, and the baby's father was a one-night stand who skipped town and has not been seen nor heard from since. You don't want the baby and can barely afford to take care of yourself, much less another mouth to feed. You are thinking about an abortion. What would you do?

Try this scenario on for size: you are a 13-year-old African American who is walking home late at night. A white man accosts you, rapes you, and gets you pregnant. Should you carry the baby full term or have the child aborted?

A preacher and his wife have 14 children. They are already living in abject poverty when she discovers she is pregnant again. Should she abort for the good of the rest of the family?

These are not fictitious stories. Each of these women wanted an abortion, but since the incidents occurred prior to 1973 it was illegal, so all four carried their babies full term. The first woman gave birth to Ludwig Von Beethoven. The second gave birth to Leonardo de Vinci. The third gave birth to Ethel Waters, the beloved soloist who sang "His Eye Is On the Sparrow" at Billy Graham crusades. The fourth delivered one of the greatest reformers and evangelists of the eighteenth century, Charles Wesley.[2] The tragic reality is that if these situations had occurred after 1973, the world might never have known the genius of Beethoven, de Vinci, Waters, or Wesley. Abortion was considered a felony for almost 200 years in American history. It was punishable for up to 20 years in prison.

How times have changed. Today, America's policy on abortion is the most permissive in the world. A baby is aborted every 22 seconds. Four thousand babies are aborted every day, more than one million every year. Given the previously mentioned stories, I cannot help but wonder who we have killed since 1973. Think about it. We have slaughtered almost 50 million innocent, defenseless babies.[3] Some of these children may have been destined to find a cure for cancer, for AIDS, or to lead the world's next spiritual awakening. Who knows? What used to be the safest place in the world has become the most dangerous place . . . a mother's womb. Statistically, the womb is more dangerous than the bottom of a coal mine, a nuclear waste dump, or even the middle of a hurricane. In fact, a soldier marching to war is more likely to come back alive than a baby conceived in an American female.[4]

Do you realize that *every year* in the United States there are more babies killed in the womb than have been killed in *all* wars fought by *all* Americans in the history of our country?[5] That's *every* year! Some cities actually have more abortions than live births.[6]

A LITTLE HISTORY LESSON

Those who promote and endorse abortion tend to consider themselves progressive and compassionate. Yet, historically, abortion has always been considered a barbaric act. The first recorded law on abortion was in Sumeria in the eighteenth century BC, where it was considered a crime and immediately punished.[7] In the sixteenth century BC, the Babylonians left behind records of punishment for abortion.[8] In the sixth century BC, the Jewish moral code stated, "Nor shall the woman destroy the embryonic child in her womb."[9] The first post-New Testament reference to abortion is found in the second century AD, which says, "Thou shalt not murder a child by abortion nor kill one after birth . . ."[10] Under English law abortion was always considered a crime. In 1250, English law stated that abortion was the same as homicide. In 1809, English law was passed that made abortion punishable by being fined, imprisoned, and whipped.[11]

A BRIEF BIBLICAL OVERVIEW

The first mention of abortion in the Bible is in Exodus 21:22, which says, "If men fight, and hurt a woman with child, so that she gives birth prematurely, yet no harm follows, he shall surely be punished accordingly as the woman's husband imposes on him; and he shall pay as the judges determine." Much of the Bible, however, is silent about abortion simply because it was unthinkable for an Israelite woman to even consider such a thing. The tone of Scripture is pro-life, especially since the Bible prohibits the taking of innocent life (Exodus 20:13). Consider Job 31:15, which says, "Did not He who made me in the womb make them, did not the same One fashion us in the womb?" Psalm 139:13-14 (NASB) states, "For You formed my inward parts; You wove me in my mother's womb. I will give thanks to You, for I am fearfully and wonderfully made; wonderful are Your works, . . ." In Jeremiah 1:5, God says, "Before I formed you in the womb I knew you, before you were born I sanctified you; . . ." So, when God looks into the womb, He doesn't see a mass of tissue. He sees a human being.

During the ministry of Jesus, "they were bringing even their babies to Him so that He would touch them, . . ." (Luke 18:15, NASB). The Greek word translated "babies" is "brephos." Here is what is interesting: "brephos" is the same word that Luke used when John the Baptist was still in the womb of his mother, Elizabeth, in Luke 1:41a (NASB): "When Elizabeth heard Mary's greeting, the baby leaped in her womb; . . ." At this time, Elizabeth had been pregnant for six months. By using the same term to describe "baby" in both chapter 18 and chapter 1, Luke does not distinguish between babies outside the womb and those inside the womb. Both were (and are) live human babies.

This is a big deal because it means that everything the Bible teaches about how to treat people also applies to the way we should treat unborn people. Thus, if one understands this all-important truth and esteems what the Bible says, then it is impossible for him or her to remain pro-choice. While the Supreme Court made the killing of unborn babies legal, it certainly does not make it morally right.

In Amos 1:13, the Lord says, "For three transgressions of the sons of Ammon, and for four, I will not turn away its punishment, because they ripped open the women with child in Gilead that they might enlarge their territory." By ripping open the pregnant women, they terminated the pregnancies of the women of Gilead. The reason given was "to enlarge their territory." They wanted more land and power. It was for selfish reasons. Likewise, a large percentage of those choosing to abort their babies do so on the faulty reasoning that rearing a child is inconvenient to their lifestyles, an interruption to their career pursuits, and financially difficult. Like the Ammonites of old, selfish agendas have taken precedence over the lives of unborn children. As with the Ammonites, the judgment of God will fall upon us.

To make another comparison with our culture of death, consider the prohibition of child sacrifices that many heathen cultures practiced during biblical times. Here are just a few examples:

> "You shall not give any of your offspring to offer them to Molech, . . ."
> —Leviticus 18:21, NASB

> "They have filled this place with the blood of the innocent and have built the high places of Baal to burn their sons in the fire as burnt offerings to Baal, a thing which I never commanded or spoke of, nor did it ever enter My mind."   —Jeremiah 19:4-5, NASB

> "And they built the high places of Baal which are in the Valley of the Son of Hinnom to cause their sons and their daughters to pass through the fire of Molech, . . ."   —Jeremiah 32:35

> "You slaughtered My children, and offered them up to idols by causing them to pass through the fire."
> —Ezekiel 16:21, NASB

The practice of child sacrifice was repulsive to God and repeatedly invoked His wrath. These pagan nations often threw their children into the fires as part of their fertility rites. It was a means of enticing their fertility gods to give them an abundant harvest. This horrific practice had nothing to do with obedience to their god. Instead, the objective was to control their gods and coerce them to give the worshippers what they wanted. Do you see it? The purpose of child sacrifice was material blessing. While it is easy to condemn such a barbaric practice that occurred centuries ago, we have simply modernized the practice and sophisticated the techniques by anesthetizing the mother as she lies on the altar. The priest enters the room wearing a surgical mask and towers over the helpless victim with cutting tools and a nice vacuum to clean up the mess. Afterwards, the mother exits the "temple" to pursue her self-centered ambitions, and the "priest" lines his pockets with thousands of dollars. Life is now easier for everyone—her boss, her school, her landlord, and her family.

A newborn baby was found in a trash can at Disney World. The mother had left him there to die and now faces criminal charges. Only moments before, a doctor could have killed the baby legally by partial-birth abortion. Not only would the doctor have been immune from prosecution; he would have been paid.[12] Surely, God's patience must be running out.

Of course, the whole question of whether abortion is right or wrong rises or falls on the question: "When does life begin?" Prior to 1973, nearly every medical school taught that conception was the beginning of human life.[13] This is an undeniable, documented fact. With today's technology, it is not even an issue because the entire process of human development can be seen. This is why pro-life advocates are infuriated by the moral relativism, liberalism, and political correctness that over-shadows this most important issue. If what's in a mother's womb is a live baby, then abortion is nothing less than murdering the most innocent and defenseless among us.

Those in the pro-choice camp have carefully selected their words so that it sounds like we are simply dealing with semantics. They have convinced much of the American public that what's in the mother's womb is nothing more than a mass of tissue. Yet, the fetus is obviously alive before the abortion, or there would be no need to kill it. You can't kill something that's not alive. So, the question is, "What is it that's alive?" Every conceivable piece of medical data confirms it is a human being. At the time when a sperm and an egg unite, there are 23 strands of DNA in the sperm and 23 strands of DNA in the egg. The uniting of these chromosomes has already determined the baby's height, eye color hair, and every other physical feature. In fact, did you know that even a trained geneticist cannot distinguish between the DNA of an embryo and that of an adult human being?[14]

DOES THIS SOUND LIKE A "MASS OF TISSUE"?

- Day 4: A special microscope can determine the sex of the child.

- Day 6: The embryo's cells begin the process of dividing into the child's body and organ systems.

- Day 20: The foundation for the child's brain, spinal cord, and nervous system has been laid.

- Day 21: The heart begins to beat and is already pumping 65 times a minute to circulate the newly formed blood through a system of tubes, which are completely separate from the mother's circulation.

- Day 28: Nearly every organ is present.

- Day 42: The baby moves his or her arms and legs. Its fingers, lips, and mouth are perceptible.

- Day 43: Doctors can pick up brain waves, which is the way the medical community determines whether a person is alive or dead.

- Day 63: The baby has fingerprints, eyelids, fingernails, and the ability to grasp an object with its hand.

- Day 84: Parents are allowed to watch their baby moving around in the uterus, even though the mother cannot yet feel the baby's movement.

- Day 140: Four-and-a-half months into the pregnancy, the baby begins to respond to outside stimuli. The baby is aware of the mother's feelings of stress, pleasure, and excitement.

- Day 161: The baby can now survive outside the mother's womb and can rest in the palm of an adult's hand.[15]

I mentioned that after only 42 days doctors can pick up brain waves. This fact exposes part of the hypocrisy surrounding the abortion issue. For example, let's say a person has a serious accident and is taken to the hospital. If brain waves are present, then the person is considered to be still alive. Why in the name of justice is the same reasoning not applied to babies who have the same brain waves after only 42 days in the womb? If what's in the womb after six weeks has brain waves, how can they call it a nonhuman mass of tissue? Scientifically, there is no stage in the process of development at which the unborn is not a living being.

Another inconsistency lies in the fact that our Supreme Court has arbitrarily implied that personhood only exists when the unborn fetus has the capability of meaningful life outside the mother's womb.[16] But Rule 73-156 in the Internal Revenue Service (IRS) Code states, "If a baby is aborted, but comes out alive by mistake, even if it dies shortly thereafter, you can claim a deduction and write it off as a dependent on your income tax."[17] So, the IRS says it is not tissue, but the Supreme Court says it is tissue.

SO, WHEN DOES LIFE BEGIN?

If the above facts do not conclusively answer this question, perhaps this will. In 1981 the U.S. Senate listened to eight full days of hearings during which testimonies from 57 witnesses were heard, many who were national and international authorities on this issue. The official report given to the Senate contained the following statement: "Physicians, biologists, and other scientists agree that conception marks the beginning of the life of a human being—a being that is alive and is a member of the human species. There is overwhelming agreement on this point in countless medical, biological, and scientific writings."[18] In the same report, they also listed a small sample of 13 medical textbooks, all of which categorically state that life begins at conception.[19]

The September 1970 issue of *California Medicine* states, "It is a scientific fact that human life begins at conception and continues until death."[20] In a special issue devoted to this subject, *LIFE* Magazine stated, "The birth of a human really occurs at the moment the mother's egg is fertilized by one of the father's sperm cells."[21]

Still not convinced? Listen to what the American Medical Association said at its annual conference held in Louisville, Kentucky back in 1859: "The Committee would advise this body, representing as it does the physicians of the land, publicly to express its abhorrence of the unnatural and now rapidly increasing crime of abortion, that it avow its true nature as no simple offense against public morality and decency, no mere misdemeanor, no attempt upon the life of the mother, but the wanton and murderous destruction of her child, and that while it would in no wise transcend its legitimate province or invade the precincts of the law, the association recommends by memorial to the governors and legislators of the several states and as representing the federal district to the President and Congress a careful examination and revision of the statutory and of so much of the common law as relates to this crime. For we hold it to be a thing deserving of all hate and detestation."[22] The British Medical Association said the same thing in 1947.[23]

Dr. Bernard Nathanson was America's most prominent abortionist in the early 1970s. He personally performed 5,000 abortions, assisted with 10,000, and oversaw another 60,000 as medical director of the world's largest abortion clinic. It was the introduction of ultrasound technology that prompted him to reconsider his position. He eventually renounced his profession and joined the ranks of the pro-life movement. He said, "There's all kinds of nonsense statements like, 'Oh, we don't know when life begins.' Of course we know when life begins; we've seen it in the laboratory. But with in vitro fertilization, we know exactly when life begins—there's no question about that."[24] Nathanson produced the groundbreaking film, *Silent Scream*, which was the first time ultrasound technology showed the public a developing baby inside the womb writhing in pain and silently screaming while being aborted. Pro-choice advocates claimed that he manipulated the film to support his new pro-life position. Dr. Nathanson replied, "Look, you don't believe my film? Make your own film and show it to me. Show me what happens in abortion clinics. . . . They never did. And you know why? You'll see the same things that you see in *Silent Scream.*"[25]

There is a perception throughout the nation that abortion is primarily a religious issue. I suppose that is understandable since it is often Christians who picket the clinics and ministers who preach against it. Yet, nothing could be further from the truth. Abortion is a scientific and biological issue. It is a scientific fact that life begins at conception. This is not merely someone's opinion, theory, or speculation. The most respected scientists in the world adhere to this fact. Here are just a few:

- "In biology and in medicine, it is an accepted fact that the life of any individual organism reproducing by sexual means begins at conception." (Professor Micheline Matthews-Roth, Harvard University Medical School)[26]

- "The beginning of a single human life is from a biological point of view a simple and straightforward matter— the beginning is conception." (Dr. Watson A. Bowes, Jr., University of Colorado Medical School)[27]

- "The standard medical texts have long taught that human life begins at conception." (Dr. Alfred Bopngiovanni, University of Pennsylvania Medical School)[28]

- "The exact moment of the beginning of personhood and of the human body is at the moment of conception." (Dr. McCarthy De Mere, Law Professor and Physician, University of Tennessee)[29]

- "Each individual has a very unique beginning, the moment of its conception." (Dr. Jerome Lejeune, world renowned professor of genetics at the University of Descarte, Paris, France)[30]

- "By all criteria of modern molecular biology, life is present from the moment of conception. Now we can say, unequivocally, that the question of when life begins . . . is an established scientific fact . . . It is an established fact that all life, including human life, begins at the moment of conception." (Dr. Hymie Gordon, chairman of the Department of Medical Genetics at Mayo Clinic)[31]

In spite of medical and judiciary precedent, on January 22, 1973 in *Roe v. Wade*, the Supreme Court ignored history, medical science, and theology by striking down every law prohibiting abortion and legalizing it in all 50 states. A part of the Court's *Roe v. Wade* ruling actually stated, "Maternity or additional offspring may force upon a mother a distressful life and future. Psychological harm may be imminent. Mental and physical wealth may be taxed by childcare."[32] In a lesser-known case, but perhaps equally as monumental, on the same day in January of '73, the Supreme Court allowed for second and third trimester abortions in *Doe v. Bolton*. The Court even made it legal for this procedure to be accomplished outside of a hospital, which helps account for the rise the number of abortion clinics throughout the United States.[33] Do you hear what the Court said in these two monumental rulings? If a woman has a baby, it may tax her physically, emotionally, and financially. What else is new? Is there any mother in America who doesn't already know that? Our Supreme Court had the arrogant audacity to suggest that babies are an inconvenience upon our time, an imposition upon our financial goals, and a burden to us emotionally. Therefore, we'll just make it legal for the mother to kill them anytime during their pregnancy. That's her right to choose. After all, it's her body, and the child is a part of her body, so what the mother chooses to do with her body is her own business. Doesn't that sound right on? When feminists boldly echo those words in front of pro-abortion rallies, the crowd wildly applauds with intense emotion. Let's set aside the emotion for a moment and look at the facts.

First of all, no one argues with the fact that a woman has the right to choose what she does with her own body, but that freedom is not absolute. For example, if she went into the middle of the street and stripped off her clothes, she would soon discover from city officials that she doesn't have the right to do that. If someone attempts suicide, they are admitted immediately to the psychiatric ward of the hospital. In other words, we are not entitled to do with our bodies whatever we like.

Furthermore, that unborn little baby has a genetic code that is totally different from the mother's cells. Since it has been overwhelmingly proven that life begins at conception, and that a separate little human being is alive within that womb, then the right of the child to live supercedes any right that a woman has to her own body. If you are still not convinced that the baby inside the womb is separate from the mother's body, consider the following scientific evidence:

- Many women carry babies with a different blood type than their own.

- A woman may be carrying a male child.

- The fetus has a DNA fingerprint distinct from the mother.

- If the embryo of black parents is transplanted into a white mother, she will still have a black baby.

- In the earliest stages of development, the fetus has its own hands, feet, heart, skin, and eyes.[34]

STILL UNSURE?

It is hard to believe that in spite of the evidence, 50% of our population remains divided over this issue. Frankly, pro-life advocates have not done the best job in dispensing the information and articulating the arguments that support their position. President Ronald Reagan made a valid observation when he said, "Anyone who doesn't feel sure whether we are talking about a second human life should clearly give life the benefit of the doubt. If you don't know whether a body is alive or dead, you would never bury it."[35] Well said. If there is uncertainty about when life begins we should err on the side of life. We don't bury those who are doubtfully dead, and we don't abandon victims of an earthquake, hurricane, plane crash, or a coal mine disaster just because we doubt they are still alive. No, rescuers will spend days on end and go without sleep in order to find any survivors. We always give life the benefit of the doubt . . . except when it comes to abortion. The burden of proof rests on the abortionist to show there is no presence of life. Scientifically and medically, it cannot be done. What's so sad is most of them know it and continue to kill babies by the millions.

I am reminded of Psalm 106:37-38 that says, "They even sacrificed their sons and their daughters to demons, and shed innocent blood, the blood of their sons and daughters, whom they sacrificed to the idols of Canaan; and the land was polluted with blood." Then, verses 40-42 say, "Therefore the wrath of the LORD was kindled against His people, so that He abhorred His own inheritance. And He gave them into the hand of the Gentiles, and those who hated them ruled over them . . . And they were brought into subjection under their hand." When Israel was attacked by a foreign power and ultimately humbled by those who hated them, I wonder if the nation ever connected the dots back to the killing of their sons and daughters? The correlation is there. We are standing where Israel stood with the innocent blood of millions of our children upon our hands.

What we are doing in America through abortion makes Hitler's concentration camps look like *Mister Rogers' Neighborhood*. Proverbs 31:8-9 says, "Open your mouth for the speechless, in the cause of all who are appointed to die. Open your mouth, judge righteously, and plead the cause of the poor and needy." In other words, we are to speak up for those who cannot speak up for themselves. For the life of me, given the weight of pro-life Scripture and warnings of judgment, I do not understand how any God-fearing Christian could ever justify voting for someone who is pro-choice. God is their judge and to Him they will give an account.

WHAT YOU MAY NOT HAVE KNOWN

A well-kept secret in the pro-choice movement is the fact that the woman who was Jane Roe in *Roe v. Wade* has since admitted that she lied to the Supreme Court in order to accommodate the feminist movement's agenda. Her real name is Norma McCorvey, and she has since received Jesus Christ as her Savior. The fabricated story she presented to the Court was that she was gang-raped and became pregnant. This means that 50 million babies have been killed, and the abortion laws of our nation have all been based upon a lie! It is just one more example of Romans 1:25, which describes how a nation exchanged the truth for the lie.

Furthermore, did you know that neither women in those landmark supreme court cases of January, 1973, Jane Roe nor Mary Doe, ever had abortions? Their two children are alive today.[36] Dr. Bernard Nathanson, cofounder of the National Abortion Rights Action League, gave Roe the ammunition she needed when appearing before the Court by contending that 10,000 women a year die in back-alley abortions. Did you know that today Nathanson is pro-life and confesses that he knew the figures were totally false?[37] Did you know that abortion is now the only surgical procedure for which a physician is not required to tell his or her patients about the dangerous complications involved after surgery, or even the truth about what they are doing: removing a baby, not a lump of tissues?[38] Did you know that abortion is based upon ignorance? The word *fetus* is constantly used, which is no coincidence. The average American does not know that *fetus* is a Latin word that means *"an unborn child."* Abortionists insist on using *fetus* instead of *baby* so people won't know what's going on. Deception is essential for the abortion industry.[39]

Yet, I am convinced that in His mercy God still was trying to get the attention of these Supreme Court justices through the presentation of convincing evidence in favor of life beginning at conception. For example, were you aware that in October 1971, two years prior to *Roe v. Wade*, a group of 220 distinguished physicians, scientists, and professors submitted an "amicus curiae" brief (advice to a court on some legal matter) to the Supreme Court? Their argument stated an unborn child from the moment of conception until the moment the child is born is a person and must be considered a person, like its mother.[40] The report actually stated, "In the seventh week, the pre-born child bears the familiar external features and all the internal organs of an adult. . . . The brain is already like the adult brain and sends out impulses. The heart beats steadily. The stomach produces digestive juices. The liver manu factures blood cells, and the kidneys begin to function by extracting uric acid from the child's blood. After the eighth week . . . everything is already present that will be found in the full-term baby."[41]

This report proved beyond any doubt that human life begins at conception. Even prior to *Roe v. Wade*, nearly every medical and biological textbook taught that human life begins at conception. Our Supreme Court was blinded to the facts and turned a deaf ear to these 220 medical and intellectual authorities. They had sufficient evidence. Medical science was not in limbo on this issue. This Court arrogantly exerted its will over the consensus of national opinion, over the medical community's expertise, over the scientific community's convincing evidence, and most importantly, over the authority of God's Word. It is hard to believe that more than three decades have passed, and with the new developments in medical technology such as ultrasound imaging and fetoscopy, we are now permitted to look into the womb and observe for ourselves fetal development from the point of conception. Yet, 4,000 innocent babies continue to be slaughtered every day. Even in the liberal country of Sweden, the fetus is recognized as a human at 20 weeks after conception, and abortion is illegal after the twentieth week. But in America, abortion is legal any time prior to birth.[42] Through *Roe v. Wade*, the Supreme Court struck down all laws against abortion and legalized it in all 50 states throughout the entire nine months of pregnancy. It is only necessary for one physician to deem it necessary for the mother's health in order to perform an abortion in the last trimester of pregnancy according the Court's definition of health as "physical, emotional, psychological and the relevance of the mother's age." It seems every woman could fit in that category.[43] In the United States of America, the leading killer of unborn babies, the womb has become the tomb. Judgment is at the door!

BUT WHAT ABOUT RAPE?

This is often the trump card of abortionists. They will present the most extreme case of some poor, helpless girl who is raped by an unknown assailant and discovers weeks later that she is pregnant. With much emotion and sympathy (and sometimes a quivering lip), the convincing abortionist asks, "Why must this poor, innocent girl be forced to go through childbirth and an unwanted pregnancy?"

The truth is that less than one percent of women get pregnant as a result of rape.[44] During a ten-year period, Chicago, St. Paul, and

Philadelphia did not report a single pregnancy from sexual assault.[45] The number of pregnancies resulting from rape or incest is roughly one in 100,000 cases.[46] In Czechoslovakia, out of 86,000 abortions, only 22 were performed as the result of rape.[47] In a medical gathering of obstetricians who had delivered more than 19,000 babies, not one had a rape pregnancy.[48] You get the point. The documentation is convincing and seemingly endless. The real truth is that 98% of all abortions are for convenience. Rape is simply the political smokescreen that pro-choice advocates hide behind in an effort to promote their cause.

METHODS OF ABORTION

I feel like putting PG-13 rating on these next few paragraphs because of their graphic nature. The methods used to kill babies are among the most barbaric imaginable. I hope you have a strong stomach because here is what's happening 4,000 times a day in our nation.

- The dilation and curettage (D & C) method is the most commonly used method during the first ten weeks of pregnancy. A catheter is inserted into the cavity of the womb, and one end is attached to a suction pump that's 25 times stronger than a vacuum cleaner. The end of the catheter is as sharp as a razor so that the baby is hacked into pieces, and then the suction tears the baby's body into smaller pieces, forcing it down a tube into a bottle.[49]

- The dilation and evacuation method is used in the first three to five months of pregnancy. The neck of the womb is stretched, and an instrument resembling a pair of pliers is placed into the womb. With those pliers the head is crushed, and the baby is torn limb from limb and then scraped into a basin. The nurse must assemble the broken parts of the body to make sure that no pieces are left in the womb.[50]

- The saline solution method is salt poisoning. After 16 weeks of pregnancy, the amniotic sac is filled with fluid. The doctor takes a large needle and injects it into the woman's abdomen, removes some of the amniotic fluid, and replaces it with salt water. The baby's skin is burned off. With such delicate skin and eyes, you can imagine how the baby must kick in agony and struggle violently to escape. Usually within 30 minutes the baby dies, convulsing and choking to death. Within 24 hours, the mother goes into labor and gives birth to a dead baby with red eyes who's covered in burns.[51]

Dr. William B. Waddill, Jr., was indicted in June of 1977 for allegedly strangling to death a baby girl following a saline solution abortion at Westminster County Hospital in California. At a preliminary hearing, Dr. Ronald Cornelsen testified that Waddill throttled the infant's neck, strangling her, while complaining of what might happen to him (lawsuits) if the baby were to live. According to Cornelsen's testimony, while he (Cornelsen) was examining the baby, Waddill again tried to strangle the baby. He complained that the baby just would not die. The trial resulted in a hung jury.[52]

Also in California, a four-pound baby was born alive after a salt injection. As reported, the doctor ordered the nurse not to use oxygen to save the baby. She replied that if she did not, it would die. The doctor replied, "Wasn't that the original idea?" She gave oxygen anyway. The baby lived and was adopted.[53]

- Another method used in later stages of the pregnancy is similar to a C-section in which the mother's abdomen is surgically opened, and the baby is lifted out alive and left to die.[54]

- The prostaglandin abortion causes such severe contractions in the woman that she goes into violent labor and gives birth to the baby, often decapitating it in the process. Most of the time the baby is born alive and left to die.[55]

Suffice it to say that if you did to your dog what a doctor does to a baby when he or she is aborting it, the authorities and animal rights activists would be down your throat. You would be imprisoned and locked up as a psycho-maniac, but you put a doctor in a hospital and let him or her do the same thing to a human being, and they're esteemed as honorable members of the medical community. The very people who are shouting, "Save the whales," are the same people screaming, "Kill the babies." They say before it's born you can chop it up and suck it out, but after it's born you can't spank it. Go figure.

MOTHER TERESA, THE PROPHET

In 1994, Mother Teresa was invited by President Clinton to speak at the National Prayer Breakfast. The last thing he was expecting was that this sweet, compassionate little lady would point her bony finger in his face and order him to repent. Hundreds of political dignitaries were present and sat with anticipation as to what this saintly ambassador from Calcutta would say. Known to be a champion for human rights and a voice for the poorest of the poor, no one expected the verbal bombshell that was about to be launched. She said, "The greatest destroyer of peace today is abortion. For if we accept that a mother can kill even her own child, how can we tell other people not to kill each other?" After her speech, she approached the president, pointed her finger in his face, and said, "Stop killing babies!"[56]

She was right on, because it wasn't long afterwards that we read about a New Jersey teen who attended her high school prom, went into the bathroom stall, and gave birth to a son. She calmly proceeded to put the newborn into a plastic bag and discarded him in a trash can. Five months later, some teenage sweethearts were charged with murder when they delivered their baby in a motel room and then stashed it in a trash bin. Two months after that, a young mother from New Jersey threw her newborn out a window. If those same teenagers had gone to a Planned Parenthood facility that evening, it would have been legal to kill the child. But since it was delivered outside the womb and separate from a medical facility, these kids were charged with murder. A little hypocritical, wouldn't you say? During the same time frame, a Maine woman gave birth in a bathroom stall at Logan Airport, then left her newborn son in a toilet covered with tissue while she boarded a flight to London to see her boyfriend. What was her punishment? She received a two-year suspension, provided she went to psychological counseling.[57]

In America, it is possible to be fined $500 for stealing an iguana egg! If you kill an unborn ugly lizard you are punished, but you are permitted to kill an unborn human being.[58] If 4000 rabbits were killed each day instead of 4000 unborn babies, there would be riots in the streets. For some strange reason animals enjoy many privileges denied to unborn babies. Here is another scenario that leaves you scratching your head. I recently heard that in California, a teenager between the ages of 14 and 18 is required to get parental consent before using a tanning bed. In fact, a minor under the age of 14 cannot use a tanning bed under any circumstance, *but* that same child can have an abortion without parental consent. [59]

A CHILLING TESTIMONY

Carol Everett was an abortion provider who owned two clinics located in the Dallas/Ft. Worth Metroplex. Here are excerpts from her speech to Cincinnati's Right to Life Educational Foundation. It is eye-opening. If you ever wondered about the viability of sex education in our public schools, the following will only add to your concerns.

"I want to tell you how I sold abortions to women and how I encouraged women to have abortions. My goal was for every young woman between the ages of thirteen and eighteen to have three to five abortions. I knew if I could get them sexually active and on a low-dose birth control pill, they would get pregnant. Then I could sell them abortions. It's called sex education—it is a tool the enemy uses. I used it because I knew any time I went into a school with my so-called 'safe sex' message, the pregnancy rate would increase by 50%. Of course, I didn't say that to school administrators. I said, 'You know these kids shouldn't have sex, but they're going to anyway, so we must teach them how to have safe sex.' Doesn't that sound caring? Sensitive?

Obviously, I don't say that anymore. Instead, I say, 'We don't take those kids out and get them drunk and try to teach them how to drive safely drunk. We give them a moral absolute: don't drink and drive. If you drink and drive, you could be killed.' Why in the world would we compromise our youth with this low moral standard to live down to? They deserve the very highest and best—abstinence—which, quite simply, still works every single time.

My goal was very simple. All I had to do was get them to laugh with me about their parents. I'd say, 'Your parents are always telling you what to do, aren't they? Oh yes. And they don't understand you, do they? They don't understand you sexually. Well, if you decided that you wanted to become sexually active, would your parents help you get on some method of contraception?' And of course the answer was no. I'd say, 'Don't worry about that. Here's my card. Come to me.'

Then I gave them a business card. I also passed out condoms, but that was not as important as getting them to come to our clinic so our doctors could prescribe a low-dose birth control pill. The next day, though many times they could not drive, they would come in that facility, and our nine doctors would prescribe that low-dose birth control pill. In order to provide any level of protection it had to be taken accurately at the same time every day. But we knew full well that there is not a teenager in the world who does anything at the same time every day.

We looked at the Planned Parenthood statistics, so we knew any time a young woman went on any method of contraception, the sexual activity went from zero or once a week to five to seven times a week. The pill would not work, and we could accomplish our agenda of three to five abortions between the ages of thirteen and eighteen. I held the hand of one young woman while she had her ninth abortion. Today, abortion is a method of birth control with almost a 50% repeat rate across the nation. So a girl gets pregnant. Of course, she's going to call me. She had that card that said, 'Free pregnancy test, licensed counselors, telephone answered 24 hours a day.' And she called that number, not understanding that we only sold one product.

We trained the people who answered our telephones as telemarketers. They used a script designed to overcome every single objection. That's what sales is about: overcoming objections. The young woman would call and confess, 'I think I may be pregnant.' And the counselor would move right in, reassuring, 'We can take care of your problem. No one needs to know. Your parents don't have to know. Your husband doesn't have to know. You don't have to drop out of school. You don't have to stop work.' They look for that fear and record it on paper. They're going to use it to reaffirm that abortion decision any time that young woman moves away.

The abortion industry has volunteers who will pay the expenses of any young woman who needs to get through the judicial process. The state pays the major portion, but transportation expenses are paid by the pro-choice movement.

Abortions in the nation cost from $250 to $8,000. To make the math easy let's just say it costs $4,000. But in the second and third trimester, the abortionist's fee is 50% of the total cost. So for that $4,000 abortion, $2,000 goes into his pocket. But he can do three an hour—$6,000 an hour. That's not bad money, is it?

Oh, but we all know that over 90% of abortions are first trimester abortions and they can't make that much money doing a $300 abortion. In the first trimester, the abortionist's fee is one third of the cost. Let's just say $100. But they use a technique which keeps them doing ten to twelve an hour. They use two teams of two assistants with each abortionist. The first team will set up the first young woman, and the abortionist will go in to do that abortion, while across the hall the second team sets up the second young woman. When the abortionist finishes abortion number one, he will go across the hall to do abortion number two. When the abortionist finishes abortion number two he can go back across the hall and do abortion number three. Ten to twelve abortions an hour at $100 is $1,200 an hour.

Then, they found another way to increase their profit line. Just sell the byproduct. You can charge a site fee for someone to harvest the babies' organs within ten minutes of death. You can charge them to be on site so they can take that little baby's body and dissect it and sell the parts. They collect $500 for a pancreas—it takes eight babies' pancreases to help one diabetic, and it's temporary so they repeat it every six months . . . Parkinson's is a horrible disease, but it takes four babies' brains at $999 for a perfect brain. My friends, an abortion clinic can easily add a $5,000 profit to their month by simply leasing a very small space."[60]

Everett went on to describe her feelings after aborting her own baby. She said, "The moment the anesthesia wore off, my first thought was, 'I'm a murderer.' You can't call your mother or your best friend and say, 'I'm depressed. I just killed my baby.' So I did what women do. I suppressed those feelings. I entered into those self-destructive tendencies and for thirteen years, I would never tell anyone that I was bad enough to kill my child."[61] Today, Everett is an outspoken Christian who takes her stand for Jesus Christ and is doing her part in persuading young girls to embrace sexual abstinence until marriage.

Likewise, Nathanson has turned from atheism to Jesus Christ. He says, "My life was spinning out of control. I had a series of failed marriages, and my only son had emotional problems. I was burned out professionally. I had the blood of 75,000 innocent babies on my hands. I was so hopeless and despairing that I searched around for all kinds of cures and healing. Eventually, I understood that there was only one place to go— and that was to go to Jesus Christ and open myself and . . . find forgiveness, absolution, and healing."[62]

For 200 years our western culture had laws specifically designed to protect the unborn. Never in modern times, except by a small group of seven physicians in Hitler's Germany and by Stalin in Russia, has there been such a holocaust of innocent lives. This nation that has more Bibles, more Christian bookstores, and more churches than anywhere in the world also has the most lenient abortion laws in the world. As the world leader in legalized abortions, Sodom and Gomorrah have nothing on America. The pulpits have been silent too long. Politicians have compromised too long. Activist judges have played the system too long. The church has been complacent too long.

The English statesman Edmund Burke was right in saying, "The only thing necessary for evil to triumph is for good people to do nothing."[63] The time has come for America to follow the examples of Everett and Nathanson . . . repent of our sin and find absolution and healing.

CHAPTER 8

Alcohol: America's Beverage of Choice

Moral Relativism's Spin: Drink Responsibly

It was 7:30 a.m. on a Monday, and Emily was sitting in her first period A.P. Statistics class. She had stayed up late the night before, so she laid her head down on her desk awaiting the enthusiastic voice of the senior class president to come over the intercom and recite the school announcements. Andrew would typically say, "Good morning, Tigers. Please take a few moments to pause for quiet reflection." But this time the voice over the intercom was Mr. Dunlap, the principal of the school. Emily lifted up her head to hear Mr. Dunlap request that the school have an extra-long moment of silence because a student was in the hospital as the result of a bad boating accident. He informed the school that Kristi's arm had been amputated. Kristi and Emily had cheered together, shared classes together, and gone to church together.

Here's what happened. The boat had stopped. There was a bunch of students on board who had been drinking, and unfortunately, Kristi was one of them. The boat was idling and Kristi was standing on the back of the boat, but she was unstable because of the alcohol in her system. She fell overboard and her body got caught in the propeller. Her arm was cut off and the rest of her body was severely mangled. With tears in her eyes, Kristi told Emily, "If I had never taken that first drink, I would not be in the condition that I'm in today. That first drink affected the crowd that I now hang out with, it affected my grades, my witness, my attitude, my conduct, and it cost me dearly." When speaking to students, I often tell them that the kind of crowd you hang around with is going to determine the direction your life takes, so before you start following some crowd, you need to first find out which direction they're headed.

Mary is another one who never planned to drink six beers at a party, get in a fight with another girl, spray hairspray in her face, get arrested, and face a lawsuit that would greatly impact her family.

Kendra never planned to wander down the beach after drinking rum with her friends, run into a group of boys, and be raped by all four of them.

Morgan never planned to get pregnant in the spring of her junior year of high school. But she drank during her junior prom, had sex for the first time, and by the end of the year, her friends were signing yearbooks, but she was expecting a baby. Her dreams of going to college and pursuing a career would never be realized.

Jessica never planned to get drunk, drive home from a party, get pulled over by the police, and have her driver's license revoked. When the University of Connecticut learned of the incident, they withdrew her basketball scholarship.

I'm sure all these students were good kids who simply made bad choices. It's a reminder once again that sin will take you further than you want to go, keep you longer than you want to stay, and cost you more than you want to pay.

The issue of social drinking is not just a huge problem within society, but in the church as well. If you go to any party, neighborhood gathering, or secular convention, alcohol is served and consumed as if it were a soft drink. The attitude is, "Everybody does it, so it's no big deal. It's just the culture in which we live." Those who do not know Jesus Christ cannot be expected to conduct themselves any other way. But for those who have been changed by the power of the Gospel and received the indwelling presence of the Holy Spirit, there ought to be something that distinguishes them from the rest of the world. As we look at this sensitive, and what has become a rather confusing issue within the body of Christ, we are going to explore the facts about alcohol: statistically, spiritually, and scripturally.

Years ago, I was contemplating the deceptive and destructive nature of alcohol. A dimension of my ministry includes speaking in public school assemblies about making wise choices. Often I am standing in the middle of the gymnasium floor looking into a sea of faces sitting in front of me. The Spirit of God often moves me with a deep compassion for these young kids. The desire to be accepted, the need to belong, and the pressure to have an identity so often takes precedence over making rational choices when it comes to chemical substances. What young person doesn't want to "be cool"? Nobody prefers rejection over acceptance. Unfortunately, the equation for acceptance often requires indulging in alcohol. Even adults who have grown up with fragile self-esteems, who were never the popular kids in school and are still searching for acceptance, will often bow to the pressures of social drinking. The term "social drinking" is really a misnomer because there is nothing social about it. Slurred speech, blurred eyes, and the inability to walk a straight line are so often the results of "social" drinking, not to mention inappropriate remarks that are made while under the influence.

Mel Gibson is a case in point. After having gained great admiration from the Christian community and the highest accolades from leaders within the church throughout the world, Gibson disappointed the very ones who sang his praises when he was arrested for a DUI and began spewing out obscenities toward the Jewish community. Afterwards, he profusely apologized and was embarrassed beyond words. While many have been quite forgiving and accepting of his remorse, others will never forget or forgive the offensive language that denigrated the Jewish world. To his credit, he immediately checked into a treatment center to deal with his drinking problem. In the hearts of millions, Gibson will remain their favorite actor and when sober, their most-loved personality in Hollywood. However, the damage that was done, at least for this moment in time, has left an unforgettable blemish on his spiritual resumé.

After returning from speaking to a school assembly, I wrote the following poem. I have a feeling Gibson would be the first to agree with these words.

AL–COHOL

Ladies and gentlemen . . .
I want to take this opportunity
To introduce you to me.
So listen up one and all
For my name is Al–cohol.

My man, before you start messin' with me,
Just let me inform you of how it will be.
I'm packaged with love and plenty of charm
And actually appear to cause you no harm.

Now that you've learned the call of my name,
I guess you should know the rules to my game.
My goal is to appeal and attract your eyes
And once in your hands, to compromise.

Tens of thousands I killed last year,
And it all started with just one beer.
"Drink responsibly" is the message I send,
But you'll never know where it will end.

Suicides and murders were in the news
Not to mention the child abuse.
Four hundred homes are destroyed each day
Cause where I am, somebody will pay.

It's my desire to make you think
That you can stop at just one drink.
But why stop now with all the fun
When you know full well, it's just begun.

From weekends to weeknights, the habit is formed,
And now you're hooked, just as I forewarned.
The hangover and vomit, it's no big deal.
It's me who now has the greater appeal.

You're a prisoner of war, though you refuse to believe.
And your potential in life, you'll never achieve.

With me by your side, your companion I'll be.
I'll walk with you to your destiny.

There's one life to live, it's yours to choose.
Whether you'll win or whether you'll lose.
It's never an easy decision to make,
But to swallow me is a big mistake.

When the music has stopped and the laughter's gone,
And you're still asking, "What went wrong?"
The party is over and you're left behind
Still searching for truth and peace of mind.

Life's too short and goes around once,
To be abused on chemical substance.
My promise to give you a home and solution
Is one big lie and attractive illusion.

Let me ease your pain and remove your depression
So that I become your only obsession.
Conflicts go up and grades will come down,
That's what happens when I'm around.

It takes more courage to make it your goal
When offered a drink, to just say "no."
So when faced with decisions, choose the best.
In the end, you'll outdistance the rest.

Ambitions and inventions, they lie before you,
With dreams and visions for you to pursue.
But through the ages I have destroyed them all,
For remember, my name is Al, Al–cohol.

ALCOHOL IS STATISTICALLY DEADLY AND DESTRUCTIVE

It is destructive; the statistics are overwhelming and alarming. Alcohol manufacturers spend more than $1 billion each year advertising their products.[1] The beer industry alone spends $700 million per year on advertising.[2] It is apparently doing a good job because within the teenage community, 80% of all high school students and 50% of all middle school students drink.[3] The average age when youth first try alcohol is 11 years old for boys and 13 years old for girls. The average age at which Americans begin drinking regularly is 15.9 years old.[4] But what the commercials fail to tell us is that for every young person who takes a drink, one in ten will become an alcoholic, which now accounts for 450,000 teenage alcoholics.[5] Beer ads show us people with healthy bodies and happy faces, holding a can of beer while projecting some macho image of success and happiness. Kids who drink are 7.5 times more likely to use illicit drugs and 50 times more likely to use cocaine than those who never drink alcohol.[6] It all starts with one social drink.

Every day an average 11,318 teens try alcohol for the first time.[7] A staggering 40% of those who started drinking at age 14 or younger become alcoholics.[8] Surveys indicate that adolescent drinking accounts for 80% of the excessive use of alcohol in the United States.[9] This issue is ranked the third most prevalent health problem in America, just behind cancer and heart disease.[10] An unbelievable 88% of people over the age of 21 (175.6 million, to be exact) are lifetime users, whereas only 11.8% (23.5 million) of people are lifetime nondrinkers.[11] Underage drinking costs the U.S. more than $58 billion every year—enough to buy every public school student their own state-of-the-art computer.[12] More than 4 million adolescents under the legal drinking age consume alcohol in any given month.[13] It is overwhelmingly documented that social drinking is destructive because it impairs a person's judgment and decision-making ability, often putting himself or herself, as well as others, in harm's way. And yet, well-meaning people and law-abiding citizens continue to vigorously defend social drinking in spite of the facts. Social drinking is not only destructive, but it is also deadly. Alcohol kills six times more youth than all other illicit drugs combined.[14] Alcohol is the leading cause of death for 16-year-olds.[15] Eighty percent of all murders in America are alcohol related.[16] Seven out of ten perpetrators of child rape are under the influence of alcohol when the rape occurs.[17] Seventy-five percent of all domestic violence cases are alcohol-related.[18] Approximately 17,000 people die on the highways in our nation every year because of alcohol, which represents 40% of all traffic fatalities.[19]

This is an average of one alcohol-related fatality every 31 minutes. Every two minutes someone is injured in an alcohol-related car crash.[20] In fact, did you know that every weekend from 10:00 p.m. to 1:00 a.m., one in every 13 people on the highways is drunk?[21] And between 1:00 a.m. and 6:00 a.m., one in seven drivers is drunk.[22] Forty-six people die daily from alcohol-related crashes, and one out of every three people will be involved in an alcohol-related traffic accident during their lifetime. The total economic cost for alcohol-related traffic accidents exceeds $50 billion each year.[23] More Americans have died in alcohol-related traffic crashes than in all the wars the United States has been involved in since our country was founded.[24] Without question, it is deadly, and it is destructive. So, why would a Christian who has been delivered from death to life and is now identified with the Prince of Peace want to be associated with, much less consume, something that is so deadly and destructive?

ALCOHOL IS SPIRITUALLY DECEITFUL AND DETRIMENTAL

Unfortunately, alcohol is not only America's beverage of choice, but has also found wide acceptance within the church. John the Baptist was strong in the Lord, and he abstained from wine and strong drink (Luke 7:33). But there's another kind of Baptist today who believes otherwise. Forty-eight percent of our Southern Baptist friends drink socially.[25] It should come as no surprise that half of all ordained ministers drink socially.[26] Needless to say, when you see spiritual leaders endorsing and participating in it, it becomes much easier for the rest of the population and congregation to justify it. So, why is this poison in a bottle so spiritually deceitful?

Proverbs 20:1 says, "Wine is a mocker, strong drink is a brawler, and whoever is led astray by it is not wise." Proverbs 23:32 says that alcohol "bites like a serpent," and in Scripture the devil is also called a serpent. The previous verse (v. 31) admonishes a person to "not look on the wine when it is red, when it sparkles in the cup, when it swirls around smoothly." The redness sparkles in the cup and flows with enticing beauty, but the appeal is deceptive. For what appears harmless, is in fact, dangerous. What appears beautiful, results in ugliness. Verse 34 says, "Your eyes will see strange things, and your heart will utter perverse things." The strong implication is that wine is a deceiver. It is interesting that Scripture also describes the devil as a deceiver. Could this be a coincidence? It is no wonder that evangelist Billy Sunday called alcohol "the devil in liquid form."

Proverbs 20:1 says that wine and strong drink will lead a person astray. Astray from what? They will be led astray from the path of wisdom. Alcohol will either lead you away from wisdom, or wisdom will lead you away from alcohol. Everybody is in agreement that drunkenness is a sin. Both the Christian and non-Christian agree that it's wrong to get drunk, so in order to market its product and maintain respectability, the alcohol industry had to come up with some ploy or slogan that would resonate with mainstream society. So, it tells young people and adults alike to "drink responsibly," and to drink in moderation. Now that sounds good until you realize that at the moment you take your first drink, your judgment has become impaired. You don't know where to draw the line. It takes an adult 10-15 years to become an alcoholic, but with that same drinking pattern, a teenager can become an alcoholic in only six months. It is spiritually deceptive. It's deceptive in that it promises much and gives back little. It's been said, "We drank for happiness and became unhappy. We drank for joy and became miserable. We drank for sociability and became argumentative. We drank for sophistication and became obnoxious. We drank for friendship and made enemies. We drank to sleep and awakened without rest. We drank for strength and became weak. We drank for medicinal reasons and developed health problems. We drank for relaxation and got the shakes. We drank for bravery and became afraid. We drank for confidence and became doubtful. We drank to make conversation easier, and we slurred our speech. We drank to forget and were forever haunted. We drank for freedom and became slaves. We drank to erase problems and saw them multiply. We drank to cope with life and we invited death." Friend, mark it down. Alcohol is a deceiver and does not live up to its promises.

But it is not only spiritually deceitful. It is also spiritually detrimental.

The sincere desire of any Christian ought to be to honor his or her Lord in every aspect of life. His or her attitude should be this: "God, I don't want to do anything that would hurt my witness for You. Lord Jesus, help me to be the person that You died for me to become." The fact is, we are not islands within ourselves. What we do, and the example we set does affect others. One Christian may say, "I can control my alcohol intake," but I would ask, "What about the person who follows your example and will not be able to control it? Do you have any responsibility for his actions?" The Bible says, "Yes, you do." You see, the question is not just "Will it hurt me?" but "Will it cause me to hurt someone else?" Romans 14:21 says that we are not to do anything that causes our weaker brother to stumble: "It is good neither to eat meat nor to drink wine nor do anything by which your brother stumbles or is offended or is made weak." In Mark 9:42 Jesus said, "But whoever causes one of these little ones who believe in Me to stumble, it would be better for him if a mill-stone were hung around his neck, and he were thrown into the sea." You have to wonder if the 80% of high school students who drink and the 450,000 teenage alcoholics in this nation are just following the example of some significant adult in their lives. After all, it is called an adult beverage.

In Leviticus 10:9, God spoke to Aaron saying, "Do not drink wine or intoxicating drink, you, nor your sons with you, when you go into the tabernacle of meeting, lest you die. It shall be a statute forever through-out your generations." So, here is God basically saying, "Aaron, I'm telling you that when you go into the temple to minister, if you do so with liquor on your breath, I'll kill you." Now listen carefully. Aaron was a priest. And if you know anything about the New Testament, you know that Christians are also called priests. Would the New Testament have any lesser standards for priests than what God had for Aaron? Where do you minister as a priest? In the temple. As a Christian, the New Testament tells us that our bodies are the temple of the Holy Spirit, and as a priest I am not going to defile my temple and bring the curse of death upon me. Habakkuk 2:15 says, "Woe to him who gives drink to his neighbor, pressing him to your bottle, even to make him drunk, . . ." God's curse is upon such behavior. I cannot help but wonder how many teenagers and young adults began drinking because their pastor said it was all right or because they saw a deacon or Sunday School teacher drinking. Or maybe they went to spend the night with a friend from church and saw a six-pack when they opened the fridge. Maybe he or she saw a stash of liquor in the cabinet next to the cereal they had for breakfast. These are church-going adults who they respect. While their parents have told them never to drink, they're getting mixed signals from the rest of the Christian community. It is spiritually deceptive and detrimental.

IS SOCIAL DRINKING CONDEMNED IN THE BIBLE?

This is really a lightning-rod issue for a lot of Christians. It is not at all uncommon to hear Christians defend social drinking under the auspices that "nowhere does the Bible condemn it." But is that an accurate representation of what the Bible says about this issue? I want to suggest that social drinking is discredited in Scripture. We all hear people say, "Well, Jesus turned water into wine, so if it was good enough for Jesus then that should settle it for the rest of us."

First of all, it's important to note that Jesus never mentioned the word "wine," much less consumed it. And what most people fail to recognize is that the wine of Jesus' day was not intoxicating. Yale University did a study on this very issue and concluded that the wine of our day and that of Jesus' day were two very different things.[28] The wine of today is not only fermented, but a mechanical process has added a minimum of 20% pure alcohol to the fermentation process.[29]

Robert Stein is a New Testament scholar who devoted a great deal of time researching the wine of the ancient world using both Jewish sources and the Bible. He discovered that the wine of Jesus' day was actually three to four parts water mixed with one part wine.[30] The water in the ancient world was unsafe to drink, so in order to make it safe they had to boil it or filter it.[31] But did you know that the safest way to purify the water and kill the germs was to mix wine with it? Stein also discovered it would take 22 glasses of wine from the first century to equal the alcohol in two of today's martinis.[32] Please understand, the wine in Bible times was totally different from the wine of today. In fact, today's wine would be considered strong drink in the Bible. In Proverbs 20:1, the word for "strong drink" is "shekir." Everywhere in the Bible that this word is used signifies that strong drink is condemned. The only time strong drink is not condemned is when it is to be used as a narcotic to help a person who is dying. We find in Proverbs 31:6 that you can give strong drink to someone who is ready to perish. But in that same chapter, using the same word, kings and national leaders are forbidden to indulge in strong drink. Verses 4-5 say, "It is not for kings to drink wine, nor for princes intoxicating drink; lest they drink and forget the law, . . ." Isaiah 28:7 rebukes the leaders of the nation for consuming strong drink. Therefore, if it is forbidden for kings to drink wine, Jesus, being the King of kings, surely did not disobey this Scripture because that would make Him a sinner. The Hebrew word for "wine" is "yayin," which is the generic word meaning either intoxicating wine or non-intoxicating wine. The context in which this word is used determines the definition.

Dr. Norman Geisler, a well-known Christian apologist, has concluded that "Christians ought not to consume wine, beer, or alcoholic beverages because they are strong drink and are forbidden in Scripture. Even ancient pagans did not drink what some Christians are drinking today."[32] What people are drinking today would always have to equate with strong drink in the Bible, which, without exception, is always condemned throughout Scripture.

Now, for clarification's sake, let's define "fermented wine." Fermentation is when you squeeze the juice out of the grapes and let it set for a few days until the grapes become putrefied or rotten. Do you think Jesus would ever compare something rotten with His sinless blood? Of course not. At the last supper, He compared the fruit of the vine with His blood. It is inconceivable that He was referring to fermented wine.

But let's go back to John 2 where Jesus turned the water into wine. Verse 10 says that when Mary asked Jesus to provide more wine, the wedding guests were already "well drunk." How do we know that? Well, Jesus commands them to fill six water pots to the brim. It's estimated those six pots would have held between 100 and 150 gallons of water. Now remember, they were already "well drunk" at this point, which means they had already drunk a lot of grape juice. So, is it even slightly possible that Jesus was producing another 150 gallons of an intoxicating beverage? Of course not. It was non-alcoholic wine that would probably be the equivalent of our purified water. Otherwise, if He was making alcoholic wine for a bunch of people who had already been drinking so much that they were drunk, He would have been helping the wedding guests get even more intoxicated. The Bible says that drunkards shall not inherit the kingdom of God. (1 Corinthians 6:10) If Jesus helped a bunch of people get drunk, He would have been sending people to hell by His miracle. In that case, He would have been sinning, and thus, He would not have been the Savior of the world.

Now it's true that in 1 Timothy 5:23, the apostle Paul instructed Timothy to "no longer drink only water, but use a little wine for your stomach's sake and your frequent infirmities." Paul never said to drink wine with your dinner or at a party. Wine was used as a medicine in those days and as a water purifier. Even today, some medicines still contain alcohol to help heal the body. Anybody who would take this statement to mean that the Bible sanctions social drinking in moderation would also have to embrace the first part of the verse that says, "No longer drink only water." He's telling Timothy to drink grape juice for his stomach ailments.

In Proverbs 13:20 the Bible says, "He who walks with wise men will be wise, but the companion of fools will be destroyed." But we're also told that those who drink wine and strong drink are not wise. A person who is not wise is a fool. A companion of fools will be destroyed. Thus, to hang around with those who drink makes that person a fool; therefore, he or she will also share in their destruction.

Yet, to make it sound respectable, we call alcoholism a disease. I do have compassion for those who are enslaved to this substance. There's no question that it creates an addiction. My heart goes out to the families and children who have to deal with an alcoholic loved one. Unbelievable abuse, poverty, fear, and emotional trauma often accompany alcoholism. To be sure, it is not politically correct to say that alcoholism is anything other than a disease. But if it is a disease, it is the only disease that the government allows to be bottled and sold to the public. It's the only disease for which the government taxes you. If it's a disease, then how do men and women who go to jail suddenly recover from it? Those who vigorously defend their right to drink socially will say, "Why don't you preachers preach against gluttony?" Well, you're right. Gluttony is a sin, and we have too many fat Christians. Yet, I've never heard of anybody being arrested for being too fat, but I've heard of a lot of people who've been arrested for being too drunk. The reality is that the moment a person takes that first drink, he or she is already under the influence of alcohol when they try to resist the second one.

I want to emphasize that the biblical word for "wine," both in Hebrew and in Greek, can mean either grape juice or intoxicating wine. The context determines which of these translations is correct, and any open-minded, objective person would have to agree that given the whole counsel of Scripture, the alcohol of today is completely different from that of the Bible and would be considered strong drink. Given this information as being as true to the principles of Scripture as we possibly can be, one can conclude that Jesus would never condone social drinking. The Bible associates strong drink with evil, and God does not lead us into evil but delivers us from it. He does not teach us to practice evil in moderation.

ALCOHOL IS SOCIALLY DISTASTEFUL AND DISTURBING

It should be noted that the great preachers of the past spoke out about the evils of social drinking. They took strong stands on this issue and did so with biblical authority. Now here is a question for those who try to defend their social drinking: do they consider themselves more spiritual and more biblically knowledgeable than those giants of the past? The last great revival that America had was in 1911. During that revival, God changed so many lives that it actually led Congress to pass a national law known as Prohibition. It prohibited the sale of alcohol because those whose lives had been changed by the Gospel demanded that alcohol be banned from our society.

There is something else about the social aspect of consuming alcohol that is seldom mentioned. Teenage girls who drink are far more likely to get addicted than teenage boys.[33] A single drink for a gal has the impact of two drinks for a guy.[34] If a teenage boy and girl both weigh the same and drink the same amount, the alcohol the girl consumes goes directly into her bloodstream because all females have a missing enzyme in their stomachs.[35] It's as if she's shooting alcohol directly into her veins.

Also, females have a higher proportion of body fat, and alcohol is not easily dissolved in fat.[36] People with more body fat will experience a higher blood-alcohol level.[37] Alcohol is more damaging to a teenage girl's brain than to a teenage boy's brain.[38] Teenage girls who drink are seven times more likely to have sex than if they had not consumed alcohol.[39]

There are 18 million alcoholics in America, and it all started with that first drink. Friend, the one thing you can do to insure you'll never become an alcoholic is to never take that first drink. Yet, each year students spend $5.5 million on alcohol, which is more than they spend on soft drinks, tea, juice, coffee, and books combined.[40]

Let's remember that alcohol is addictive, and Jesus would never advocate anything that would lead you into bondage. He came to set people free. As Christians, we are sanctified, which means that we are set apart for the express purpose of glorifying Jesus Christ. Since we are to glorify God in our bodies, and knowing what we know about alcohol, it's difficult to fulfil that Scripture while drinking socially.

No doubt there are many sincere and well-meaning Christians who drink socially, but they've just never taken the time to examine the biblical case for total abstinence. It's easier to understand how this can happen when a person comes from a family that drinks socially, joins a church where it's commonly accepted, and never hears anybody teach otherwise. God's preachers and the church today have done an injustice to our nation by being silent on this issue.

Natalie Holloway was a vibrant, healthy, happy, and beautiful young lady who was a senior in high school in Birmingham, Alabama. She and her friends were excited about planning a senior trip to the island of Aruba. Little did she know that her much-anticipated trip would result in her name appearing in the headlines of every major media outlet in America. To this day, her disappearance remains a mystery. There are lots of unanswered questions, but this much we do know: alcohol played a role in her decision-making on the night of her disappearance. Some say she was drunk, and others say she had been drinking quite a bit socially. One can only speculate as to where Holloway would be today if alcohol had not been involved.

Alcohol is statistically deadly and destructive. It is spiritually deceptive and detrimental. It is scripturally discouraged and discredited. And it's socially distasteful and disturbing. The Bible says whether we eat, drink, or whatever we do, do it all for the glory of God. (1 Corinthians 10:31) The Bible says that whatever is not of faith is sin. (Romans 14:23) The very fact that a Christian has a question about this issue ought to raise a red flag that says, "Do not proceed."

I find it interesting that Ephesians 5:18 commands us not to be drunk with wine, but to be filled with the Spirit. God is saying that we should not allow ourselves to be controlled by some foreign substance, but instead we should allow the indwelling presence of God's Spirit to control us. Getting drunk is the devil's substitute for being filled with the Spirit. It's a cheap substitute. Why settle for a drink that serves as an anesthetic designed to deaden the pain of life when Jesus came to give us abundant life 24/7?

CHAPTER 9

Random Chance or Intelligent Design?

Moral Relativism's Spin: Natural Selection and Evolution

It is a fascinating world that God has created. Wherever life is found, there you will also find the undeniable fingerprints of God. It is impossible to observe any living thing without being forced to acknowledge there is an unbelievable design and intricate detail to life-forms as we know them. Take your eyes for example. Did you know that on a clear night, you can see the flame of a candle 30 miles away? The iris is what gives your eyes color, and it has 266 DNA-controlled characteristics. Did you know that your retina has over 120 million rods that allow you to see at night and give you peripheral vision? The retina also has 7 million cones, which allow you to distinguish millions of shades of color. In addition, each eye has one million nerve fibers that electronically connect the photoreceptors in the retina to the visual cortex of the brain.[1]

John Stevens is a biomedical engineer. Stevens says the Cray supercomputer would need several minutes to do the work that a single nerve cell in your retina completes in ten milliseconds. There are at least ten million nerve cells in your retina that interact with each other. It would take the Cray supercomputer 100 years to simulate what takes place in your eye many times every second![2] And you never even have to wash your eyes. Your tear ducts are sterile and have bacteria-destroying enzymes that do the job for you. You blink your eyes every two to ten seconds, 400 million times during your lifetime, and every time you blink you are lubricating your eyes.[3] So, whenever you watch TV or read a book, you are experiencing a miracle. Psalm 94:9 asks the question: "He who formed the eye, shall He not see?"

Did you know that your body has 600 muscles, which account for

40% of your total weight?[4] We also have automatic muscles that control our eyelids, breathing, heartbeat, and digestion. Automatic muscles are like the cruise control button on a car. They are built in and do the work for us.[5] For example, we breathe 23,000 times a day, 630 million times in an average life span. We take in more than one billion trillion molecules of air with each lungful, which adds up to seven quarts of air every minute. Now, if you were to weigh all of that air, it would equal about 22 pounds a day.[6]

Keep in mind that 25% of the oxygen we breathe goes to the brain, 12% to the kidneys, and seven percent to the heart. In fact, without any conscious effort on your part, your heart pumps blood through 60,000 miles of blood vessels in your body and back again. Every day, your 10-ounce heart muscle contracts 100,000 times without missing a beat. In a year's time, the average human heart circulates between 770,000 and 1.6 million gallons of blood through the body. That's enough to fill 200 train tank cars, each with a capacity of 8,000 gallons! In an average lifetime, the heart beats 2.5 billion times and pumps 60 million gallons of blood.[7]

Your brain weighs about three pounds and contains over 10 billion neurons, each of which has contact with 10,000 other neurons, requiring a total of 100 trillion neurological interconnections. If all the neurons and threadlike connections of the brain were laid end to end, they would circle the equator four times.[8] Your brain can hold the same amount of information as the content of 20 million books, which would fill a bookshelf 500 miles long.[9] By the time a person reaches the age of 30, he or she will have a mental videotape library of about three trillion visualized experiences.[10] The brain is capable of thinking at a rate of 800 words per minute in one of the world's more than 5,000 languages.[11]

If a team of scientists and computer programmers were to try to assemble a brain of comparable intelligence and complexity, using the most sophisticated digital and electronic technology known today, it would require a structure the size of the Empire State Building to house it, and would require more electricity to run than it takes to power a city the size of New York.[12] Machines can process information, can calculate and retrieve data and apply it to solving problems, but they cannot think. Unlike humans, regardless of their intelligence level, machines are incapable of producing one single original thought on their own. It is a physical impossibility. Yet, we originate thoughts every day in the blink of an eye. Only God could have conceived and created such a creature.

The way that you digest your food is equally amazing. Did you know that if you were to unravel the alimentary canal (comprised of the esophagus, stomach, and large and small intestines) in your body, it would reach the height of a three-story building?[13] Your three-pound liver performs over 500 functions. It detoxifies substances, guards vitamins and minerals, stockpiles sugar for quick energy, and manufactures new proteins.[14] We could go on and on about the amazing design of the human body. We can only agree with the Psalmist who said that we are all "fearfully and wonderfully made" (Psalm 139:14).

But the same is true in the animal kingdom. Owls can hear sounds ten times softer than humans can hear. Dogs can detect high-pitch sounds with frequencies up to 40,000 vibrations per second, which is twice what humans can hear. A German shepherd or golden retriever has 220 million smell cells compared to a mere five million for humans. An eagle's eyes are six times sharper than the human eye. A seagull has built-in sunglasses that enable him to look directly into the sun.[15]

A flea can jump 100 times the height of its own body. That's the equivalent of a six-foot man jumping over a 40-story building. Fleas can accelerate 50 times faster than the space shuttle.[16] The fastest-moving animal is the falcon, which has been clocked at 217 miles per hour.[17] Humans have 600 muscles while a caterpillar has over 2,000 muscles.[18]

An ant can lift its own weight, and a bee can handle 300 times its own weight.[19] That's the equivalent of a human pulling a ten-ton trailer. Seals can dive to depths up to 2,600 feet and stay underwater for as long as two hours without coming up for air.[20] Camels can travel three days without needing a drop of water, and some birds can fly 22,000 miles a year with their own built-in navigation system.[21]

So, here is the question: is all this stuff the result of spontaneous energy or creative genius? How you answer that question will ultimately determine everything else in your life. The question of origins is one of the most fundamental questions anyone can ask. How you answer that question will determine the basis of your morality, how you value life, how you derive meaning from life, and will ultimately dictate your destiny in life.

Consider first the presuppositions of evolution. A presupposition is a foregone conclusion in your mind which serves as a starting point or the foundational building block upon which you form a worldview. It is a preconceived paradigm that you bring to the table in forming your opinion about the origins of life. Evolution begins with the presupposition that there is no God. Therefore, man and all other living things are products of mere chance. In other words, this world is the result of an accident, a cosmic coincidence. We are all the product of random, chaotic, impersonal, un-intelligent design. The evolutionist would say that to believe otherwise is ignorant, naïve, and fanatical.

That's why many Christian students sit silently in biology classrooms feeling intimidated while the professor eloquently spouts off his neat little discourse on the origins of life. Let's listen in on such a classroom now: the professor states, "Science has proven that we all evolved from lower life-forms, and like so many of them, Homo sapiens will also one day be extinct. Oh, I know that some people still believe the myths from Genesis, but personally, I can live with the facts."

But then a student like my son, Josh, raises his hand and says, "Professor, is there scientific evidence that substantiates the claim that life arose from nothing and then went through the changes represented on the evolutionary ladder?" Maintaining his composure, the professor responds, " Well, young man, I'm sure in your lifetime scientists will create life in a test tube." With persistence, Josh replies, "Sir, with all due respect, if that happens then wouldn't that be creating life by intelligent design?" The professor then gets defensive and personalizes the argument, "Are you one of those Bible-believing Christians?" Josh respectfully says, "Yes sir, I am, but that doesn't mean I'm not interested in getting the correct information." In irritation and disdain, the professor replies, "This is biology, not a religion class. Now let's move on to the next chapter."

Make no mistake about it. There are only two presuppositions in approaching the origins of life. It's either divine creation or spontaneous generation; purposeful design or random accidental order; infinite God or infinite odds; life from life or life from nothing; God as creator or time as creator.

So, the presupposition of evolution says there is no God. We are all the product of random chaos. We are just an accident that came together as a result of the Big Bang. If that is the case, let's look at the process of evolution because that's what it is, a process. Evolution says that billions of years ago there was a large inorganic soup of nitrogen, ammonia, salts, and carbon dioxide, and out of this primeval caldron arose the first single cell. And over the process of time, we have now entered the information and computer age of this evolutionary process. Of course, evolution has no explanation as to where this bubbling inorganic soup came from. That's just something you must accept by faith!

In layman's terms, here is how the process of evolution works. Out of nothing, this universe suddenly and accidentally came into existence. At first, the material was inanimate. But then, over billions of years animate life came out of inanimate life, the living from nonliving. It all started as a single cell. After millions of generations, simple plants and animals accidentally appeared and became more complex with the passing of time. Finally, this process gave rise to man as we now know him. You see, the mask that the evolutionist hides behind is Father Time. The contention is that anything can happen over billions and billions of years. That is the layman's explanation, but here's the same explanation, only with the scientific jargon added to give it more credibility and believability.

The Public Broadcasting Service's (PBS) award-winning television broadcast entitled *The Miracle of Life* gave this explanation for how life began: "Four-and-a-half billion years ago, the young planet Earth was a mass of cosmic dust or particles. It was almost completely engulfed by the shallow primordial seas. Powerful winds gathered random molecules from the atmosphere. Some were deposited in the seas. Tides and currents swept the molecules together. And somewhere in this ancient ocean the miracle of life began . . . The first organized form of life was a tiny protozoan (a one-celled animal). Millions of protozoa populated the ancient seas. These early organisms were completely self-sufficient in their seawater world. They moved about their aquatic environment feeding on bacteria and other organisms . . . From these one-celled organisms evolved all life on earth."[22]

Evolutionists believe that chance plus time will generate life, and when they run into problems with their theories, they just add more millions and billions of years to their hypothesis. That is the heart of the evolutionary process. Have you ever stopped to consider this absurdity? Unknown chemicals through unknown processes produced unknown life forms through unknown reproductive methods in an unknown atmospheric composition in an unknown oceanic soup complex at an unknown time in an unknown place. Then, there are other evolutionists who embrace the popular theory that everything you see around you happened by a super explosion called the Big Bang. My question is, "Since when do explosions ever produce order?" That's not a complicated question requiring a lot of thought. If you blow up a pile of lumber with a stick of dynamite, it's not going to result in a plush office building no matter how much time passes.

Yet, it is this process that has gained incredible prominence in the world of academia. On August 11, 1999, the Kansas State Board of Education made headlines around the world by proposing to delete evolution from state assessment tests since it was still an unproven theory.[23] There was a collective cry of outrage from the scientific community that said, "How dare you question the absolute certainty of our explanation for the origin of life?" For example, Robert Palazzo, an associate professor of molecular biosciences from Kansas protested, "The concept of evolution is inextricable from the language of all life sciences and is a cornerstone for learning by all those who seek an education in basic science, medicine, and ecology."[24]

Others chimed in such as Maxine Singer, president of the Carnegie Institution of Washington. She wrote a column in the *Washington Post* that said, "Omitting evolution from biology is comparable to leaving the U.S. Constitution out of civics lessons. Evolution is the framework that makes sense of the whole natural world."[25] Are you kidding me? What is sensible about life resulting from the nonliving, something resulting from nothing, or unintelligence producing intelligence? Evolution contends that nothing plus chance equals everything. For Singer to call this sensible makes no sense to me.

As a result of these protests, in 2001 the Kansas Board of Education reversed their decision by allowing evolution to be presented in the classroom as a foundational fact of biology.[26] Evolution has become the basis of education throughout most of the world today. I don't know that it's possible to attend a biology class at any state university or public school without being exposed to the theory of evolution. And that's fine, as long as it is presented as a theory, but more times than not, it is presented as a fact. And anyone who believes otherwise is just not in step with the times. Almost every textbook presents evolution as the only intellectual possibility for life.

Before embracing such a theory, you need to first consider its ramifications. Let's suppose there is no God, and thus, no one to whom we must answer. That means there is no such thing as absolute right and wrong. After all, since there is no God then there is no objective standard by which we can measure right and wrong. Why have rules if there is no rules enforcer? Why have morals if there is no moral governor ruling the universe? Since we are all the product of a random collision of impersonal particles, that means we have no real purpose for existing. The foregone conclusion is that there are no lasting consequences for our actions. Since we have no rules, we are free to do as we please. Since there is no God, we do not need to worry about eternal accountability because there is no such thing as an eternal afterlife. There you have it, the perfect formula for anarchy and the collapse of a nation: no rules, no authority, no consequences, and no God. Do whatever you want.

Interestingly enough, it's not just the creationists who make this charge, but even those evolutionists who are honest enough to admit it agree there is very little scientific evidence to support their claims. Sir Arthur Keith, the Scottish anatomist and anthropologist, said, "Evolution is unproved and unproveable. We believe it because it is the only alternative to special creation, and that is unthinkable."[27]

Another teacher of evolution was honest enough to say, "I know evolution is scientifically impossible, but I'm still going to teach it because it is morally comfortable."[28] Dr. George Wald, a former professor of biology at Harvard University and Nobel Prize winner said, "The idea that life arose from nonliving matter was scientifically disproved by Louis Pasteur in 1860. One has only to contemplate the magnitude of this task to concede that the spontaneous generation of a living organism is impossible."[29] And when contemplating that magnitude, Albert Einstein said, "Is it any wonder why mathematicians have serious doubts about evolution?"[30]

Sir Frederick Hoyle is one of the world's leading astronomers and mathematicians. While speaking before the British Academy of Science, he said, "The probability of life arising by chance is the same probability as throwing a dice and having a six come up five million consecutive times . . . Let's be scientifically honest. We all know that the probability of life arising to greater and greater complexity and organization by chance through evolution is the same probability as having a tornado tear through a junkyard and form out of the other end a Boeing 747 jetliner."[31]

There are hundreds of eminent scientists who hold prestigious degrees and have attained the highest honors of recognition within the academic community who declare that evolution is a scientific impossibility. To watch the documentaries on TV or read the textbooks in today's curricula, we are led to believe that anyone who adheres to intelligent design and creationism does so in blind faith without the support of science. This is not the case, and what they don't want to admit is that it takes more faith to believe in evolution that it takes to believe in creationism.

WHY IS THE MISSING LINK STILL MISSING?

First of all, evolution has a major problem with the absence of any transitional life forms in the fossil record. You see, evolution claims that through thousands of generations life developed from simple to more complex forms. If that is true, why don't we see transitional life forms in the fossil record to confirm that claim? In other words, evolution contends that we are all descendents from monkeys. You've seen these charts speculating that apes came from monkeys, chimpanzees came from apes, and the gorilla came from the chimpanzee, and man evolved from the gorilla. Now, if all that were true, you would think that somewhere in the fossil record we would see this transition taking place. But instead, the fossils show just the opposite. When monkeys appeared, they were full-blown monkeys. When apes appeared, they were full-blown apes.

The oldest fossilized bat skeleton is said to be 50 million years old, but the skeleton is precisely the same as those of modern bats. *National Geographic* published an article about a fossilized cockroach that is supposedly 300 million years old, and there is no change in its appearance from today's cockroaches.[32] We also have an ant that has been perfectly preserved and is said to be 100 million years old that is exactly the same as today's ant.[33] We have a praying mantis that is 40 million years old and is precisely the same as its descendents.[34] So, here is the question: if evolution was taking place in even the slightest measure, then wouldn't these fossils show some evidence of transition?

Newsweek magazine published an article that said the inability to find the fossils of transitional life forms between species is a professional embarrassment for paleontologists.[35] Even Charles Darwin himself admitted in his memoir, *My Life and Letters,* "Not one change of species into another is on record . . . we cannot prove that a single species has been changed."[36] Over a century has passed with paleontologists devoting their entire careers to looking for examples of gradual transitions over time, and their efforts have been a total failure.

However, what the fossil record does show is the sudden appearance of fully formed invertebrates such as snails, clams, and jellyfish. The fossil record also shows the sudden appearance of fully formed fish of every kind.

Dr. Gary Parker is a biologist and former evolutionist. He says, "In most people's minds, fossils and evolution go hand in hand. In reality, fossils are a great embarrassment to the evolutionary theory and offer strong support for the concept of creation. If evolution were true, we should find literally millions of fossils that show how one kind of life slowly and gradually changed to another kind of life."[37]

But the cover of *TIME* magazine carried the headline, "When Life Exploded." The article simply claims that new discoveries now show that life as we know it appeared suddenly, and there has been little change since. The article went on to say that "scientists delicately slide across thin ice, suggesting scenarios that are based on intuition rather than solid evidence."[38] Make no mistake about it. The clear evidence from the fossil record shows that the origin of life began with God, just as the Genesis record tells us. But even in the face of convincing evidence, that's not an option to the evolutionist. His or her presupposition is based upon the assumption that there is no God. There are those today who still make wild assertions that life has evolved from one distinct species to another and another and another, but they cannot prove it or demonstrate it. They cannot even give a logical explanation for it, but they demand that it be taught as a cornerstone of our children's education.

THE SECOND LAW OF THERMODYNAMICS

The second problem with evolution is its contradiction to the second law of thermodynamics, which says that everything as we know it is winding up and wearing down. But evolution teaches that everything is evolving upward to greater and greater complexity. That is contradictory to the laws of physics. Everything we know about our universe shows that in every single case all energy and matter are governed by the laws of thermodynamics. That second law clearly states that everything in the universe is going from a state of organization and complexity to a state of disorganization and chaos. Everything loses energy, but not according to evolution. Its premise that things are moving upward to complexity contradicts everything we know about the universe. In fact, of all known forms of animal life to ever inhabit the earth, only ten percent still exist today, and 100,000 animal species have become extinct since 1980.[39] The current rate of extinction is anywhere from one per day to five species per hour.[40] The point is that decline and extinction are the rule, not evolution. There is not one example of self-generation or self-organization that can be found in the entire realm of nature. So, it's no surprise that Dr. Michael Cuenot, a French biologist of international fame, says, "The classical theory of evolution belongs to the past. Even if they do not publicly take a definite stand, almost all French specialists hold today strong mental reservations as to the validity of natural selection."[41]

But do you know what is amazing? On page 410 of his book, *Origin of the Species,* Darwin himself wrote these words: "To suppose that the eye (with so many parts all working together) . . . could have been formed by natural selection seems, I freely confess, absurd in the highest degree."[42] When you have Darwin himself admitting that portions of his theories on evolution appear to be "absurd in the highest degree," don't you think it would cause people to step back and say, "You know, maybe this theory is not true after all? Maybe I ought to look at the evidence for creation."

THE SIMPLE CELL

A third problem with evolution is the simple cell. In Darwin's time, it was thought that cells were just blobs of protoplasm, but we now know that the outside of cells are studded with sensors, gates, pumps, and identification markers. Some have rotary outboard motors. But it's on the inside that we see power plants, recycling units, and miniature monorails that have caused the most hardened atheists to marvel at such intricate design.[43]

Of course, one has to ask, "How did this single cell come into existence in the first place?" The evolutionist will avoid that question as quickly as possible because he or she has no plausible answer. You see, a living cell requires hundreds of protein molecules coming together to perform the necessary functions for supporting life. So, the question once again is, "What are the chances of all those molecules randomly coming together to form a single cell?" Sir Frederick Hoyle, the esteemed astronomer and mathematician from Cambridge University says, "The chance of this randomly happening is one with 40,000 zeros behind it."[44] Now, our finite minds cannot fathom numbers of that magnitude, but it would be comparable to winning a large lottery six times in a row. Or think of it this way: it would take only 10^{17} of silver dollars to cover the entire state of Texas two feet deep in silver dollars.[45] Yet, Hoyle is talking about 10^{40} instead of 10^{17}. Did you know that the number of snowflakes that have fallen on earth since the beginning of time is only 10^{35}?[46] Here's another way to compare it: if a billion continents, each the size of North America, were totally covered with sacks of dimes that were 239,000 miles high (the distance of the earth and the moon), the possibility that a blind-folded person could pick out the one dime that had been painted red on the first try would be roughly equivalent to one in 10^{40}. So, is it any wonder that Hoyle concluded that "this improbability is big enough to bury Darwin and the whole theory of evolution"?[47]

Another scientist said that for the last several decades there has been a thundering silence in attempting to explain the origin of the cell. He said, "Absolutely no one—not one scientist—has published any detailed proposal or explanation of the possible evolution of any such complex biochemical system (like the cell structure)."[48]

THE PROTEIN MOLECULE

Another problem with evolution is answering the question of where the protein molecule originated. The evolutionist will probably say that amino acids randomly assembled together, and all of these gases were struck by lightning and just mysteriously exploded into a molecule. Dr. James Coppedge, who is an expert on statistical probability, says that the chances of that happening are one in 10^{161}.[49] That's a one with 161 zeros behind it. Considering that a "simple" cell contains at least 239 molecules, each containing 445 amino acids, all of which are made up of 10 to 20 atoms, it can easily be seen that the simple cell is anything but simple. Given the fact that all 445 amino acids must be lined up single file in perfect sequential order for the protein to function, it also would cause any thinking person to question the "random chance" theory of evolution. Think about it. For a single cell to spring to life, 445 amino acids would have to accidentally line up perfectly not once, but 239 times to form 239 proteins that would spontaneously become a living cell. A single "simple" cell contains as much data as all the individual letters in the world's largest library—that's about a trillion tidbits of information.[50] Random chance or intelligent design? I know where I'm casting my vote.

Dr. Michael Behe illustrated the improbability of this occurrence by saying, "Let's imagine that someone hid a grain of sand and marked it with a tiny 'x' somewhere in the Sahara desert. After wandering blindfolded for several years in the desert, you reach down, pick up a grain of sand, take off your blindfold, and find it has a tiny 'x'. Suspicious, you give the grain of sand to someone to hide it again, and again you wander blindfolded into the desert, bend down, and the grain of sand you pick up has an 'x'. You do this a third time and pick up the marked grain. The odds of finding that marked grain of sand in the Sahara desert three times in a row are about the same as finding the one new functional protein structure."[51] These guys are only confirming what Darwin himself admitted about portions of his own theory: to believe in evolution is absurdity in the highest degree.

THE QUESTION OF DESIGN

The fifth problem with evolution concerns the question of design. How do you explain the fact that every living thing shows evidence of intelligent design rather than random chance? The DNA molecule is just one of thousands of examples. Did you know that a single fertilized egg in a human being is no larger than a pinhead, and yet it contains enough DNA information to fill 500,000 printed pages? That pinhead of information determines the color of your hair, shape of your nose, color of your skin, height, and every other detail about your physical body.[52]

But then that fertilized cell will divide into 30 trillion cells, 12 billion of which are in your brain and will go on to form over 120 trillion connections. The complicated set of instructions that guide that process is more than three billion letters long, and all of that information is contained in a single DNA molecule.[53] When you see the complexity of the DNA information system, wouldn't you think that there must be an intelligent Designer behind it? Yet, Sir Francis Crick, the very person who discovered the DNA molecule, refuses to admit such a possibility. Instead, he theorizes that the DNA was sent to earth by an advanced civilization from another planet. I would have to agree with author Phillip Johnson, who says, "When a scientist of Crick's caliber feels that he has to invoke undetectable spacemen, it is time to consider whether the field of pre-biological evolution has come to a dead end."[54]

You see, programmed into the DNA of every species of every living thing is a genetic code that defines its characteristics. But it's that genetic code that makes it impossible to crossbreed between species. For example, DNA programming does not make animals talk, and the DNA programming of reptiles does not equip them to fly.

God used 110 elements such as iron, oxygen, hydrogen, and helium to create the entire universe and more than a trillion galaxies. Only an intelligent Designer could have turned out such a variety by using the same components.

Did you know that your body contains 10^{28} atoms, which is more than the number of grains of sand on all the world's beaches?[55] Atoms are what constitute cells, and your body contains between 10 trillion and 100 trillion cells, each of which has about one trillion atoms that are constantly being torn down, remodeled, and replaced. Ninety percent of the atoms in your body are being replaced every year, and every five years, 100% of your atoms are replaced. Even in the last hour, one trillion of your atoms have been replaced.[56] When you stop to think about it, you are a walking miracle. Your body is constantly rebuilding itself, repairing itself, and regulating itself.

Let's go back to cells for just a moment. All cells are made up of molecules, which are comprised of atoms, which contain protons, neutrons, and electrons, along with 200 other particles that are even smaller. Every cell has its own internal biological clock that switches on every 22 to 26 hours. Each cell's nucleus contains a digitally coded database larger in content than all 30 volumes of the *Encyclopedia Britannica* put together.[57] And that's just for one cell!

In order for life to occur, three kinds of molecules need to work in perfect harmony. DNA molecules hold the blueprints for the construction of life molecules. Protein molecules build and repair life molecules. RNA molecules carry the blueprints from the DNA to specific protein molecules. All of these are interdependent of one another. The genes within DNA manufacture proteins that do everything necessary to keep you alive. A typical cell contains countless thousands of different types of proteins that make it possible for you to live. Each gene knows how to make one protein, so 100,000 genes make 100,000 different proteins. All this incredible amount of information that is stored in the DNA molecule did not come from the DNA. It came from an outside source. Which is more feasible and believable? Random chance or intelligent design?

Evolution raises far more questions than it answers. This godless theory fails to explain why we don't see examples of species changing before our eyes today. I mean, why don't we see animals and humans in various stages of evolution? Why has evolution failed to produce one mammal from the fossil record that is in the process of evolving, such as half man and half animal? If evolution is so true that we're going to portray pictures of apes becoming men, then why don't we have one scientifically documented specimen of monkeys turning into men? Why doesn't evolution have an explanation for the first atom? How does the theory of evolution justify its violation of the second law of thermodynamics? How can the theory of evolution insult the intelligence of others by suggesting that an orderly universe with the fingerprint of design all over it could possibly have been the result of random chance?

Dr. Wernher Von Braun was a leading scientist in the U.S. Space Program. Before his death in the early '70s, he said, "One cannot be exposed to the law and order of the universe without concluding that

there must be design and purpose behind it all. The better we understand the intricacies of the universe and all it harbors, the more reason
we have found to marvel at the inherent design upon which it is based."[58]

To be forced to believe only one conclusion—that everything in the
universe happened by chance—challenges the very objectivity of science
itself. What random process could produce the brain of a human or the
system of the human eye? Evolutionists challenge science to prove the
existence of God. But must we really light a candle to see the sun? They
say they cannot visualize an electron. What strange rationale makes some
physicists accept the inconceivable electron as real while refusing to
accept the reality of a Designer on the grounds that they cannot con-
ceive Him? In scientific honesty, it would be an error to overlook the
possibility that the universe was planned rather than happened by
chance.

Sadly enough, the official 1995 position from the American National
Association of Biology teachers states: "The diversity of life is the outcome of evolution: an unsupervised, impersonal, unpredictable and natural process of temporal descent with genetic modification that is affected by natural selection, chance, historical contingencies and changing
environments."[59]

Did you catch that wording? "Unsupervised . . . impersonal . . . unpredictable . . . natural . . . chance?" This is the godless indoctrination that
our children are being taught. It is the official stance of our public school
curricula. Is it any wonder that so many youth have low self-esteems?
Being told that you're an accident originating from some amoeba in a
pool of primeval slime doesn't do much for your self-image. The ramifications of this can be seen in violent behavior, suicides, indecent dress,
radical music, lax work ethic, and on it goes.

It must be remembered that those who embrace evolution do so, not
because the evidence for intelligent design is weak or because the
evidence for evolution is so convincing. Granted, some believe evolution
because it is the only thing they have been taught, but many choose to
be evolutionists in spite of the absurdities and improbabilities of the

theory. Romans 1:20 reminds us, "For since the creation of the world His invisible attributes are clearly seen, being understood by the things that are made, even His eternal power and Godhead, so that they are without excuse." Yes, the evidence for a Creator is clearly seen and clearly understood by observing the very things He created, but when a culture exchanges the truth of God for the lie, the mind is darkened and reality is hidden from those who choose to worship the creature rather than the Creator. Romans 1:22 says, "Professing to be wise, they became fools."

Agnostic scientist Robert Jastrow sums it up quite well. He says, "For the scientist who has lived by faith in the power of reason, the story ends like a bad dream. He has scaled the mountain of ignorance, and is about to conquer the highest peak. As he pulls himself over the final rock, he is greeted by a band of theologians who have been sitting there for centuries."[60]

THE WORLD'S MOST RENOWNED SCIENTISTS REFUTE EVOLUTION

The above heading is a shock to those who are products of our public school systems, liberal churches, and a cooperative media. Millions have been led to believe that anyone who still embraces creationism is out of step with the times, uninformed, and uneducated. For example, biologist Ernst Mayr says, "No educated person any longer questions the validity of the so-called theory of evolution, which we now know to be a simple fact."[61] I mentioned a cooperative media because PBS aired a seven-part series on evolution and asserted that "all known scientific evidence supports (Darwinian) evolution as does 'virtually every reputable scientist in the world.'"[62] That is simply a bald-faced lie. What these very people do not realize is that they're the ones who have been brainwashed. Evolutionists continue to believe that given enough time their theory will be proven, but in fact, just the opposite is occurring. As Father Time marches on, our science becomes more precise, and our technology becomes more advanced, all of which have thrust a dagger into the heart of this well-worn theory. It is time to cast it out to the dump heap. Evolution has run its course. Just as modern science can now look into the womb and see a baby in its earliest stages of development, we can now also peek into the vast expanse of our universe and see that evolution is so improbable it is not even worth consideration. Yet, because we live in a culture of truth decay and because we have exchanged the truth for the lie, those in high places continue to expose the innocent minds of our children to such an unproven theory as though it were true.

What these children do not know is that the most brilliant minds in the world stand in the corner of creationism, fully persuaded that the case for intelligent design outweighs the theory of evolution. After the above statement was broadcast on PBS, 100 renowned scientists stepped forward and published a two-page advertisement in a national magazine under the banner, "A Scientific Dissent From Darwinism." They were direct and defiant. These men and women were biologists, chemists, zoologists, physicists, anthropologists, molecular and cellular biologists, bioengineers, organic chemists, geologists, astrophysicists, and other scientists. Their doctorates came from such prestigious universities as Cambridge, Stanford, Cornell, Yale, Rutgers, Chicago, Princeton, Purdue, Duke, Michigan, Syracuse, Temple, and Berkeley. They included professors from Yale Graduate School, the Massachusetts Institute of Technology, Tulane, Rice, Emory, George Mason, Lehigh, and the Universities of California, Washington, Texas, Florida, North Carolina, Wisconsin, Ohio, Colorado, Nebraska, Missouri, Iowa, Georgia, New Mexico, Utah, Pennsylvania, and elsewhere. All of these men and women wanted the world to know that they were in direct disagreement with the information disseminated by PBS.[63]

Reading the above list is somewhat like reading the biblical genealogies—not the most inspirational but necessary to give an overview of the quality and quantitative impact their rebuttal held. You have the best of the best in your corner. Here are just a few:

- Allan Rex Sandage is known as the greatest observational cosmologist in the world. He has been showered with prestigious honors for his genius discoveries. Even the *New York Times* called him "The Grand

Old Man of Cosmology." Sandage had been an atheist since child-hood. In 1985 he was on the platform for a conference on science and religion. The panel was divided among those scientists who believed in God and those who did not. As Sandage approached the platform, he set the room buzzing with whispers, gasps, and turning heads as he took a seat on the side of the theists. When he arose to speak, there was silence as the audience awaited his words of wisdom. He told them the universe was the result of a supernatural event. The sudden emergence of matter, space, time, and energy pointed to the need of some kind of transcendence. He said, "It was my science that drove me to the conclusion that the world is much more complicated than can be explained by science. It was only through the supernatural that I can understand the mystery of existence."[64]

- American astronomer Robert Jastrow said, "The essential element in the astronomical and biblical accounts of Genesis is the same: the chain of events leading to man commenced suddenly and sharply, at a definite moment in time, in a flash of light and energy."[65]

- Dr. D. James Kennedy reports that 90% of today's astronomers believe in God.[66]

- Pierre Simon de La Place, one of the greatest of all astronomers, does not hide his emphatic dogmatism in favor of a Creator. He says, "The proof in favor of an intelligent God as the author of creation stands in infinity to unify against any other hypothesis of ultimate causation; it is infinitely more probable that a set of writing imple-ments thrown promiscuously against parchment would produce Homer's Iliad, than that creation was originated by any cause other than God."[67]

- Sixty notable scientists, including 24 Nobel Prize winners, wrote a classic volume on science entitled *Cosmos, Bios, Theos*. The co-editor of the book, Yale physicist and Nobel Laureate Professor Henry Margenau concluded, "There is only one convincing answer for the intricate laws that exist in nature. That is, creation by an omnipo-tent-omniscient God."[68]

- Sir James Jeans, one of the greatest of modern astronomers, said that the more he examined the vast expanses of space and the tremendous complexity of these things, the more the universe seemed to be one gigantic thought of a great mathematician.[69]

- Dr. Dean Kenyon was a biology professor at San Francisco State University. He received his PhD in biophysics from Stanford University and was the co-author of *Biochemical Predestination*, which is considered one of the finest texts available on how a living cell might have emerged from the primeval state. After years of study, Kenyon's lab work led him to conclude that chemicals simply could not organize themselves without outside guidance. Thus, the concept of spontaneous generation is fatally flawed. The university forbade him from sharing his findings with the students, and he was eventually fired because of his creationist position.[70]

- Dr. H.S. Lipson, a physicist and self-avowed agnostic, concludes, "I think . . . the only acceptable explanation is creation. . . . I know that this is an anathema to physicists, as indeed it is to me, but we must not reject a theory we do not like if the experimental evidence supports it. . . . To my mind the theory (evolution) does not stand up at all."[71]

Consider these distinguished men who founded modern science. Without exception, all of them were creationists believing that the scientific evidence for intelligent design far outweighed the theory of evolution: Johannes Kepler – Astronomy; Blaise Pascal – Hydrostatics; Robert Boyle – Chemistry; Isaac Newton – Physics; Nicolas Steno – Stratigraphy; Michael Faraday – Magnetic theory; Charles Babbage – Computers; Louis Agassiz – Ichthyology; Louis Leigh Simpson – Gynecology; Gregor Mendel – Genetics; Louis Pasteur – Bacteriology; Lord Kelvin – Thermodynamics; Yoseph Lister – Antiseptic surgery; James Clerk Maxwell – Electrodynamics; and William Ramsay – Isotopic chemistry.[72]

- Scientist Walter Bradley, co-author of *The Mystery of Origin*, writes, "Evidence for an intelligent designer becomes more compelling the more we understand about our carefully crafted habitat."[73]

- Paul Davies, the former professor of theoretical physics at the University of Adelaide, has now changed his position to that of intelligent design. In his book, *The Mind of God,* he writes, "I have come to believe more and more strongly that the physical universe is put together with an ingenuity so astonishing that I cannot accept it merely as a brute fact. I cannot believe that our existence in this universe is a mere quirk of fate, an accident of history, an incidental blip in the great cosmic drama."[74]

- Cosmologist Edward Harrison has also arrived at this conclusion: "The fine tuning of the universe provides *prima facie* evidence of deistic design."[75]

- Harvard astronomy professor Owen Gingerich, a senior astronomer at the Smithsonian Astrophysical Observatory, comments, "A common sense and satisfying interpretation of our world suggests the designing hand of a superintelligence."[76]

Have you heard of Blaise Pascal's famous wager? Although he lived in France 200 years ago, his legacy as a theologian, mathematician, and scholar lives on. One day he told a skeptic, "If I am wrong about God existing, then neither of us would ever know it, because we would both die and cease to exist, and all consciousness would disappear. But, on the other hand, if I am right and you are wrong, when we both die, I will go to heaven and you will go to hell. Now," he added, "it seems to me than any intelligent man would bet on the right side of that wager."[77]

An educational system is being built upon the sands of evolution, and it's producing a nation of fools along with a moral foundation that is unstable. Jesus warned that it is foolish for any man or any nation to build upon a foundation that is devoid of God. He prophesied that the result would be destruction. Yet, that is the path our nation has chosen. While new discoveries produce new theories that change with each passing year, we have a constant, steadfast anchor that is immovable and unshakable.

When we tell our children that they evolved from animals, why are we surprised when they behave like animals? When we teach that they are products of random chance and a cosmic accident, why are we shocked by their purposelessness, depression, and suicide attempts? My friend, you are no accident! The Great Architect of the universe designed you with a purpose in mind. He declares, "For I know the thoughts that I think toward you, says the LORD, thoughts of peace and not of evil, to give you a future and a hope" (Jeremiah 29:11).

CHAPTER 10

The Glut of Smut

Moral Relativism's Spin: Adult Entertainment

It was a Saturday afternoon and I was traveling through the hills of eastern Kentucky admiring the beauty and enjoying the music on the Christian radio station when my cell phone interrupted the tranquility of the moment. I cheerfully answered, but there was a garbled response. As annoying as cell phones and dead zones can be, it was obvious that this was not static from outside interference. I turned off the radio in an attempt to better understand the voice on the other end. It became apparent that this person was emotionally distraught and choked up with convulsive weeping. He again tried to identify himself. I said, "I'm sorry, but can you repeat your name once more?" This time he said, "Steve, this is Terry Henderson." (Name has been changed to conceal identity.) I said, "Terry, what in the world has happened?" With a trembling voice and broken spirit, he simply said, "I need help."

As the conversation unfolded, I discovered that Terry had been involved with Internet pornography. He served as the minister of music at a large and growing church in Alabama where his wife was the pianist. He was the father of two beautiful children. While he and his family were on vacation, Terry's pastor apparently had reason to be suspicious and enlisted a technician to check his computer for any pornographic history. The pastor's suspicions were confirmed by documented chat room conversations, which included language that was not becoming to any Christian, much less a minister of the Gospel. When Terry and his family arrived home from vacation, the pastor and a couple of deacons were standing on his front porch asking for his resignation. This man's world was rocked, his wife was deeply disillusioned, and his children were utterly confused. After a year of counseling and restoration, Terry eased back into ministry and now, years later, he is serving in a wonderful church and is again using his incredible talents for the Lord. However, the journey has been long and gruesome. To this day, trust has not been fully restored with his wife. Terry is fortunate to have kept his family intact through this hellish and anguishing experience. Most do not.

It is difficult to overstate the marital discord, domestic destruction, teenage depression, and dysfunctional lifestyles that have resulted from pornography. The battle is real. The addiction is severe. The scars are there to prove it. The statistics are there to document it. So why the silence? Why are bookshelves barren on this subject? Under the banner of free speech and moral relativism, the desire to be politically correct seems to outweigh any risk of speaking up on this issue. I must tell you, doing research for this chapter has been eye-opening. Living in metro-Atlanta, I have access to several Christian bookstores and large secular bookstores. However, none of the stores stocked any books on pornography. The sales clerk at the Christian store pulled up three on the computer screen; one was unavailable. Next, I went to Barnes & Noble and Borders bookstores. With thousands of books written on every conceivable topic imaginable, I had no doubt that current statistics and relevant documentation could be found. Boy, was I wrong! Neither of these stores had one book on pornography in stock. I went to the information desk to see what could be pulled up on the computer. Surprisingly, most of the stuff was unavailable from the warehouse. I left knowing that I would be traveling to other cities in the next few weeks and could just as easily patronize those stores. I was still under the assumption that this huge topic was being addressed in countless volumes. Again, I came up empty.

Finally, I ordered 14 books from Barnes & Noble with the understanding that I could return them if they did not contain the pertinent information that I needed. Two of the books, however, were college textbooks that were non-returnable. When I reviewed the other 12, without exception they were written from a pro-pornography point of view. When I approached the information desk to return them, I was told that they could not sell them because people were not interested in the subject. What invoked additional concern was that the two college textbooks I was required to keep were also sympathetic toward pornography and even contained pornographic pictures. Perhaps I am naïve, but it is baffling to hear the strange silence of our pulpits and to view the vast vacuum of information that exists in our bookstores regarding this epidemic.

A few years ago, a meeting took place at the Justice Department with Attorney General John Ashcroft in which Dr. James Dobson of Focus on the Family, Chuck Colson of Prison Fellowship, and Dr. Richard Land of the Southern Baptist Convention's Ethics and Religious Liberty Commission were each asked to identify the single greatest threat facing America. Surprisingly, they each gave a different answer. Colson pleaded his case for the sanctity of life. Still believing that abortion is the key battleground, Colson convincingly described the horrors of how human life is being cheapened in our society.[1]

Dobson, although sympathetic to Colson's position, disagreed. He declared that the greatest single threat facing America is the assault on marriage, led by the radical homosexual movement. He then proceeded with an eloquent discourse in defense of the family.[2]

It must have come as a surprise to both of these men when Land failed to side with either of their positions. "No one argues with how our whole culture of death has devalued life, and until a few years ago I would have said without hesitation that the greatest single threat facing America is the sanctity of human life. . . . However, I recently changed my mind, not because the sanctity of human life issues has [sic] gotten any better, but it has been overtaken by hard-core pornography and its full-blown offensive for a fully pagan sexuality in which anything goes. I believe hard-core Internet pornography is destroying more lives every day than the four-thousand killed each day through abortion."[3]

This is not the time or place to split hairs on which of these men is right. Realistically, all three issues are wreaking havoc and destruction on our nation. Certainly, there is no shortage of those who would just as passionately disagree by contending that "right-wing" politicians, along with the religious right, have sensationalized these issues in order to further their own self-serving agendas. Let's put aside our political persuasions and theological convictions for a moment and just consider the facts. No doubt, the common ground we share is the fact that we are Americans who love this nation and want to see it prosper. Anthropologist J.D. Unwin conducted an extensive study on the 86 different societies throughout human history and found that the one common denominator leading to their destruction was sexual immorality. He said, "Sexual fidelity was the single most important predictor of a society's ascendancy. In human records there is no instance of a society retaining its energy after a completely new generation has inherited a tradition which does not insist on prenuptial and postnuptial continence."[4] What makes Unwin's study more intriguing is the fact that he was not a Christian and was puzzled by his findings. He had no explanation for such irrefutable data. Yet, Romans 1 clearly delineates the decline and destruction of a civilization. Sexual sin is at the heart of it. If we do not learn from history, then we are bound to repeat it.

PORN IS BIG BUSINESS

Pornography generates $12 billion a year in the United States, making it a larger producer of revenue than the NFL, NBA, and Major League Baseball combined.[5] There are 4.2 million pornographic Web sites and 372 million pornographic pages, which generate 68 million daily search engine requests. Those 68 million daily search engine requests account for 25% of *total* search engine requests per day on the Internet.[6] About 200 sex-related Web sites are added to the Internet each day.[7] In previous generations it was difficult for a respectable citizen to maintain anonymity when buying a porn magazine at a convenience store or to risk being seen at an adult video store. Those days are gone. With the invention of the World Wide Web, high-speed cyber connections can be accessed in the privacy of one's office or home, connecting millions with live pornographic footage and interactive chat rooms all with the simple click of a button. Sadly enough, in her Department of Justice study, Judith Reisman asserts that the porn industry targets 12- to 17-year-old boys so that they will become regular consumers, ensuring a lifetime of addiction.[8] This is confirmed by the fact that the average age of Internet exposure to pornography is 11 years old.[9] An unbelievable 80% of 15- to

17-year-olds have had multiple hard-core porn exposures, and 90% of 8- to 16-year-olds have viewed porn online, most often while doing homework.[10]

In his book, *Battle Cry For a Generation*, Ron Luce cites that pornography is a booming $57 billion dollar industry, generating more money than the revenue of television networks ABC, CBS, and NBC combined. Its revenue totals more than the revenue of all professional sports teams put together.[11] Consider the following:

- $20 billion is spent worldwide on adult pornographic videos.

- $2.5 billion is spent worldwide on cable pay-per-view pornography.

- $3 billion is generated annually by child pornography.

- 4.2 million pornographic Web sites exist on the Internet, accounting for 21% of total Web sites.

- 2.5 billion pornographic e-mails are sent daily, which is eight percent of total e-mails.

- 4.5 pornographic e-mails are sent daily per Internet user.

- 100,000 Web sites currently post illegal child pornography.[12]

If the above statistics don't cause your head to spin, then maybe this will get your attention. According to the trade publication *Adult Video News,* in 1986 one in every five videocassettes were categorized as "adult," and 1,500 new adult movies hit the market every year.[13] Between 1985 and 1992, the adult movie industry expanded its revenues from $75 million to $490 million.[14] Today, one in four American adults admits to having seen an X-rated movie in the past year. Four billion dollars a year is spent on video and DVD pornography in the United States. Americans rent over 800 million pornographic videos and DVDs per year. This accounts for one in five of all rented movies. To put it in perspective, Hollywood pumps out about 400 feature films each year, but 11,000 porno films are produced annually with total revenue for the adult film industry running between $5 billion and $10 billion.[15]

Of course, the reason for this huge discrepancy is obvious. It does not take a lot of talent or money to produce a porn film. The cost to produce most pornographic films is between $5,000 and $10,000, compared with the $150 million budgets for Hollywood's blockbusters. Even the highest quality smut films cost only $100,000, a mere fraction of the cost for a quality Hollywood film.[16] A staggering 25% to 30% of all pay-per-view revenue is generated by pornography. In 2002, Comcast reportedly made $50 million on pornographic programming.[17] Analysts estimate that AT&T Broadband makes between $8 million and $20 million per month on adult entertainment.[18]

The statistics continue to be alarming. For instance, were you aware that half of all hotel guests order pornographic pay-per-view movies? This accounts for 80% of in-room entertainment revenue and 70% of total in-room revenue.[19] Today, 73% of all movie searches on the computer are for pornography, and 24% of all image searches are specifically for child pornography.[20] Type "XXX" into an Internet search engine like Google, and 106 million pages appear, up from 76 million just six months ago. A 2004 study found that pornographic sites are visited three times more often than Google, Yahoo!, and MSN Search combined.[21] Sixty-six percent of all men between the ages of 18 and 34 view pornography every month.[22]

If you are 50 years of age or older, you probably read this stuff and shake your head in disbelief. Those who are younger most likely don't blink an eye. They have been so desensitized by sexual innuendos and R-rated movies that it has become an accepted part of their culture. In the '50s, pornography was relegated to run-down adult movie theaters on the wrong side of town. Even as recent as the '80s, porn was obtained primarily through mail-order catalogs or watched in the back rooms of video stores. There was a time when people were ashamed and embarrassed by it. There was a time when respectable people didn't look at dirty pictures. There was a day in our history when it would have been unthinkable for the president of the United States to have sexual liaisons in the White House. When President Ronald Reagan served the nation, he held the Oval Office in such high esteem that he refused to take off his coat and tie while sitting behind his desk. Less than a decade later,

Americans were shown two vans delivering 36 boxes of materials that documented the sexual affair President Bill Clinton had with his intern, Monica Lewinsky. Excerpts from the infamous Starr Report contained explicit descriptions of their sexual rendezvous. While under oath, Lewinsky vividly described the sordid details of the when, where, and how of it all. The report itself could easily be considered pornographic. Yet, in spite of the evidence, an NBC poll showed that 70% of Americans did not think that he should be impeached but merely slapped on the wrist with a censure.[23]

YES, TIMES HAVE CHANGED

What was considered pornography in yesteryear has now found mainstream acceptability and respectability. Hugh Hefner, the creator of *Playboy* magazine, is now treated like an elder media statesman. On the 50th anniversary of *Playboy*, Hefner was given a front-page profile in the arts section of the *New York Times*. In 2003, Victoria's Secret prime-time TV specials attracted a record nine million viewers. During the 2004 Super Bowl halftime show, a duet by Janet Jackson and Justin Timberlake resulted in what was later described as a "wardrobe malfunction." As Timberlake sang the words, "I'm going to get you naked by the end of this song," he was true to the lyrics by ripping Jackson's blouse and exposing her breast. The point to be made, however, is not that a mere 56% of Americans thought it was disrespectful, but that the next day Janet Jackson's breast became the most-searched-for image in online history. It also set records on Yahoo!, where it accounted for 20% of all searches.

Sports Illustrated has always been acclaimed as a leader for reporting the best and most accurate news in the world of athletics. Yet, once a year it pushes the envelope to print its most popular issue, the swimsuit issue. Ironically, there are fewer swimsuits than ever, as one-fourth of the photographs in the last issue depicted women who were topless or completely naked. The magazine's 40th anniversary issue even included a nude "centerfold."

Ron Jeremy, who has starred in more than 1,800 X-rated films, was given a VIP pass to Disney World in Orlando, Florida, where he was mobbed by "clean-cut dads and moms and their kids who took turns snapping pictures with him all day."[24] In fact, in March 2003, the University of Alabama hosted a debate between Jeremy and anti-pornography activist Susan B. Cole. Jeremy was greeted with cheers from students dressed in T-shirts boasting, "I love porn," while Cole was booed and jeered by the audience.[25]

One poll shows that the majority of men no longer consider *Playboy* to even qualify as porn.[26] Are you kidding? Sociologist Michael Kimmel, who studies pornography and teaches sexuality at the State University of New York, said, "Twenty years ago, my female students would say, 'Ugh, that's disgusting,' when I brought up pornography in class. Today, they'll admit using it themselves."[27] In February 2004, Harvard University officials approved the launch of a student publication that included naked pictures of Harvard students and other sexual content.[28] A female student at Boston University has announced the launch of a new magazine, *Boink*, which she admits is pornography.[29] Female students at Smith College host a pornographic Web site called "Smithiegirls."[30] From the highly successful *Girls Gone Wild* videos to strategically placed camcorders in girl's dorm rooms, which are designed for private Web sites, porn has found wide acceptance across gender lines. In fact, 32 million women were tracked visiting at least one adult Web site in January 2004. Seven million of them were ages 35 to 44. What's even more interesting is that almost a million women over the age of 65 were tracked to be intentionally viewing adult Web sites.[31] The combination of all these examples give a clear and undeniable picture that porn has entered into mainstream America. From Ivy League schools to Disney World, from the sports world to college classrooms, porn looms much larger than any of us can imagine.

The indifference (and perhaps ignorance) toward pornography among the American public can easily be seen by these "real-life" quotes:

- "Porn is harmless; it's just looking at pictures. What's wrong with fantasy?"

- "If we women want to be naked and be proud of our bodies, what's the problem? We're in control, and it's our choice."

- "All men look at porn. It's human nature. Men are biologically programmed to be visually stimulated."

- "If you believe in civil liberties and freedom of the press, you've got to be in favor of porn."

- "Pornography just isn't that big a deal. It's like scratching an itch."[32]

This is the culture in which we live. These statements are strictly from a morally relativistic perspective with no hint of a biblical worldview. Apparently, the above assertions are not the exception, but the norm. For example, a 2004 poll of 15,246 men and women conducted by MSNBC.com and *Elle* magazine documented that 75% of men said they had viewed or downloaded erotic films and videos from the Internet, and 41% of women did as well.[33] According to comScore, an Internet-traffic-measuring service, 70% of 18- to 24-year-old men visit a pornographic site in a typical month. Furthermore, 66% of all men between the ages of 18 and 34 look at Internet pornography every month.[34]

STRAIN ON THE BRAIN

Pornography poisons the brain with erototoxins that create neuro-chemical pathways that are impossible to delete. Putting it in layman's terms, pornographic images imprint and alter the brain by creating a biochemical memory trail that remains with a person throughout life. Pornography triggers a myriad of internal, natural drugs that imitate the "high" derived from street drugs. I suppose this is why Dr. James Dobson says that pornography is just as addictive and destructive as cocaine.[35] Brain scientists tell us that "in 3/10 of a second a visual image passes from the eye through the brain, and whether or not one wants to, the brain is structurally changed and memories are created. We literally grow new brain cells with each visual experience."[36] Professors Satinover, Weaver, Layden, and Reisman testified about the destructiveness of pornography's erototoxins before a Senate investigative committee on November 18, 2004. They explained that the human brain obeys a "law of strength." This means that "arousing, pornographic images will always dominate, occupy, and colonize the brain and displace cognition, despite any disclaimers used in sex education."[37] Science is now proving that the human brain is restructured, altered, and permanently changed by each pornographic image. Neurologist Richard Restak further explains: "Thanks to the latest advances in neuroscience, we now know that emotionally arousing images imprint and alter the brain, triggering an instant, involuntary, but lasting biochemical memory trail. Once our neurochemical pathways are established they are difficult or impossible to delete."[38]

This information becomes an even greater concern when applied to a teenager's brain. In less than one-one thousandth of a second, pornography's erototoxins shape the teenage brain on three levels. First, the brain perceives pornography as "reality." Secondly, the brain "stores" pornography as viable information. Thirdly, pornography injures the teenager's mental health.[39]

We also know that the more men watch porn, the less satisfied they are with their partner's looks and sexual performance.[40]

PORN ON THE JOB

With the advent of the Internet, pornography is so accessible that it has become a major distraction in America's workforce. A 2004 survey by the Web-filtering company Cerberian found that 75% of people have accidentally visited a pornographic site while at work; 15% have done so more than ten times. Forty percent said they'd seen their coworkers surfing pornography on the job.[41] In another 2004 survey by the Employment Law Alliance, one in four workers said they or their coworkers visited pornographic Web sites or engaged in sex talk or other sexually oriented Internet activities on their work computers during office hours.[42]

In 2004, 43 employees in Kentucky's state transportation department were suspended or fired for viewing pornography on their office computers. A 24-hour monitor found that 212 computers were used to view pornography on any given day.[43] In 2002, a computer-abuse sweep at the

Virginia Department of Transportation found that 17 employees were accessing the Internet on their computers for more than two hours each day to look at pornography online.[44] One can only imagine the thousands of hours that are being wasted by the American workforce, and one way or another the American taxpayer and consumers are paying for such a lack of productivity.

THE SILENT EPIDEMIC

Within the Christian community, pornography is the silent and secret sin. It is rarely discussed and seldom preached. Promise Keepers can be credited with bringing the issue to the forefront of the church. Increasing numbers of men's conferences are addressing this issue, but given the enormity of the problem, little is being done. Jonathan Daugherty, founder of Be Broken Ministries in San Antonio, Texas, claims that at least half of the men sitting in churches on Sunday morning struggle with pornography at some level. He says that it has become the leading factor in divorce.[45] Pastor and author Ted Roberts also concurs by estimating that 50% of the men in every congregation where he has had the opportunity to minister are struggling with pornography.[46] According to a 2000 survey of clergy members conducted by *Christianity Today* and *Leadership* magazines, 40% of clergy acknowledge visiting sexually explicit Web sites.[47] Another poll, conducted by Pastors.com in 2002, found that 50% of pastors admitted to viewing pornography in the previous year.[48] According to Henry Rogers, a corporate chaplain who researches pornography, between 40% and 70% of evangelical Christian men say they struggle with pornography.[49]

When you add to this the fact that 53% of Promise Keeper men viewed pornography last week, and 47% of Christians say that pornography is a major problem in their homes, we must sadly admit that this tsunami of smut has flowed into the evangelical world and is sweeping many away in its powerful undertow.[50] In fact, one survey showed that when it comes to being faithful to our spouses, there is only a two percent difference between conservative Christian men and those who do not know the Lord.[51] This is all the more reason for admonishing preachers to abandon their silence on this issue. Sexual bondage in the church is one of hell's primary strategies, and the Internet has become its stealth bomber. Every Sunday morning we have men sitting in our congregations who are headed for heaven, but living in hell. One denominational survey found that almost one-third of the pastors were sexual addicts. They weren't just struggling with pornography—they were addicts![52]

The Psalmist said, "I will walk within my house with a perfect heart. I will set nothing wicked before my eyes; . . ." (Psalm 101:2b-3a). Job made a covenant with his eyes not to look lustfully upon a young woman (Job 31:1). It would serve us well to remember that the word "fornication" is derived from the Greek word "porneia," where we get the word "pornography." Fornication refers to any illicit sexual activity outside the confines of marriage. So, while it does not specifically refer to pornography, it most certainly includes it. First Corinthians 6:18 admonishes the Christian to flee fornication, while 1 Thessalonians 4:3 instructs us to abstain from it. Once again, God has not come to rain on our parade. He is protecting us from the deceitfulness and destructiveness of sin.

THE DESTRUCTIVE RESULTS

Advocates for pornography will argue that porn is a harmless, extracurricular, recreational activity that relieves stress and releases sexual tension. Jim Weaver, a professor of communication and psychology at Virginia Tech, has taught a course on pornography for years. I am fearful that his experience reflects most of the guys in our nation. He says, "Young men in my classroom today don't even understand why we should be talking about it. They see it as harmless entertainment. Their attitude is, 'it's a free country and I've been watching porn on the Internet since middle school and there's nothing wrong with it.'"[53] Welcome to the world of moral relativism. It is their contention that it helps overcome sexual inhibitions and makes them more comfortable with their own sexuality. Interestingly enough, one nationwide poll showed that while 47% of the women polled believed pornography to be harmful to relationships, only 33% of the men agreed.[54] But to argue that pornography has no negative effect on those who consume it is like arguing that the multibillion-dollar advertising business is all for naught. Yes, people are influenced by what they see, read, or hear. Here are just a few adverse effects that pornography brings to a person's life:

- According to a large-scale 1994 report summarizing 81 research studies, 70% of the studies found that exposure to non-aggressive pornography had a clear negative effect.[55]

- Gary Brooks, a psychologist at Texas A&M University, claims that porn teaches men to view women as objects rather than to be in relationships with women as human beings.[56] Pornography gives men the false impression that sex and pleasure are divorced from relationships. Through porn, women become another product to consume.

- Pornography leaves men insecure with the need for continual validation through ongoing conquests.[57]

- Pornography reduces sexual drive and can lead to impotence. In a study by James L. Howard, Myron B. Reifler, and Clifford B. Liptzin, men who were shown pornographic films for 90 minutes a day, five days a week experienced less sexual arousal and interest in similar materials with the passage of time.[58]

- Pornography is highly addictive. Like a drug, the effect wears off. The user searches for better porn. It becomes repetitive with increased viewing, prolonged visits to certain Web sites, and a tendency to fall into a routine. Once they get through what's available for free, they'll move on to the paid services, which means more action, more intensity, and more extreme situations. Users find themselves veering off into pornographic arenas that they never thought they would find appealing. By this time, they are hooked.

- Porn numbs people's sensibilities toward sex. The user becomes increasingly desensitized and dissatisfied. A husband's expectations of his wife are affected by the images he sees in porn. Her appearance and performance cannot measure up to the fantasy of airbrushed images on a screen. Real life women can seem boring when compared to the euphoria viewed in pornography. It creates tremendous marital dissatisfaction and insecurity within the wife.

- Porn is an unproductive use of time. Psychiatrist Jennifer P. Schneider conducted a study of porn's effect on families. Thirty-seven percent of those families studied reported that children lost parental time and attention due to a parent's online sexual activities.[59] In a 2004 *Elle*-MSNBC.com poll, men confessed that online pornography was eating up hours formerly devoted to other things. One in five said pornography took time away from their work, and another fifth said it took time away from their wives or children.[60] Take your average husband or father. A full-time job often means he's up at 6:00 a.m. and out of the house by 7:30 a.m. Sometimes he goes to the gym after work, but usually he comes straight home for dinner. He would like an hour with the kids at night, to spend more time with his wife, or to get in some reading. But there's always something that needs to be done. The dog needs to be walked, bills need to be paid, and a bit of housework needs to be finished. On weekends, he's running between the kids' soccer games, Home Depot, and an occasional round of golf. An extra two or three hours for pornography every week takes away from something.

- The user of porn commits adultery. In the 2004 *Elle*-MSNBC.com poll, only one-third of women said they considered their husband's online activities to be cheating, compared to the 13% of men who saw it as cheating.[61] Yet, public opinion polls are not the standard for truth. Jesus makes it very clear that adultery occurs whenever a man looks at a woman with lust in his heart. As the groom stands at the marriage altar, he says something like, "I take you to be my wedded wife, to have and to hold from this day forward, for better, for worse, for richer, for poorer, in sickness and in health, to love and to cherish, till death us do part, according to God's holy ordinance." Quite simply, he is saying, "You have my word that I'm going to keep my promises to you." What promises? Forsaking all others and sharing the wealth. Anyone who draws the sexual affections of a husband or wife away from his or her spouse desecrates the seal of their covenant.

- Pornography is a contributor to divorce. In the *Elle*-MSNBC.com poll, 25% of divorced respondents said that Internet pornography had contributed to their split.[62] At the 2003 meeting of the American Academy of Matrimonial Lawyers, a gathering of the nation's divorce lawyers, attendees documented a startling trend. Nearly two-thirds of the attorneys had witnessed a sudden rise in divorces related to the Internet. The association's president, Richard Barry, said, "Eight years ago, pornography played almost no role in divorces in this country, but today there are a significant number of cases where it plays a definite part in marriages breaking up."[63]

- Porn can lead to criminal activity. Between 1996 and 2004, the total number of child porn cases handled by the FBI's cyber-crime investigators increased 23 fold.[64] By 2003, there were more than 80,000 reports of Internet-related child pornography made to CyberTipline, having increased by a staggering 750% in five years.[65] A recent study of 101 sexually abusive children documented increased aggressiveness in boys who use pornography.[66]

To illustrate, while I was writing this chapter, my wife, Debbie, had lunch with a Christian friend who has a precious little eight-year-old girl. One day her little girl, along with another neighborhood child, was playing dress up and pretending to be a plumber. They were playfully going from house to house wearing their plumber hats and taking their plungers with them. Coming from godly families and knowing all of their neighbors, it seemed like harmless fun . . . until a drastic turn of events occurred. They approached the house of a committed Christian family who were good friends with the girls' parents. However, their 21-year-old son came to the door in his parent's absence. He invited the girls inside and escorted them to his bedroom. He showed them nude pictures and exposed himself to them. Upon interviewing both girls separately, the police confirmed that their stories matched, even to the extent of describing the guy's genitals. As you can imagine, his parents were totally oblivious to their son's secret life. The case is now in a one- to two-year court proceeding in which this young man is looking at between 10 and 20 years in prison, not to mention the fact that he will now carry the stigma of being a child predator for the rest of his life. It all started "harmlessly" with the first click of the mouse on his computer screen.

- Pornography leads to earlier premarital sexual activity, which, in turn, results in more teen pregnancies and STDs. The largest consumers of Internet pornography are kids 12- to 17-years old.[67] When a kid views pornography, his or her hormones are already in overdrive. Porn is just adding fuel to a fire that's already simmering. Being taught in sex-ed classes that condoms are synonymous with safe sex, he or she is more inclined to experiment with disastrous results. The average age of first-time sexual intercourse is 15.8 years old, with 25% of those being "one-night stands." The average length of first-time sexual relationships is 3.8 months.[68] This is the quick-fix mentality promoted by pornography. The emotional pain, financial hardships, unfulfilled dreams, rejection from peers, and more can often be traced to a teenager's obsession with pornography. For grown adults, the cost is often divorce in which they lose everything, including their own children.

- Pornography can contribute to rape crimes. Various studies have shown a strong connection between rape statistics and pornography statistics. There are two that are especially worth mentioning. In 1983, two University of New Hampshire sociologists, Murray Straus and Larry Baron, studied the correlation between rape and readership of pornography. What they discovered was chilling. Studying the FBI's annual Uniform Crime Report for rapes reported to and recorded by police, Straus and Baron found that Alaska and Nevada were first and second in the nation for occurrences of rape. The researchers then turned their attention to the Audit Bureau of Circulation and studied circulation rates for the most widely read sexually oriented magazines in the United States. After compiling the total circulation figures, Straus and Baron found that Alaska and Nevada once again led all other states in the nation, this time in readership of pornography.[69] The fact that Alaska and Nevada have the highest rape rates and highest pornography readership rates is no coincidence. Straus and Baron also found that states that had the lowest readership had the lowest rape rates.[70] A 1987 study found that women who were battered and subjected to sexual aggression had partners who viewed "significantly more pornography than" that of an average university student.[71] Three separate studies demonstrate that exposure to violent pornography did increase males' laboratory aggression toward women.[72]

- Pornography is a financial drain on the American economy. In the United States, the annual cost of teen pregnancies from lost tax revenues, public assistance, child health care, foster care, and involvement with the criminal justice system is estimated to be about $7 billion.[73] Likewise, more than one-third of all teenage pregnancies in the U.S. end in abortion.[74] Abortionists' fees for 45,014 abortions in the fiscal year of 1992-93 cost taxpayers more than $5 million.[75] In addition, the annual comprehensive cost of STDs in the United States is estimated to be in excess of $10 billion.[76]

- Most importantly for the Christian, pornography is sin that severs fellowship with his or her Savior, sets up a beachhead for demonic activity, and diminishes power in prayer. The list could continue endlessly. Pornography is anything but harmless, recreational activity that has no repercussions or emotional implications. It is more than a "free-speech" issue, because the thrill of the moment often leads to a lifetime of addiction. The pornographic images are permanently burned into the brain by a mixture of hormones that are released when sexually explicit materials are viewed. This imprinting process is linked to fear, violence, and shame . . . the antithesis of godly character. Like LSD flashbacks, the recurrences of pornography draw the user into a world of fantasy. The lines between fantasy and reality become blurred and he or she becomes a shell of a human being. Now addicted to porn, he or she wanders aimlessly through life seeking only one thing: fulfillment of the lust that has taken complete control of their life.

The gateway to the soul is the eye. In Matthew 6:22-23, Jesus said, "The lamp of the body is the eye. If therefore your eye is good, your whole body will be full of light. But if your eye is bad, your whole body will be full of darkness. If therefore the light that is in you is darkness, how great is that darkness!" A person who feasts their eyes on pictures that have been made by exploiting others is plunging themselves into darkness. In short, pornography kills the soul, steals the heart, and destroys the mind. Such self-destructive behavior applies to nations as well. America is quickly losing its soul and selling out to momentary gratification without the wisdom to discern the long-term destructive repercussions.

AMERICA'S DOWNWARD SPIRAL
INTO THE WORLD OF PORN

In just a few short decades, consider how our nation has continued its moral freefall.

- 1953: *Playboy* magazine was launched.[77]

- 1960: The birth control pill was introduced. At this time, 5.3% of babies were born to unwed mothers and the divorce rate was 9.2 per 1,000 marriages.[78]

- 1965: *Penthouse* magazine was first published.[79]

- 1970: Eleven percent of babies were born out of wedlock.[80]

- 1972: *Playboy* magazine grew to 7.2 million readers.[81]

- 1973: The U.S. Supreme Court affirmed the right of a woman to obtain an abortion.

- 1978: An estimated 75 percent of all rented videos were X-rated.[82]

- 1981: The first diagnosed HIV case in the United States was reported.[83]

- 1982: *Hustler* magazine circulation hit more than 1.1 million, *Penthouse* magazine circulation hit more than 3.7 million, and *Playboy* hit 4.5 million per month.[84]

- 1992: U.S. viewers rented 490 million adult videos.[85]

- 1994: *Playboy* received 4 million hits a day on its Web site.[86]

- 1995: 31 million Americans had genital herpes.[87]

- 1996: 15 million cases of STDs were reported.[88]

- 1997: 32% of babies were born to unwed mothers, 69% within the African-American population. This was a 600% increase since 1969.[89]

- 1998: U.S. viewers rented 686 million adult videos.[90] An estimated 70,000 porn sites were posted on the Internet.[91]

- 2000: Nearly a thousand X-rated videos were being produced each month.[92] Also, 18.9 million new STD cases were reported, and 9.1 million of those cases were found in 15- to 24- year-olds.[93]

- 2001: Pornography was a bigger business than professional football, basketball, and baseball combined. People paid more for pornography in America in a year than they did on movie tickets and on all the performing arts combined.[94] Also in this year, 3,000 new Internet porn sites were added each week to the N2H2 filtering list.[95]

- 2002: 65 million Americans had an incurable STD.[96] Adult movie rentals were available in 500,000 hotel rooms and accounted for 80% of in-room movie profits.[97]

- 2003: Sales and rentals of adult videos totaled more than $4 billion. Internet porn generated another $2 billion annually.[98] Also, this was the year that the number of commercial pornography Internet sites reached 1.3 million, an 1,800% increase since only 1998.[99]

- 2004: The STD of human papillomavirus was found to be the primary cause of almost all cervical cancer.[100] The Gay Pride parade in San Francisco, California, drew 1 million people.[101]

You can see why I was astounded by the void of material in our nation's largest bookstores. This issue is eroding the moral fiber of our country. So, where is the outrage? Several explanations can be proposed. Perhaps it is a "cast-the-first-stone" mentality in which those who could and should address the issue are guilty themselves. Or, maybe it is a "who-are-you-to-judge" mentality that falls under the banner of tolerance and diversity. Maybe it is a satanic conspiracy or a legal catch-22. Regardless, like a stealth bomber, the attacks are being done with pinpoint accuracy, and the American landscape is littered with casualties.

WHERE ARE YOUR KIDS AND WHO ARE THEY WITH?

I am convinced many parents are naïve and completely unsuspecting when it comes to sexual abuse against children. A major reason for this is due to the computer illiteracy of most parents who grew up prior to the invention of the Internet. For example, child porn was virtually nonexistent in 1970, but with the invention of the Internet there has been an explosion of sex crimes against children that has increased by 750%.[102] As a parent, you may be wondering, "Who are these perverts?" Everyday in America more than 50 newspapers contain stories about child pornography.[103] The purpose of including the following excerpts from actual newspapers is not to scare you, but to raise your awareness of the problem and correct any stereotypical profile that you may have of a child predator.

"Harold Shaw, 59, was a regular church-goer, a 'good guy' according to neighbors. The former gymnastic coach worked as a volunteer at a summer camp run by the Mormon church. Fellow church-goers affectionately called him 'Brother Shaw'. In February of 2004, Shaw was arrested on charges of child pornography. The walls of his Las Vegas home were lined with photographs of girls between the ages of 11 and 15, featuring close-up shots of their genitalia while performing gymnastics. The police also discovered a videotape of Shaw performing sex acts on an 11-year-old girl, who appeared to be drugged or drunk in the footage."[104]

"In March 2004, Joseph Thomas Nurek, 54, a school principal on Chicago's north side, was arrested for possession of child pornography. Federal authorities found more than 100 images on Nurek's computer with pictures of boys as young as 12 performing sexual acts."[105]

"David Deyo, 43, was a Sunday School teacher and youth group leader in North Palm Beach, Florida. He was also a pedophile and child pornographer who had more than 100 images stored on his computer and computer disks."[106]

"In February 2004, Kerry Dwayne Stevens, 48, of Aberdeen, Mississippi, pleaded guilty to charges of child pornography. Stevens photographed his daughter and two of her friends' genitalia while they slept, and uploaded the images to his computer for distribution. Prior to this incident, Stevens worked as a radio show producer for a children's program on American Family Radio, a Christian radio station."[107]

With 3,500 child pornography sites being added to the World Wide Web each year, the problem is only going to get worse.[108] A parent can never be too cautious.

SIGNS OF SEXUAL ADDICTION

- Do you routinely spend significant amounts of time viewing pornography?

- Do you hide your online transactions from your spouse or parents?

- Do you anticipate your next online session with the expectation that you will find sexual arousal or gratification?

- Do you feel guilt or shame from your online use?

- Did you accidentally become aroused by Internet sex at first, and now find you actively seek it out when you are online?

- Do you masturbate while online?

- Are you less involved with your spouse because of your experience with Internet sex?

Experts say that anyone who answers "yes" to any of the above questions may very well be a sex addict.[109]

Let us be reminded again that all of this is a reflection of God's judgment upon the nation. Our Scriptural premise for *Truth Decay* is based upon Romans 1, where the nation exchanged the truth of God for the lie. In such a twisted society, men and women leave the natural use of sex to do those things that are unnatural and shameful (v. 27). The nation is given over to the lusts of their hearts, to dishonor their bodies among themselves (v. 24). Gradually, the degenerate nature of this society succumbs to a debased mind to do those things that are not fitting or inappropriate (v. 28). The end result is a nation filled with all kinds of sexual immorality (v. 29). Remaining pure, living blamelessly, and walking undefiled through the sewer of our world's obsessions with sex is the challenge for today's Christian. Be encouraged by 2 Peter 1:3-4, which says that "His divine power has given to us all things that pertain to life and godliness, . . . by which have been given to us exceedingly great and precious promises, that through these you may be partakers of the divine nature, having escaped the corruption that is in the world through lust."

CHAPTER 11

The Abnormality of Homosexuality

Moral Relativism's Spin: Alternative Lifestyle

The 2006 Oscar-winning movie *Brokeback Mountain* challenged the gay stereotyping in America by telling the story of two rugged cowboys, both of whom were married, but fell in love with one another. Perhaps the most notable observation about this movie was not its critical acclaim at the Oscars, but the fact that in an increasingly gay tolerant culture, heterosexual consumers flocked to the theaters to support the production. Naturally, the gay community could not have been more thrilled because *Brokeback Mountain* is only one of many recent groundbreaking developments that have given gay-rights groups cause to celebrate. Bravo, the cable channel owned by NBC Universal, has launched OUTzoneTV.com as the first broadband entertainment channel for gay viewers. Sony Music is teaming up with Matt Farber, founder of Logo, MTV's gay-themed cable channel, to create a label featuring singers who are popular with gays, such as Beyonce' and Melissa Etheridge. Warner Books, a division of Time Warner, published a romance novel for gay men entitled *Hot Sauce*.[1] Programs such as *Will & Grace, Queer as Folk, Queer Eye for the Straight Guy,* and the hit drama on Showtime called *The L Word* are only a few examples of shows designed to desensitize Americans to the homosexual agenda. Likewise, IBM, Microsoft, Apple Computers, Hewlett-Packard, Eastman Kodak, Xerox, the *New York Times*, Time Warner, and the Walt Disney Company are just a few of the major corporations that have integrated gay friendly policies for their employees.

The gay market, as never before, is a top draw for advertisers. It is a known fact that gays, generally speaking, have more discretionary income due to the fact that most do not have children. Their annual spending this year alone is estimated at $641 billion.[2] A survey from the mid-1990s revealed that the annual income of homosexual households was as much as 41% higher than the national average. *Business Week* magazine reported that homosexuals are five times more likely than the average American to earn salaries higher than $100,000 a year.[3] According to Simon Market Research Bureau, a consumer-tracking firm, the average homosexual is better educated and has a higher income than the typical heterosexual.[4] A 1990 Simmons study found that 53% of homosexuals hold professional or management jobs, compared with the national average of 34% in the general population; 61% have graduated from college, compared with only 24% nationally; and the average homosexual household income is $53,000 compared with $35,000 nationally.[5] "Homosexual households," the researchers said, "are twice as likely as the typical household to have incomes over $60,000, and they're also twice as likely as the general populace to have incomes over $250,000."[6]

Twenty-five years ago, alcohol and tobacco firms targeted gays for advertising revenue. In the 1990s, it was airlines and financial services. Today, everyone from Firestone to Ford Motor Company is courting the gay dollar. This trend will only continue as long as the crossover appeal remains high with such programs as *Queer Eye for the Straight Guy* and NBC's *Will & Grace*.

Progress for gays is more than one-dimensional. In medical circles, homosexuality was removed from the American Psychiatric Association's list of emotional disorders in 1973.[7] In religious circles, some of the largest denominations in the nation have embraced the gay community by ordaining them into the ministry. In the political realm, gay candidates have been elected and appointed to major offices, ranging from governors to members of Congress. Between 1972 and 1978, at least 40 state legislatures granted "civil rights" to homosexuals comparable to those accorded to ethnic minorities.[8] In fact, at least 20 states have repealed their sodomy laws.[9]

I can hear the critics shouting, "What's the big deal? Who are you to judge? If they love each other, then that's their business. Chill out, be tolerant, and get off your self-righteous bandwagon. Gays and lesbians are like everyone else, with the same hopes, dreams, and desires." That's the lie they want us to believe. The reality is, we've all been caught up in a highly strategic, well-thought-out plan designed to desensitize the American public in such a way that the homosexual lifestyle is presented in the most positive light possible. However, there is a dark side to this equation of which few people are aware.

THE STRATEGY

A pamphlet entitled *After the Ball: How America Will Conquer Its Fear and Hatred of Gays in the 1990's*, presents in shocking detail a blueprint for brainwashing the American public. This treatise was written by two Harvard-educated sociologists, Marshall Kirk and Hunter Madsen. Kirk and Madsen describe a variety of brainwashing techniques that were used during the late 1960s to successfully transform the nation of China into a revolutionary "people's republic." It was Kirk and Madsen's belief that with enough time, money, and influence within the media and popular Hollywood culture, the homosexual community could force its goals and values upon America, regardless of whatever opposition stood in its way.[10]

In the article, "The Overhauling of Straight America," Marshall Kirk and Erastes Pill describe several strategies to push the gay agenda on America. This includes:

- Talk about gays and gayness as loudly and as often as possible.

- Portray gays as victims, not as aggressive challengers.

- Give protectors a just cause.

- Make gays look good.

- Make the victimizers look bad.[11]

A casual observer can easily see that gay opponents are often portrayed as racists and right-wing religious fanatics. To say anything against the gay lifestyle is considered hate speech. Gay advocates compare their opponents to Nazis, Klan members, and ignorant homophobes. Of course, the heart of the strategy is to perpetuate the big lie that homosexuality is simply an alternative lifestyle, and anyone who believes otherwise is intolerant.

Kirk and Pill advocate the following: "Portray gays as victims, not as aggressive challengers. In any campaign to win over the public, gays must be cast as victims in need of protection so that straights will be inclined by reflex action to assume the role of protector. . . . Straight viewers must be able to identify with gays as victims. Our campaign should not demand direct support for homosexual practices, but should instead take antidiscrimination as its theme."[12]

Kirk and Pill continue by saying, "Make the victimizers look bad. The public should be shown images of ranting homophobes whose secondary traits and beliefs disgust Middle America. These images might include: the Ku Klux Klan demonstrating that gays be burned alive or castrated; bigoted southern ministers drooling with hysterical hatred to a degree that looks both comical and deranged."[13] Recently, the front page of USA Today featured an article depicting a "hateful" Baptist minister calling gays "fagots" who would burn in hell. Rev. Fred Phelps from Westboro Baptist Church in Topeka, Kansas, has been notorious for attending these kinds of rallies and displaying provocative signs such as, "God Hates Fags." In my view, he does more harm than good. He certainly does not represent the spirit of the Christian community. Yet, I see no reason why this insignificant and little-known incident should have made the front page of one of the nation's most popular newspapers other than to cast gays in the role as victim.[14]

Kirk and Pill, in "The Overhauling of Straight America," gives this counsel to the gay community: "You can forget about trying to persuade the masses that homosexuality is a good thing. But if only you can get them to think that it is just another thing with a shrug of their shoulders, then your battle for legal and social rights is virtually won. And to get to the shoulder-shrug stage, gays as a class must cease to appear mysterious, alien, loathsome and contrary. A large-scale media campaign will be required in order to change the image of gays in America."[15]

The gay community recognizes that almost any behavior begins to look normal if you are exposed to it enough. Once the public is desensitized, homosexuality begins to be viewed with indifference. Once this happens, it is only a matter of time before it is fully embraced and given legal standing within the culture.

I want to make it clear that God loves the homosexual as much as He loves anyone. It is not my intent whatsoever to approach this subject with a "holier-than-thou" attitude. We are all sinners standing in need of God's forgiveness. Too often, preachers are guilty of preaching the truth in anger, and more damage than good is done. In Mark 10:6-9 Jesus identified in the most specific terms what God's original intent was for human sexuality: "But from the beginning of the creation, God 'made them male and female.' 'For this reason a man shall leave his father and mother and be joined to his wife, and the two shall become one flesh'; . . . Therefore what God has joined together, let not man separate." Jesus was taking us back to the Genesis account of creation and could not have made it clearer: God joined male to female. To assume otherwise is either blatant defiance of holy Scripture or a twisted and deceived approach to biblical hermeneutics. There is a place for kindness and gentleness. In fact, these are expressions of the indwelling presence of the Holy Spirit in a believer's life (Galatians 5:19-22). Yet, kindness and gentleness are never to be sacrificed at the expense of truth.

Christians in the twenty-first century are, for the most part, biblically illiterate, so if you want to find a "Christian" who endorses the gay lifestyle, you'll have no problem. A *USA Today* survey found that of the 56% of Americans who attend church, 45% did so because "it's good for you," and 26% went for peace of mind.[16] In other words, the majority attend church with a consumer mentality that asks, "What's in it for me?" What a church teaches or believes is not on the radar screen. Couple that with the fact that two-thirds of Americans no longer believe there is such a thing as "absolute truth," then you can easily understand why homosexuality is increasingly accepted as a normal way of life. It is most distressing, however, to learn that 53% of those not believing in absolute truth identified themselves as born-again Christians, 75% of whom were mainline Protestants.[17] In spite of these depressing stats, 66% of Americans still oppose same-sex marriages.[18]

Violating God's laws always carry consequences. The greater the violation, the greater the consequence. Consider the following, and then ask yourself, "What's wrong with this picture?"

IS THIS NORMAL?

Remember that Romans 1:26-27 states that it is unnatural for a man to burn in lust toward another man or for a woman to burn in lust toward another woman. Those verses state that such a lifestyle is in error to the truth, brings shame, and will result in a penalty to be paid. With that in mind, there is a little-publicized dark side to the gay lifestyle on which the media is strangely silent.

According to research by Dr. E.L. Goldman, 30% of currently 20-year-old gay men will be HIV positive or dead from the AIDS virus by the age of 30.[19] The average age of death for HIV-infected men is 39, while the average age of death of homosexual men from all other causes is just 42.[20] Just two percent of homosexual men will ever reach old age (defined as age 65 or older). Even when AIDS is not present, fewer than 12% of homosexual men will ever reach old age.[21] This is not normal.

Domestic violence occurs at a rate twice that of heterosexual couples.[22] Another study published in the law review of Valparaiso University reported that from 50,000 to 100,000 lesbians and as many as 500,000 homosexual men are battered each year in this country.[23] In a survey of 1,099 lesbians, more than half said that they had been abused by a female lover/partner.[24] This is not normal.

Forty-three percent of white male homosexuals estimate having had sex with 500 or more different partners, while 28% reported more than 1,000 sexual partners. Incredibly, 79% of those surveyed admitted that at least half of their partners were strangers. A study in the early 1980s revealed that only about two percent of homosexuals are "monogamous or semi-monogamous," which means that they've had 10 or fewer partners in their lifetime.[25] If these figures sound a bit exaggerated, then listen to a study by the U.S. Centers for Disease Control and Prevention (CDC). They found that 1,100 sexual partners is about *average* for gay men. Some reported as many as 22,000 partners in their lifetime![26] This is not normal.

Statistics from two different credible organizations reveal emotional and mental abnormalities within the gay community. The CDC and the National Institute of Mental Health found that homosexuals have higher rates of depression, anxiety disorders, and substance abuse. There is also a higher use of mental health services in men and women with same-sex partners.[27] This is not normal.

In a study of 153 self-confessed homosexual pederasts, they had assaulted a total of 22,981 victims—that's approximately 150 boys per offender! The study concluded that the incidence of molestation among homosexual offenders is a rate five times greater than that for heterosexual offenders.[28] This is not normal.

Gay men smoke twice as much as straight men.[29] Gay men are nine times more likely to have a drinking problem than straight men.[30] The *Journal of Consulting and Clinical Psychologists* found that homosexual women were more than twice as likely to be involved in heavy drinking than heterosexual women.[31] This is not normal.

David McWhirter and Andrew Mattison, a psychiatrist and psychologist, respectively, studied 156 homosexual couples whose relationships had lasted from one to 37 years. They discovered that not a single couple living together more than five years was able to sustain a monogamous relationship—not one.[32] This is not normal.

The Netherlands is probably the most gay friendly country on earth. Homosexuality is considered the norm there, so we might expect a more accurate reading of the gay lifestyle. A study released in 2003 found that the average duration of a relationship was between nine and 27 months.[33] What's even more interesting is that the study revealed that even those who were in a steady relationship still had an average of eight casual partners a year in addition to the significant other.[34] This is not normal.

Social scientific journals are now presenting unbiased research revealing that kids who are reared in same-sex marriages experience the following:

- poorer physical health
- poorer emotional health
- increased risks of suffering physical abuse
- poorer school performance
- lower self-confidence
- less compassion for others
- less respect for women
- high rates of criminal behavior
- higher rates of sexual experimentation
- earlier onset of sexual experimentation.[35]

This is not normal.

More than half of all people diagnosed with AIDS in the United States, and as many as 56% of new HIV infections, are homosexual males.[36] Homosexuals account for 80% of the serious STDs in the United States.[37] AIDS was first diagnosed as a disease of homosexual men, it was spread by homosexual men, and Family Research's long-term study confirms that it is increasingly a "gay disease."[38] This is not normal. If taxpayers are forced to foot the bill for the cost of medical care for everyone who has contracted AIDS, HIV, or the dozens of STDs associated with homosexual practices, the resulting price tag will cripple our economy.[39]

If, indeed, the above information is accurate, then why isn't the American public more informed? Why are lawmakers putting our nation at risk? Why are judges ignoring the facts of credible research? Why would our government allow public schools to sympathize with the homosexual lifestyle and promote it to our children as something to be normalized? Why would the legalization of same-sex marriage even be up for debate? The reason is because of a powerful, pro-active homosexual lobby coupled with a slumbering, indifferent church that needs to be awakened.

WHAT IS NORMAL?

I could not say it better than Glenn Stanton, an employee of Focus on the Family. He says, "Rarely have the social sciences come to a surer conclusion than on the question of how heterosexual marriage benefits men, women, and children. When men and women marry, they live longer lives. They enjoy higher levels of physical and mental health. They are less likely to suffer from substance abuse. Husbands and wives are less likely to abuse each other sexually or physically. Married people miss fewer days at work, hop from job to job less often, and save and invest more money. . . . Likewise, children with a married mother and father . . . have less need to visit doctors for physical or emotional problems. They do markedly better in intellectual and educational development. They are more sympathetic toward others and less likely to be in trouble at school, home or with the police. . . . Just as a male and female are needed to create new life, they are both needed to bring a young life to healthy maturity. It is uncompassionate to deny children mothers and fathers in order to fulfill adult desire."[40] This is not one man's biased opinion. Study after study has verified the truth of these words. The simple truth is that marriage has not been imposed on society by some religious institution or governmental power. God established it. For a nation to try and reinvent what God has already perfected is asking for social calamity.

WHAT ABOUT A GAY GENE?

While homosexual propagandists want us to believe that gays are "born that way," scientific evidence points to the opposite. In fact, most homosexuals do not believe that their orientation is genetic and inborn. Of course, it is politically expedient to view sexual orientation as inborn. Homosexuality will be viewed much more favorably if the public can be convinced it is an inherited trait. It is no surprise to hear such rabid claims coming from the homosexual community, which are then reported by the liberal media. It reminds me of whenever archeologists discover a bone fragment and then give it a name, a date, and hail it as further evidence for supporting the theory of evolution. Just as these "evolutionary" digs have proven to be hoaxes, the media and public schools continue to expose the public to false information that has absolutely no scientific support whatsoever. Yet, when you read it in a biology textbook and see an artist's rendition of the evolutionary charts or hear about it on PBS television, then it must be true. So, it is with the homosexual agenda. Yet, we must turn a deaf ear to those clamoring for political correctness and approach this issue with objectivity by looking at the unbiased scientific evidence. Even homosexual advocate and researcher Alfred Kinsey administered a questionnaire to 979 homosexuals regarding this very question. Only ten percent of the respondents believed they were "born that way." Over 80% attributed their orientation to childhood trauma or other environmental influences.[41]

It cannot be stated strongly enough that never has any research institute, any school of medicine, any journal of medicine, or any of the major therapeutic organizations ever said that medical researchers have found a "homosexual gene." Although there is no conclusive science that shows any correlation whatsoever, that hasn't stopped the homosexual community from making these false claims. The research is unequivocal: there is no such thing as a gay gene. Homosexual researcher Dean Hamer had to admit, "There is not a single master gene that makes people gay . . . I don't think we will ever be able to predict who will be gay."[42] Another well-known homosexual researcher, Dr. Simon LeVay, had to acknowledge, "It's important to stress what I didn't find. I did not prove that homosexuality is genetic, or find a genetic cause for being gay. I didn't show that gay men are born that way, the most common mistake people make in interpreting my work."[43] Even lesbian author and activist Dr. Camille Paglia reluctantly said, "Homosexuality is not 'normal.' On the contrary it is a challenge to the norm. . .Nature exists whether academics like it or not. And in nature, procreation is the single relentless rule. That is the norm. Our sexual bodies were designed for . . .No one is born gay. The idea is ridiculous . . . homosexuality is an adaptation, not an inborn trait."[44] One observer gave the "gay gene" argument this humorous spin: "My point is, homosexuality is an idea. You have never heard a doctor say, 'Mr. and Mrs. John Doe, you have a bouncing baby homosexual.' It's an idea."[45] As author Louis Sheldon says, "The body parts don't fit!"[46]

WHERE ARE WE HEADED?

In the past four decades America has managed to turn an ancient sin once punishable by death into a celebrated and protected right. By embracing the worldview of moral relativism, we are calling right wrong and wrong right. I have often said we can know what will work in the future by seeing what has worked in the past. Conversely, we can determine what will fail by looking at the historical documentation of what has caused civilizations to collapse. Can I be blunt for a moment? We are stupid and deserving of whatever consequences come our way if we refuse to learn from history and repeat the same destructive mistakes of the once-great empires of the past. It is time for someone to stand up and speak out with moral clarity on these issues.

For hundreds of years historians have chronicled the fate of empires and have found some common denominators that led to their collapse. Empires that once rose to greatness and collapsed in shame all fell because they chose to depart from the very values that made them great. So, what does history tell us? Nations die when sexual immorality runs rampant. Anthropologist J.D. Unwin studied 86 different empires in recorded history. What he discovered should send chills down our spines. He found that no nation that rejected premarital sexual chastity and monogamy in marriage survived longer than a generation after it had embraced sexual hedonism.[47]

Russian sociologist Pitirim Sorokin wrote another classic, *The American Sex Revolution,* in which he reaffirmed Unwin's conclusion. He claimed that America's downfall began in the late 1960s when we abandoned traditional values, and that we are committing "voluntary suicide" through unrestrained sexual indulgence. Sorokin accurately predicted that as premarital sex increased, the birth rate would decline, and our nation would be depopulated. He also accurately predicted the increase in divorce and an epidemic of sexual promiscuity resulting in a rise in illegitimate births and abortions. Sorokin's exhaustive study of decadent cultures convinced him, just as it did Unwin, that a society can only survive so long as strong families exist, and sexual activities are restricted to marriage.[48]

Another researcher traced the decline of great empires and found seven distinct characteristics:

1. Men rejected spiritual and moral development as the leaders of families.

2. Men began to neglect their families in search of material gain.

3. Men began to engage in adulterous relationships or in homosexual sex.

4. Women began to devalue the role of motherhood and homemaker.

5. Husbands and wives began to compete with each other, and families disintegrated.

6. Selfish individualism fragmented society into warring factions.

7. Men and women lost their faith in God and rejected all authority over their lives.[49]

Jim Nelson Black, in his book *When Nations Die,* identified ten factors that result in a civilization's collapse:

- Increase in lawlessness

- Loss of economic discipline

- Rising bureaucracy

- Decline in education

- Weakening of cultural foundations

- Loss of respect for traditions

- Increase in materialism

- Rise in immorality

- Decay in religious belief

- Devaluing of human life[50]

It is Black's conviction that only a few of these characteristics are enough to destroy a culture. According to Black, for the first time in history, a single culture—the United States—possesses all of these characteristics simultaneously.[51] It is no wonder that many of today's perceptive leaders are sounding the alarm and saying that apart from divine intervention in a massive spiritual awakening, America is destined to fall.

It deeply saddens me, but given the facts and looking at history, I see no other sensible conclusion. One day America will be forced to admit that homosexuality is wrong, and it was a tragic mistake to legitimize it. The only question is, "Will it be too late?"

WHERE IS THE CHURCH'S VOICE?

When it comes to addressing the moral issues of our day, I have been stunned by the deafening silence coming from the pulpits of churches that claim to believe the Bible. As a revivalist/evangelist, I only have a limited number of opportunities to speak to congregations in a normal four-day revival format. By the time I preach evangelistically in a few services, speak in school assemblies, conduct a strong youth night emphasis, and address specific needs in the church, there is little time left to speak on the variety of topics covered in *Truth Decay*. Since college days, these hot-button issues have been close to my heart, and I have seen the writing on the wall for decades. In fact, my wife will sometimes say, "You said that would happen 20 years ago."

I have to agree with Pastor Chuck Smith who says, "The very fact that we're arguing over homosexuality is evidence of a weak church. It should not even be a question because the Bible is very clear on the subject."[52] The truth of the matter is, the church represents the last voice of protest against the gay rights movement. If that voice is silenced or compromised, then we have lost the battle and, in essence, lost America. As I travel across the nation, it is apparent that ministry as we have known it in the past is in transition and has been for several years. Church as we have done it in the past is rapidly changing. There is cause for concern. I am not a deadhead traditionalist, but it seems that many "good" churches are letting immorality go without confronting it because the spirit of this age has invaded our congregations. We want to be more tolerant, so how does that translate in the pulpit? It often means putting a priority on being nice and making everybody feel comfortable. Don't misunderstand, I am not suggesting that God's preachers should be obnoxious, but neither should we soft-peddle sin. Granted, God uses all kinds of styles and personalities in the pulpit. But truth should never take a backseat to one's style or personality. In my opinion, we must awaken the church's prophetic spirit because as it now stands, we have surrendered our moral authority. It is baffling that the annual Gallup Poll of religion in America has shown for more than 40 years that at least 85% of Americans identify themselves as Christians.[53] But what difference does it make if the ungodly are the ones who make all the rules?

The Barna Research Group claims the trend for the foreseeable future is that popular culture will have a much greater influence on American society than the Christian church. The name of Jesus Christ means little to many young people today, and evangelical Christianity no longer ranks among the top ten "change agents" in our society.[54] What a sad commentary.

Robert Sheldon nails it when describing the status of today's church. He says, "Our churches have grown large and comfortable. We have programs. We have expansion plans. We have baseball tournaments and potluck suppers. We have gifted teachers and speakers, tapes and television, and full-color brochures that sparkle in the racks at the door. But what about the men and women who fill the pews? Do they understand Christ's command to work before the night comes when no one can work? Are they concerned about the eradication of our godly heritage by the schools and the courts? Do they understand what's happening to their children and the world they inhabit? Or are they, perhaps, too busy to notice?"[55]

If there is a silver lining in this dark cloud, it is that evangelical, Pentecostal, and independent Bible-believing churches have been growing at a record pace since the mid-1970s, largely at the expense of mainline denominations that have turned away from biblical inerrancy. Michael Medved observes that evangelicals enjoy unprecedented influence in government at all levels, a fresh array of educational alternatives, soaring enrollment at evangelical colleges, huge sales for religious music, novels, radio programming, and even motion pictures.[56]

I am convinced that these moral concerns could be largely overcome if the church would wake up and let its prophetic voice be heard. Thankfully, the God of history is not bound by surveys. In his book, *The Gay Agenda,* Ronnie Floyd quotes from a letter sent by the archbishop of the Anglican Church of Uganda to the presiding bishop of the Episcopal Church in the United States. The letter was a response to the shameful installation of Rev. Gene Robinson as the first openly gay bishop in the Episcopal Church. Please weigh each word carefully:

"Considering those things, we were shocked to receive a letter from you informing us of your decision to send a delegation to the enthrone- ment of our new Archbishop in January, and your intention for the delegation to bring aid and assistance for the people who live in desperate conditions in the camps in Gulu that you have ignored for years. Recent comments by your staff suggesting that your proposed visit demonstrates that normal relations with the Church of Uganda continue have made your message clear: If we fall silent about what you have done—promoting unbiblical sexual immorality—and we overturn or ignore the decision to declare a severing of relationship with ECU-SA, poor displaced persons will receive aid. Here is our response: The gospel of Jesus Christ is not for sale, even among the poorest of those who have no money. Eternal life, obedience to Jesus Christ, and conforming to His Word are more important. The Word of God is clear that you have chosen a course of separation that leads to spiritual destruction. Because we love you, we cannot let that go unanswered. If your hearts remain hardened to what the Bible clearly teaches, and your ears remain deaf to the cries of other Christians, genuine love demands that we do not pretend that everything is normal. As a result, any delegation you send cannot be welcomed, received, or seated. Neither can we share fellowship nor even receive desperately needed resources. If, however, you repent and return to the Lord, it would be an occasion of great joy."[57] May his tribe increase.

CHAPTER 12

Bring Back The Glory

Much of what you have read in the preceding chapters may have been unfamiliar to you. It may be that the research and statistical documentation has simply confirmed your suspicions that something is frightfully wrong with our beloved nation. America is not merely in the midst of a moral freefall; we are spiraling downward at a speed much faster than any of us could have imagined. I have quoted historians, politicians, military leaders, anthropologists, sociologists, educators, and theologians, all who proclaim a consistent message that the path we have chosen leads to inevitable destruction. The alarm they are sounding, however, is being drowned out by other cultural voices competing for our attention and appealing to our sensual nature. I cannot escape Alexis de Tocqueville's observation: "It was not until I stepped inside her pulpits and found her pulpits aflame with righteousness. Then, I discovered the source of America's strength."[1] It is not being nostalgic to call for a return of "the old-time religion." I am not advocating preachers who foam at the mouth with shouting, stomping, spitting, and sweating. The appeal being made does not concern style and methodology as much as it concerns the fundamentals of theology. Our pulpits have been strangely silent on most of the issues undermining the foundation of our nation. It is time for God-called men to be men of God in humility, standing tall, speaking in power, and submitting in grace to God rather than cower to the intimidating opinions of men. When we return to calling sin what it is, confront our congregations with an uncompromised Gospel that incorporates repentance, and preach with a passion that doesn't lull people to sleep, I believe the Holy Spirit will awaken the slumbering giant called the church, bring cleansing to our wicked ways, and begin to heal our land. It all starts with God's people and specifically, God's preachers.

THE 20/60/20 RULE

This rule simply means that usually there are 20% of people who are committed to one set of beliefs, and another 20% who are committed to the opposite ideology or worldview. In between, however, there is another 60% who lean in the direction of the most assertive twenty percent. We especially see this during elections. Through the years, I have been astounded at the fickleness of the American public. Instead of voting on principle, most of the nation is easily swayed by persuasive rhetoric or a fluctuating economy that strikes an emotional cord at the appropriate time of the year. All it takes is one miscue by a political administration, and the public, with the help of a powerful media, can be convinced to change party lines. It often becomes personality rather than principle on which people base their vote.

The 20/60/20 rule states that 60% of the population are followers who don't usually speak or embrace strong personal convictions. Those who see danger ahead and share the same moral concerns *must* let their voices be heard. We can accomplish this in multiple ways, such as frequently contacting your senator and state representatives to voice your opinions or working on behalf of a political candidate who stands for your causes. Identifying with a church that represents your concerns and serving in the community (i.e., crisis pregnancy centers, drug rehabs, and other support groups) are also avenues where each of us can make a difference.

Let us not overlook the key ingredient of prayer. Massive spiritual awakening will not come except through prayer. In fact, every spiritual awakening in America's history has had two things in common: prayer and youth. The often-quoted 2 Chronicles 7:14 mandates prayer as being essential for the spiritual healing of a nation. Our youth are often overlooked as a resource for restoring moral sanity in our nation. We are often prone to think they are the problem, but it is more than coincidental that the spiritual awakenings in the past have been initiated and perpetuated by youth.

Let's consider a thumbnail sketch of some of the great spiritual awakenings in history. The First Great Awakening is considered to have taken

place from 1734 to 1760. It was this divine visitation that laid the for-
mation of our system of government.[2] The Second Great Awakening
occurred from 1790 to 1840. Characterized by a host of circuit-riding
preachers, social reforms and the modern mission movement were
birthed out of this powerful awakening.[3] In 1857 and 1858, there was
the Great Prayer Revival, which occurred after a stock market crash.[4]
Prayer meetings sprang up from the eastern Seaboard to the coast of
California. It was reported that as many as 50,000 people a week were
being converted to Christ.[5] In 1904, the Great Welsh Revival, the result
of a reaction to liberal theology and the teaching of evolution, spread to
America.[6]

While each of these highlighted the integral role of youth, I want to
highlight the awakening in Wales that sparked revival in many of
America's cities. Evangelist Gypsy Smith called it the "Acts of the
Apostles up-to-date."[7] Dr. George T.B. Davis exclaimed that "this is
a picture of what must have occurred in the early church in the first
century of the Christian era."[8] On Christmas Eve 1904, in the city of
Abercarn (population 21,000), there were no arrests. The jails stood
empty on Christmas Day. Since coal miners stopped using profanity,
their workhorses stood still in confusion not knowing how to respond in
the absence of obscenities.[9] A young preacher named Evan Roberts was
the primary catalyst who God used. The Lord woke Roberts at a little
after 1:00 a.m. night after night and took him into a prolonged prayer
time lasting four hours. This pattern continued for three months.[10]
Roberts envisioned himself preaching to his former classmates and
seeing them come to Christ in salvation. Not long thereafter, his vision
was fulfilled and many of those who confessed Christ as Savior became
flaming evangelists. In two months, 70,000 came to Christ. In five
months, 85,000 had made professions of faith.[11]

While easily overlooked, youth were the spark that got the fire going
and kept it going. Jonathan Edwards remarked that the First Great
Awakening affected the youth more than anyone else.[12]

THE ASBURY REVIVAL

In more recent times, two great spiritual movements have occurred, though not nearly with the magnitude of those mentioned previously. Dr. Robert Coleman cites the Asbury Revival that took place in February 1950 on the campus of Asbury College in Kentucky. Classes had to be suspended because for nearly a week they waited upon God day and night. It was such a manifold presence of God that NBC network cameramen came on campus to film the proceedings. One of them commented, "It seemed that we were an intrusion to be present."[13]

THE JESUS MOVEMENT

The Jesus Movement touched thousands of youth in the late '60s and early '70s. Although it lacked the theological depth and societal impact of previous awakenings, its impact upon America cannot be understated. In the Southern Baptist Convention alone, baptisms surpassed 400,000 for five consecutive years, the only time this has ever happened.[14] Although high standards of morality accompanied this movement, its organization was minimal. Nevertheless, Marches for Jesus began spontaneously springing up throughout the nation. In Fort Worth, Texas, more than 13,500 youth marched down Main Street carrying signs saying, "Turn on to Jesus," "Jesus is Real," as well as others. The chief of police in Fort Worth called it "one of the best things I had seen in years."[15]

Dr. Alvin Reid, professor of evangelism at Southeastern Baptist Theological Seminary stated, "The history of great revivals demonstrated the vital role of youth. More and more I meet youth pastors and other leaders who comment on their youth who really believe they can change their world. Studies show the coming generation may be prime for a touch from God."[16] I concur.

Richard Ross, a professor at Southwestern Baptist Theological Seminary and the creator of the True Love Waits campaign, says, "I can already see a spark in the eyes of students who are coming to believe this may be the revival generation."[17] Ross is so convinced of this that Southwestern has actually created a new course describing the role of students in past revivals and spiritual awakenings.

From God's vantage point, I believe they are an integral part of His plan for America's future. Their numbers exceed the Baby Boom generation. Their energy, expressive worship, heart for missions, and passion for God are unsurpassed by any previous generation of teenagers. We must fan the flame that is within them. Rather than criticize their body piercings, tattoos, backward caps, and baggy pants, let's look into their hearts and praise them for what they do right instead of accentuating what we think is inappropriate and wrong. Too often they interpret adult's criticisms as frivolous, pharisaical, and narrow. It is this very attitude that is a turn-off to them ever wanting to come back to church. I understand that adults mean well when they instruct a student to tuck in his shirttail or take off his cap, but such comments often major on the minors. The spirit by which the reprimand is given can all too often be one of superiority. That's not the spirit of Jesus. I can testify from crisscrossing the nation year after year, there is incredible complacency and apathy among adults. While the same can also be said for many students, often they are responsive to God's call and desire to know the One who created them. This generation of young people is not turned off to God, only to the hypocrisy they often see within the church.

A GENERATION THAT DOES NOT KNOW GOD

In Judges 2:10 we are told that "another generation arose after them who did not know the Lord nor the work which He had done for Israel." This is my concern for today's youth. A great percentage of them are oblivious to the Christian heritage of our nation, to the faith of our fathers, and to the hand of God intervening on our behalf. Take this story about George Washington, for example.

Christian attorney David Barton cites this story recorded in an 1856 history textbook that was once used in virtually every classroom in America. Washington and his troops were involved in the French and Indian War and were marching toward Duquesne, which is now Pittsburgh, Pennsylvania. Suddenly, they were ambushed and hit from all sides. It was a lopsided, two-hour battle in which the American troops were soundly defeated. Washington was the only officer who remained on his horse. He returned home and wrote this letter to his family:

> "I took off my jacket and had four bullet holes in my jacket but I was not harmed. I brushed my hair and had fragments of bullets in my scalp but I was not scathed. God's hand was upon me. God protected me."[18]

The story in the textbook goes on to say that 15 years later, Washington and a close friend rode back through those same Pennsylvania woods where that battle had been fought. An old Indian chief heard that Washington was returning to those same woods, and he traveled from a long distance to meet with Washington. They sat down face-to-face, and over a council fire the chief said, "You don't know me, but 15 years ago you and I were in those woods together. I was the chief of the Indians who attacked you that day. We knew that you were one of the leaders and if we could kill you, then the rest of your troops would scatter. So, I told my boys to single you out and fire at you. I personally fired my rifle at you 17 times. When we saw that none of our bullets were having any effect on you, I told my boys to stop firing at you. I traveled all this way just to meet the man whom God would not let die in the battle."[19] God's hand has supernaturally rested upon our nation. He has protected us in the past when we have sought to honor Him. Yet, like the passage in Judges, we have a generation that does not know the Lord or the work that He has done for us. In fact, this is likely the first time most adults have heard the above story about Washington.

A MEASURE OF REVIVAL IN OUR BONDAGE

During a recent devotional time, I came across Ezra 9:8 that says, "And now for a little while grace has been shown from the Lord our God, to leave us a remnant to escape, and to give us a peg in His holy place, that our God may enlighten our eyes and give us a measure of revival in our bondage." For the past several decades God has given us a space of grace that we might escape His judgment. As in Ezra's day, He is enlightening our eyes and showing us our need for repentance. Hopefully, the result will be "a measure of revival in our bondage." This is the pressing need of the hour.

After the terrorist attacks on September 11, 2001, I wrote this poem that reflects our nation's need in this desperate hour.

When Lady Liberty Wept

In New York Harbor there stands a lady
With liberty's Light held high.
A symbol of freedom, a haven of peace,
"God bless America"—her battle cry.

Her majestic appearance, her torch of hope
Has won the applause of men.
From kings and presidents, parliaments and popes
She shouts, "Let freedom come in."

In bold splendor, with sheer delight,
Her message is loud and clear.
Calling the world, both day and night,
"All who love freedom come here."

Her dignity, poise, and stately resolve
Hold the dreams of the nations she's kept.
On 9/11 the Twin Towers dissolved
And the Statue of Liberty wept.

For across the harbor she watched aghast
As planes plunged from the sky.
"We will win. We'll get them back,"
She heard the nation cry.

But deep in her heart she knows the truth
That America's left her God.
From courts to schools, from old to youth,
Will we walk where our fathers once trod?

We've defied His laws, cursed His name,
And aborted millions in violence.
We point to others to cast the blame
While turning our heads in silence.

Prayers are being made, and soldiers being sent
With workers cleaning up the rubble.
But God is waiting for us to repent
Keeping us safe from any more trouble.

It's a defining moment, a point in time
To look to the God of our past.
That the flame of freedom will brightly shine
And the pursuit of happiness will last.

In horror we saw those plane crashes,
With evil unfolding before our eyes.
And now we're digging through the ashes,
Wondering why such men should needlessly die.

History reminds us time and again
That when great nations fall,
It's not from without; it's from within.
Let's heed the Spirit's call.

In disbelief through blinding tears
We watched the unthinkable occur.
A nation held captive, enslaved to fears,
Wondering "Will freedom endure?"

Ten thousand children now left without fathers,
Never again their Dad to see,
A void not filled by mothers or daughters,
What will these children grow up to be?

Just when we hope things will get better,
We're told, "There may be more attacks."
It's sad when you can't open a letter,
For fear of germs and death by anthrax.

The soul of the nation has been assaulted,
Death and destruction is all we can see.
But the name of our God shall be exalted
As the nation humbly bows the knee.

"Call unto Me," says the Lord.
"The plans for you I know.
Plans to prosper and reward,
Just follow Me wherever you go."

"I'll take the tragic, sad things in life,
And all that happened on that date,
Transforming hatred, bitterness, and strife
With the promise of Romans 8:28."

So Lady Liberty, wipe your tears.
The terrorist's actions were insane.
But perfect love casts out all fear.
Our citizens will not have died in vain.

If 9/11 was a wake-up call
For the church to arise from her sleep,
Then the time is now for one and all
To pray our liberties to keep.

Our history is filled with similar occasions
To lift up high the red, white, and blue,
In fighting nations of other persuasions,
And asking God to see us through.

A return to God is what we must hear.
Anything less is to miss the point.
Wake up America, to your God draw near.
Only repentance will He anoint.

"It's not too late to heed My voice,
But My mercy will not always strive."
To obey or rebel, that's your choice.
Will it be to die or survive?

For about three weeks after 9/11, church attendance rose substantially but then returned to its previous numbers. I remember someone commenting right after 9/11 that a large number of people across the nation went back to churches looking for answers as to what happened, but when they walked out of the sanctuaries, they remembered why they had left church in the first place. No doubt, many have vowed never to return because all too often the church is seen as irrelevant, boring, money-grubbing, and hypocritical. It is only healthy to ask ourselves, "Are we answering questions that no one is asking?" The church's voice must be on the cutting edge with the cultural issues of our day, allowing the Word of God to speak for itself whether it be exposing sin or offering hope and healing. The contemporary music group Casting Crowns has a popular song entitled, "We Are The Body." The chorus asks, "If we are the body, why aren't His arms reaching? Why aren't His hands healing, why aren't His words teaching? And if we are the body, why aren't His feet going, why is His love not showing them there is a way? There is a way."[20] Of the more than 200 nations on this planet, only 26 actually enjoy a way of life that includes political and social freedom.[21] Unless we have absolute standards of truth, there is no way to maintain law and order. If we cannot stop this avalanche of relativism, we will continue to lose one generation after another until our connection with God becomes a faint memory from the distant past. Many of our policies in government, education, and media are so diametrically opposed to the principles upon which the nation was built that we can only pray for God's intervention. The Bible reminds us in 2 Corinthians 3:17 that "where the Spirit of the Lord is, there is liberty." But the reverse is also true: where the Spirit of the Lord is absent, there is bondage and enslavement.

As much as I would like to say otherwise, I have to agree with Dr. D. James Kennedy when he says, "Unless we regain the moral authority upon which the nation was founded, and unless we return to the godly principles that allow society to function in harmony, there is very little hope that this nation can avert imminent disaster."[22] It is true, my friend. A nation without moral restraint cannot exist.

THE PRAYER THAT SENT RUMBLES
THROUGHOUT THE NATION

When someone is called upon to pray, seldom does the prayer or pray-er become the focus of attention. When the prayer has been punctuated with an "amen," attention is then given to the next activity or item on the agenda. Not this time. When Pastor Joe Wright was asked to open the new session of the Kansas Senate, everyone was expecting the usual politically correct generalities. Instead, what they heard was a stirring prayer, passionately calling our nation to repentance.

The response was immediate as a number of legislators walked out during the prayer. In six short weeks, the Central Christian Church of Wichita, Kansas where Wright was pastor had logged more than 5,000 phone calls, and only 47 of those callers responded negatively. Commentator Paul Harvey aired the prayer on his radio broadcast and received a larger response to this program than any other program he's ever aired. The Central Christian Church continues to receive international requests for copies of this prayer from places like India, Africa, and Korea. Here is the prayer that sent rumbles throughout the nation:

"Heavenly Father, we come before You today to ask Your forgiveness and seek Your direction and guidance. We know Your Word says, 'Woe on those who call evil good,' but that's exactly what we have done. We have lost our spiritual equilibrium and inverted our values.

We confess that:

We ridiculed the absolute truth of Your Word and called it pluralism.

We have worshipped other gods and called it multiculturalism.

We have endorsed perversion and called it an alternative lifestyle.

We have exploited the poor and called it the lottery.

We have neglected the needy and called it self-preservation.

We have rewarded laziness and called it welfare.

We have killed our unborn and called it choice.

We have shot abortionists and called it justifiable.

We have neglected to discipline our children and called it building self-esteem.

We have coveted our neighbor's possessions and called it ambition.

We have polluted the air with profanity and pornography and called it freedom of expression.

We have ridiculed the time-honored values of our forefathers and called it enlightenment.

Search us, O God, and know our hearts today; cleanse us from every sin and set us free. Guide and bless these men and women who have been sent here by the people of Kansas, and who have been ordained by You to govern this great state. Grant them the wisdom to rule, and may their decisions direct us to the center of Your will. I ask it in the name of Your Son, the Living Savior, Jesus Christ, Amen."[23]

Let's reflect on this for a moment. Here is a man who took a stand in an atmosphere charged with political correctness, but like Daniel of old, he refused to bow. Instead, with backbone he stood before Almighty God and voiced a prayer that sent shock waves through the Kansas Senate that day, provoking many to walk out and compelling others to chime in with their own hearty "amens." Once the dust settled, Wright's prayer brought to the surface the fact that millions of Americans are angry at the moral decline of this country and want their voices to be heard. From the 5,000 unsolicited calls made to the church, 90% were positive affirmations. Can you imagine, from a repertoire of countless thousands of programs, the legendary Paul Harvey receiving more response to this broadcast than any other? What does this tell us? I believe there is a ground swell of support for conservative causes, and there is a generation of adults who recognize the truth and are willing to rally behind anyone, whether it is a preacher, a politician, or an institution that refuses to compromise truth's integrity. We have a generation of Boomers and senior adults who understand that America's destiny hangs in the balance, and we must do whatever we can to empower those who are in the trenches and fighting for our survival.

WHY HAS GOD BLESSED AMERICA?

It is certainly not because we deserve it, but there are some identifiable, tangible reasons for why God has blessed our nation. First, the nearest and dearest thing to the heart of God is reaching others with the Gospel so they may know Him and spend eternity in heaven. America has had the distinction of producing 75% of all Christian missionaries over the last century.[24] Second, America has been a friend of the Jews. Of the 13 million Jews in the world in the year 2000, half of them lived in America.[25] Third, America has been a laboratory of freedom on display for the world to see that liberty works. Fewer than one in five people in our world are free. We are among the 20% of the world's population who enjoy the blessing of liberty.[26] Finally, America has historically honored the Word of God. The Bible was our founding document, and we have been the beneficiaries of the blessing our founding fathers set in motion.

The Book of Judges contains 21 chapters in which a four-fold cycle appears 13 times: rebellion, retribution, repentance, and restoration. America seems to parallel that pattern. We must always be reminded, however, that whenever God addresses the subject of national repentance, He speaks primarily to His own people. Likewise, national awakening begins with one person. If God chooses to bring revival to America, He will do it through a person—someone yielded to Him, someone with a strong conviction, someone who discerns the signs of the times, someone whose loyalty is first and foremost to God, and someone who embraces absolute truth as found in holy Scripture.

THE IMPORTANCE OF OUR RELATIONSHIP WITH ISRAEL

As I write this closing chapter, Israel is engaged in war with Lebanon and the Hezbollah regime. Her air force is dropping bombs at strategic military command posts, but Hezbollah bases much of its operation within the homes and communities of civilians, thus protecting itself against the enemy onslaught. As a result, Hezbollah is winning the public relations war. Commentators are condemning Israel for the deaths of innocent civilians while ignoring the fact that Israel did nothing to provoke these attacks. Nevertheless, as a longtime friend of Israel, America once again finds itself in the heat of conflict centered in the Middle East.

One of the clearest messages contained in Scripture is found in Genesis, which promises that those who bless Israel are blessed, and those who curse Israel are cursed. This truth is also repeated in Deuteronomy 28:7, 30:7; Isaiah 41:10-12; Jeremiah 10:25, 30:16; and Micah 5:9. Egypt, Syria, Babylon, Rome, Spain, Germany, and Russia can all testify that God will indeed curse any nation that turns away from the Jews. During this defining moment in world history, America must never forget this principle. We are indebted to Israel for our spiritual heritage. Israel gave the world the Ten Commandments, and it was through the Jews that God brought our Savior into the world. America's alliance with Israel is perhaps our strongest line of defense. The world court will never understand this principle, but we must never let our political leaders forget it.

The fact that America is not mentioned by name in the Bible is of concern. Perhaps it can be explained in prophetic terms. Through the rapture, God will remove Christians from the world scene, and then He will begin to unfold the futuristic events described in His Word, including the Great Tribulation and the emergence of the Antichrist. Since there are more Christians in America than anywhere else in the world, this may explain our absence from the prophetic picture. However, an even more sobering thought is that America's moral decay will become so imbedded and our departure from truth so prevalent, that we will go the way of past great empires and cease to exist altogether.

None of us can predict the outcome of this moral crisis. We have survived the Civil War, the Spanish-American War, two World Wars, the Korean War, Vietnam, the Persian Gulf War, and now we are engaged in the ongoing war against terrorism, which many are calling the third World War. But the question remains, "Will we survive the internal cultural war for values?" Deep within, many are wondering, "Is God on our side?" The real question is: "Are we on God's side?" While God is our greatest hope, He is also our greatest threat. He doesn't need a majority to accomplish His purposes. In fact, He doesn't need a minority. One old preacher of yesteryear said, "Snowflakes are frail, but if enough of them stick together they can stop traffic." Together, we can bail out the water, turn this ship around, and avert the iceberg of disaster that is staring us in the face.

This book is not about what Christians are against. That is not what defines us or the church of the living God. We are pro-life, pro-America, pro-freedom, pro-God, pro-family, etc. I have no political drum to beat and no self-serving agenda to promote. Like you, I am just an American who is privileged to have been born in the greatest nation on earth, and who has been given the freedom to make a difference. I am deeply concerned with the state of our nation. Yet, there is still hope. These things I believe:

- *I believe the Bible is the Word of God.*

- *I believe in absolute standards of morality.*

- *I believe Jesus Christ is the one way to salvation.*

- *I believe the unborn fetus is a human being with rights.*

- *I believe sex outside of marriage is wrong and constitutes fornication and adultery.*

- *I believe homosexuality is one of the final stages of moral perversion.*

- *I believe America was established as a Christian nation, founded by Christians on the principles of the Bible.*

- *I believe God will judge America, not in heaven, but in this life, for its sin.*

- *I believe in a real heaven and a real hell.*

Here we stand, immersed in a culture that promotes relativism and tolerates an anemic church that rarely holds high the standard of absolute moral truth. Without a solid moral foundation, churches and their congregants are affected by the culture more than they are affecting the culture's views and behavior. To put it in biblical language, the salt has lost its flavor. God help us.

Endnotes

Preface

1. Barna Research Group, "Americans Are Most Likely To Base Truth on Feelings". www.barna.org September 2002.

Chapter 1
A NATION IN CRISIS

1. Richard Whitmire, "1987: The Year America Changed" (USA Today; January 19, 1993).

2. *Ibid*

3. Engle v. Vitale; 370 U.S. 421,422 (1962).

4. Richard Whitmire, "1987: The Year America Changed" (USA Today; January 19, 1993).

5. Abington v. Schempp; (1963).

6. Reed v. Van Hoven; (1965).

7. Roe v. Wade; (1973).

8. Stone v. Graham; (1980).

9. Graham v. Central, (1985); Kay v. Douglas, (1986); Jager v. Douglas, (1989); Lee v. Weisman, (1992).

10. John Eidsmoe, *Christianity and the Constitution* (Grand Rapids, MI: Baker Book House, 1987), p. 406.

11. William J. Murray, "America Without God," The New American, June 20, 1988; p. 19.

12. D. James Kennedy, *Character and Destiny: A Nation in Search of Its Soul* (Grand Rapids, MI: Zondervan Publishing House, 1994), p. 247.

13. "The Tonight Show with Jay Leno" (NBC Productions; Fall 2004).

14. National Commission on Excellence in Education, A Nation at Risk: *The Imperative For Educational Reform* (Washington, D.C.: U.S. Government Printing Office; 1988), p. 13.

15. Phyllis Schlafly, *Child Abuse in the Classroom* (Alton, IL: Marquette Press, 1984), p. 400.

16. William J. Bennett, Secretary of Education, *American Education – Making IT Work* (Washington, D.C.: U.S. Government Printing Office; 1988), p. 13.

17. National Center for Educational Statistics,

Department of Education, *The Condition of Education*, 1987 (Washington, D.C.: U.S. Government Printing Office; 1987), p. 145.

18. *Ibid*, pp. 7-8.

19. *Ibid*, p. 34.

20. David Gyertson, ed., *Salt and Light* (Word, 1993), pp. 52-54.

Chapter 2
MORAL RELATIVISM

1. Thom S. Rainer, *The Millennnial Generation: America's Second Largest Generation, What They Believe, How to Reach Them* (Nashville, TN: Broadman & Holman Publishers, 1997).

2. Robert Jeffress, *Hell? Yes!* (Colorado Springs, CO: WaterBrook Press, 2004), p. 5.

3. Barna Research Group, "Americans Are Most Likely To Base Truth on Feelings".

4. Rev. Barbara Cawthorne Crafton, "Can You Believe It?" ("The Protestant Hour"; June 2, 1996, www.prtvc.org.)

5. Barna Research Group, "Americans Are Most Likely To Base Truth on Feelings".

6. Kennedy, *Character and Destiny: A Nation in Search of Its Soul*, pgs. 15 – 17.

7. Josh McDowell and Bob Hostetler, *Right from Wrong* (Dallas, TX: Word Publishing, 1994), p. 5.

8. Kennedy, *Character and Destiny: A Nation in Search of Its Soul*, p. 18.

9. James Patterson and Peter Kim, *The Day America Told the Truth: What People Really Believe About Everything That Really Matters* (New York, NY: Prentice Hall, 1991), p. 8.

10. William J. Bennett, *The De-Valuing of America: The Fight for Our Culture and Our Children* (New York, NY: Summit Books, 1992), p. 25.

11. McDowell and Hostetler, *Right from Wrong*, p. 7.

12. *Ibid*, p. 3.

13. George Barna, *Generation Next* (Venture, CA: Regal Publishing, 1996), page 77.

14. Patterson and Kim, *The Day America Told the Truth: What People Really Believe About Everything That Really Matters*, p. 25-26.

15. *Ibid*, p. 27.

16. *Ibid*, p. 49.

17. *Ibid*, p. 73.

18. *Ibid*, p. 8, 89.

19. *Ibid*, p. 94-97.

20. *Ibid*, p. 172.

21. *Ibid*, p. 170.

22. *Ibid*, p. 173.

23. *Ibid*, p. 120.

24. *Ibid*, p. 155.

25. *Ibid*, p. 199-200.

26. *Ibid*, p. 203.

27. McDowell and Hostetler, *Right from Wrong*, p. 19.

28. Peter Kreeft, *Making Choices* (Cincinnati, Ohio: St. Anthony Messenger Press, 1990), p. 502.

Chapter 3
TRUTH MATTERS

1. Norm Geisler & Frank Turek, *I Don't Have Enough Faith To Be An Atheist* (Wheaton, IL: Crossway Books, 2004), p. 37-38.

2. *Ibid*, p. 175.

3. Erwin Lutzer, *The Truth About Same-Sex Marriage* (Chicago, IL: Moody Publishers, 2004), p. 18.

4. Ryan Dobson, *Be Intolerant* (Sisters, OR: Multnomah Publishers, 2003), p. 52.

5. Bob Woodward, *Bush at War: Inside the Bush White House* (New York, NY: Simon & Schuster, 2002), p. 131.

6. George Barna, "Morality and the Church" (2002 videotape, quoted in Barna Research Online, "Americans Are Most Likely.")

7. Allan Bloom, *The Closing of the American Mind* (New York, NY: Simon & Schuster, 1987), p. 25.

8. Charles Colson, *Lies That Go Unchallenged* (Wheaton, IL: Tyndale House Publishers, 2005), p. 255.

9. *Ibid*, p. 255-256.

10. *Ibid*, p. 33-34.

11. "Dr. Phil Show", February 2, 2006.

12. Frank Peretti, *The Wounded Spirit* (Nashville, TN: W. Publishing Group, 2001), p. 31-35.

13. Frank Moore, *Dismantling The Myths* (Kansas City, MO: Beacon Hill Press, 1997), p. 88-89.

14. Kennedy, *Character and Destiny: A Nation in Search of Its Soul*, p. 34.

15. *Ibid*

Chapter 4
THE WAY WE WERE

1. Citizen magazine, July 2005, p. 24.

2. *Ibid*

3. *Ibid*, p. 25.

4. *Ibid*

5. David Limbaugh, *Persecution* (Washington, D.C.: Regnery Publishing, Inc., 2003), p. 69.

6. *Ibid*, p. 72.

7. *Ibid*, p. 70.

8. David T. Moore, *Five Lies of the Century* (Wheaton, IL: Tyndale House Publishers, Inc., 1995), p. 9.

9. Delaware Constitution of 1776, Art. 22, quoted in Francis Newton Thorpe, ed., The Federal and State Constitutions, Colonial Charters, and Other Organic Laws of the States, Territories, and Colonies Now and Heretofore Forming the United State of America, 7 vols. (Washington, DC: Government Printing Office, 1909), p. 566. www.press-pubs.uchicago.edu/fiybders/documents/a6_3s2.html.

10. Ken Woodward and David Gates, "How the Bible Made America," (Newsweek; December 27, 1982). Found at www.shakinandshinin.org/OurChristianHeritage-TheFoundingOfAmerica.html.

11. Moore, *Five Lies of the Century*, p. 10.

12. Quoted in John Eidsmoe, *Christianity and the Constitution* (Grand Rapids, MI: Baker Book House, 1987), p. 4.

13. *Ibid*, p. 8.

14. *Ibid*, p. 11.

15. Tim and Beverly LaHaye, *A Nation Without a Conscience* (Wheaton, IL: Tyndale House Publishers, Inc., 1994), p. 60.

16. Eidsmoe, *Christianity and the Constitution*, p. 11 – 12.

17. Kennedy, *Character and Destiny: A Nation in Search of Its Soul*, p. 34, 76.

18. David Barton, "America's Godly Heritage" VHS. (Aledo, TX: Wallbuilders, Inc., 1990).

19. LaHaye, *A Nation Without a Conscience*, p. 57.

20. Russ Walton, *Biblical Principles* (Plymouth, MA: Plymouth Rock Foundation, 1984),p. 357.

21. David Barton, "Separation of Church and State" VHS. (Aledo, TX: Wallbuilders, Inc., 1992).

22. Kennedy, *Character and Destiny: A Nation in Search of Its Soul*, p. 125.

23. Rod Parsley, *Silent No More*, (Lake Mary, FL: Charisma House, 2005), p. 13-14.

24. Henry Steele Commager, ed., *Documents of American History* (New York, NY: Appleton-Century-Crofts, Inc., 1949).

25. Congress, Senate, Joint Committee on Printing, *Washington's Farewell Address to the People of the United States*, prepared by the Legislative Reference Service, 96th Congress, 1st session, 1979, Senate Document No. 5.

26. Parsley, *Silent No More*, p. 16.

27. Limbaugh, *Persecution*, p. 158.

28. Thomas Jefferson quoted in Merrill D. Peterson, ed., *Jefferson Writings* (New York, NY: Literary Classics of the United States, 1989), p. 510. www.religious freedom.lib.virginia.edu./sacred/ danbury_1802.html.

29. Roger Williams, *Mr. Cottons Letter Lately Printed, Examined and Answered* (London, 1644), in Reuben Aldredge Guild, ed., The Complete Writings of Roger Williams, vol. 1 (New York, NY: Russell & Russell, 1963), p.108. William Sierichs Jr., "Ye Olde Walls of Separation," (Freethought Today, March 2001, www.ffrf.org/fttoday/march01/ sierichs.html).

30. Jeffress, *Hell? Yes!*, p. 177.

31. *Ibid*

32. Barton, *The Myth of Separation* (Aledo, TX: Wallbuilders, Inc., 1996), p. 50.

33. Moore, *Five Lies of the Century*, p. 25.

34. Engle v. Vitale; 370 U.S. 421,422 (1962).

35. David Barton, *America: To Pray or Not To Pray?* (Aledo, TX; WallBuilders, Inc.; 1995), pp. 20-21.

36. The People v. Ruggles 8 Johns 545 (Sup. Ct. N.Y., 1811), quoted in Church of the Holy Trinity v. U.S., 143 U.S. 470-471 (1892)

37. Vidal v. Girard's Executors; 43 U.S. 126, 132 (1844), quoted in Christian Defense Fund, "One Nation Under God" (1977). www.leaderu.com/orgs/cdf/onug/deci- sions.html.

38. Jeffress, *Hell? Yes!*, p. 181.

39. Everson v. Board of Education, 330 U.S. 1, 1947.

40. *Ibid*

41. Daniel Dreisbach quoted in Witham, "Church, State 'Wall' Not Idea of Jefferson." www.washingtontimes.com.

42. Philip Hamburger quoted in Witham, "Church, State 'Wall' Not Idea of Jefferson." www.washingtontimes.com

43. Kennedy, *Character and Destiny: A Nation in Search of Its Soul*, p. 125.

44. Chief Justice Earl Warren, quoted in "Breakfast in Washington" (Time maga- zine; 63, no. 7; February 15, 1954), p. 49.

45. Limbaugh, *Persecution*, p. 61.

46. State Senator Chip Rogers, quoted in The Towne Lake Ledger, December 2005, p. 12.

47. John Gibson, *The War On Christmas* (New York, NY: Sentinel Publishing, 2005), p. 58.

48. *Ibid*, p. 87.

49. *Ibid*, p. 102.

50. *Ibid*

51. *Ibid*, p. 113.

52. *Ibid*, p. 43.

53. Limbaugh, *Persecution*, p. 5.

54. *Ibid*, p. 6.

55. *Ibid*

56. *Ibid*, p. 37.

57. Moore, *Five Lies of the Century*, p. 19.

58. Barton, "Separation of Church and State" VHS, 1992.

59. Jeffress, *Hell? Yes!*, p. 185.

60. Barton, "Separation of Church and State" VHS, 1992.

61. April Shenandoah; *History of America's Education, Part II: Noah Webster and Early America, The Progressive Conservative*; Volume IV, Issue #34; April 3, 2002.

62. Limbaugh, *Persecution*, p. 321.

Chapter 5
AMERICA'S FAVORITE PASTIME

1. William Bennett, *Index of Leading Cultural Indicators* (New York, NY: Simon and Schuster, 1994), p. 103.

2. *Ibid*

3. www.tvturnoff.org/images/facts&figs/fact-sheets/FactsFigs.pdf.

4. Frank Moore, *Dismantling The Myths* (Kansas City, MO: Beacon Hill Press, 1997), p. 80.

5. *Ibid*, p. 80.

6. *Ibid*, p. 81.

7. Charles Swindoll, *Growing Strong in the Seasons of Life* (Portland, OR: Multnomah Press, 1983), p. 326-327.

8. Rod Parsley, *Silent No More* (Lake Mary, FL: Charisma House, 2005), p. 156.

9. *Ibid*, p. 157.

10. *Ibid*

11. Media Analysis, May 1997.

12. Ron Luce, *Battle Cry for a Generation*, Colorado Springs, CO: Cook Communication Ministries, 2005), p. 37.

13. Bennett; *Index of Cultural Indicators*; p. 104.

14. David Chagall, *Surviving the Media Jungle* (Nashville, TN: Broadman and Holman, 1996), p. 75.

15. Luce, *Battle Cry for a Generation*, p. 37.

16. "Violence and Promiscuity Set The Stage for Television's Moral Collapse," Issue 248 www.lfrc.org/get.cfm?i=ISO2E4

17. Bennett; *Index of Leading Cultural Indicators*; p. 145.

18. *Ibid*, p. 132.

19. *Ibid*, p. 143.

20. *Ibid*

21. *Ibid*

22. *Ibid*

23. *Ibid*

24. *Ibid*

25. *Ibid*

26. *Ibid*, p. 144.

27. *Ibid*

28. *Ibid*

29. *Ibid*

30. *Ibid*

31. Media Analysis, May 1997.

32. www.parentstv.org/ptc/facts/mediafacts. asp, www.newjerzee.com and www.tvturnoff.org.

33. Media Analysis, May 1997.

34. Bennett, *Index of Leading Cultural Indicators*, p. 112.

35. Media Analysis, April 2003.

36. Reported by Rob McGann in an article titled, "Internet Edges Out Family Time More than TV Time"; January 5, 2005 www.clickz.com/stats/sectors/demographics/article.php/3455061

37. Family Safe Media, Pornography Statistics 2003. www.familysafemedia.com/pornography_statistics.html

38. *Ibid*

39. Parent TV Council, p. 4, n.d.

40. See pages 22-23 of Report 6 article. Footnoted in that article to Family Pride Canada;www.familypride.uwo.ca/teens/teenbk2.html.

41. Judith A. Reisman, PhD., report "Pornography Targets the Teenage Brain, Mind, Memory, and Behavior: America's Children v. the Impotence Industry" for the Institute for Media Education. (n.d.)

42. Moore, *Dismantling the Myths*, p. 153-154.

43. Ron Luce, *Inspire the Fire* (Orlando, FL: Creation House, 1994), p. 41.

44. *Ibid*, p. 42.

45. *Ibid*

46. *Ibid*

47. "New Survey Reveals Shocking Values Among Children" (*Educational Newsline*; September/October 1990), p. 1. Quoted in McDowell, *McDowell Research Almanac*, p. 310.

48. Moore, *Five Lies of the Century*, p. 256.

49. Randy Alcorn, *Christians in the Wake of the Sexual Revolution* (Portland, OR: Multnomah Press, 1985), p. 94.

50. Drs. L. Rowell Huesman and Leonard Eron, quoted in "Violence Goes Mainstream" (Newsweek; April 1, 1991), p. 51.

51. Chuck Colson, *Break Point*,(Wheaton, IL: Tyndale House, 2005), p. 1.

52. The Desert Sun; May 24, 1993; B1.

53. Moore, *Five Lies of the Century*, p. 266-267.

54. *Behind The Screen: Hollywood Insiders on Faith, Film, and Culture*, edited by Spencer Lewerenz and Barbara Nicolosi; Chapter by Karen and Jim Covell (Grand Rapids, MI: Baker Books, 2005), p. 86.

Chapter 6
THE DANGER OF SAFE SEX

1. Allen Bloom, *The Closing of the American Mind* (New York, NY: Simon & Schuster, 1987, p. 25.

2. Luce, *Battle Cry For a Generation*, p. 92.

3. *Ibid*, p. 97.

4. Pam Stenzel, *Sex Has a Price Tag* (El Cajon, CA: Youth Specialties, 2003), p. 73.

5. *Ibid*, p. 97.

6. *Ibid*, p. 78.

7. *Ibid*, p. 77.

8. Stenzel, *Sex Has a Price Tag*, p. 46.

9. Josh McDowell, *The Myths of Sex Education* (San Bernardino, CA: Here's Life Publishers, Inc., 1990), p. 49.

10. "Teen Pregnancy, 16.6 Billion." (Chicago Tribune, February 19,1986)

11. *Ibid*

12. Dr. Harvey Fineberg, Dean, Harvard School of Public Health, "*Prevention Better Than Cure*" (AIDS Protection 3:1, May 1989).

13. Nora Zamichow, Times Herald, n.d.

14. Boston Herald; July 13, 1989.

15. George Grant, *Grand Illusions: The Legacy of Planned Parenthood* (Brentwood, TN: Eolgemuth & Hyatt Publishers, Inc., 1988), p. 30.

16. Asta Kennedy, "School-Based Clinics: A National Conference"(Family Planning Perspectives 18:1, January/February 1986).

17. Consumer Reports, March 1989.

18. "*Will Safe Sex Education Effectively Combat AIDS?*" (Paper written by staff of Department of Education, January 22, 1987).

19. Theresa Crenshaw, M.D., (Condom Advertising; February 10, 1987.)

20. "Condoms: Experts Fear False Sense of Security" (New York Times, August 18, 1987.)

21. The Common Appeal; November 7, 1988.

22. McDowell, *The Myths of Sex Education*, p. 54.

23. *Ibid*

24. Reginald Bibby and Donald Posterski, *The Emerging Generation—An Inside Look At Canada's Teenagers* (Toronto: Irwin Publishing, 1985).

25. Lewis Lord, "Sex With Care" (U.S. News & World Report, June 2, 1986), p. 53.

26. Jean Seligmann, "A Nasty New Epidemic" (Newsweek, February 4, 1985), p. 73.

27. From the report: "Tracking the Hidden Epidemic Trends in STD's in the United States 2000"; published by the Centers for Disease Control and Prevention; p. 1.

28. Virginia's Family Life Education program, chapter 20---part four, Resource #1.

29. Roberta Weiner, ed., *Teen Pregnancy: Impact on the Schools* (Alexandria, VA: Capitol Publications, 2000), p. 17.

30. Bill Reed, M.D. Position paper, October 23, 1985, p. 1.

31. *Family Planning Perspectives* 12:5:229 (September/October 1980)

32. "Does Contraception Prevent Abortion?" (Human Life Center, 1983)

33. Figures for 1970-1978 from Susan Roylance testimony before U.S. Senate Committee on Labor and Human Resources, Washington, D.C., 1986.

34. Jacqueline Kasun, "Teenage Pregnancy: What Comparisons Among States and Countries Show" (A position paper, Department of Economics, Humboldt State University, Arcata, CA., 1986).

35. William Bennett, "Our Children"

(Address to the National School Board of Education; January 22, 1987).

36. Ibid

37. Stenzel, *Sex Has a Price Tag*, p. 54.

38. Ibid

39. Harris, *American Teens Speak*, p. 7.

40. Anne Marie Morgan, "Comprehensive Sex-Ed: Ten Fatal Flaws." (Virginians for Family Values, n.d.)

41. Gregory Fossedal, "Dartmouth's 'Safe Sex Kit' is Far From Morally Neutral" (Orange County Register, February 10, 1987).

42. Marsha Goldsmith, "'Silent Epidemic' of 'Social Disease' Makes STD Experts Raise Their Voices" (*Journal of the American Medical Association* 261:24 (June 23/30, 1989).

43. *AIDS and the Education of Our Children: A Guide for Parents and Teachers* (U.S. Department of Education, October 6, 1987).

44. Phyllis Schlafly, *Child Abuse in the Classroom* (Alton, IL: Marquette Press; 1984), p. 278.

45. Ibid, p. 294.

46. Barbara Vobejda, "Right and Wrong and the Three R's—Consensus Supports a Return to Teaching Values in Public Schools" (Washington Post, April 4, 1987).

47. Stephanie J. Ventura, William D. Mosher, Sally C. Curtin, Joyce C. Abma, Stanley Henshaw, "Trends in Pregnancy Rates for the United States, 1976-97: An Update" (*National Vital Statistics Reports* 49, no. 4; June 6, 2001).

48. Anastasia Toufexis, "What to Do When Priests Stray" (Time; September 24, 1990), p. 79.

49. Rutgers, The State University of New Jersey, The National Marriage Project, "Should We Live Together?" Online at http://marriage.rutgers.edu/Publications/swlt2pdf.

50. Ibid

51. "Sex in America" (U.S. News and World Report; October 17, 1994), p. 77.

52. D. James Kennedy, *Why The Ten Commandments Matter* (New York, Boston, Nashville: Warner Faith, 2005), p. 124-125.

53. Bradley Greenberg, Robert Abelman, and Kimberly Neuendorf, "Sex on the Soap Operas: Afternoon Delight" (Journal of Communication, Summer, 1981).

54. McDowell, *The Myths of Sex Education*, p. 39.

55. "A Thumbs Down for Music Videos" (USA Today; November 14, 1988.)

56. McDowell, *The Myths of Sex Education*, p. 194.

57. Barna Research Group, "Americans Are Most Likely To Base Truth on Feelings".

58. Luce, *Battle Cry for a Generation*, p. 15.

59. J.D. Unwin, *Sex and Culture* (London: Oxford University Press, H. Milford; 1934), p. 37.

Chapter 7
ABORTION: THE AMERICAN HOLOCAUST

1. Sean McDowell, *Ethix* (Nashville, TN: Broadman & Holman Publishers, 2006) p. 89.

2. Parsley, *Silent No More*, p. 15.

3. D. James Kennedy, *What If America Were a Christian Nation Again?* (Nashville, TN: Thomas Nelson Publishing, Inc., 2003), p. 101.

4. John Powell, *abortion: the SILENT HOLOCAUST* (Allen, TX: Argus Communications, 1981), p. 50.

5. John Anderson, *Cry of the Innocents* (South Plainfield, NJ: Bridge Publishing, Inc., 1984), p. 121-122.

6. Ibid, p. 5.

7. Dr. Margaret White, *Two Million Silent Killings* (Basingstoke, UK: Marshall, Morgan and Scott Publications, 1987), p.4.

8. Ibid

9. Ibid

10. Ibid

11. Ibid, p. 5.

12. N. Allan Moseley, *Thinking Against The Grain (Developing a Biblical Worldview in a Culture of Myths)*, (Grand Rapids, MI: Kregel Publications, 2003), p. 235.

13. John Ankerberg and John Weldon, *The Facts on Abortion* (Eugene, OR: Harvest House Publishers, 1995), p. 7.

14. Dr. & Mrs. J.C. Willke, *Handbook on*

Abortion (Cincinnati, OH: Hays Publishing Co., 1979), p. 10.

15. *Ibid*, p. 18-22.

16. Lawyer Cooperative, U.S. Supreme Court Reports, p. 183, 410 US 113 at 163.

17. Internal Revenue Service, *Exemptions, Standard Deduction and Filing Information*, Publication 501, cat. #15000U, p. 12.

18. White, *Two Million Silent Killings*, p. 17.

19. *Ibid*

20. *Ibid*

21. *Ibid*

22. *Ibid*, p. 42-43.

23. *Ibid*

24. Citizen magazine; August 26, 1996; p. 7.

25. *Ibid*, p. 7.

26. Ankerberg and Weldon, *The Facts on Abortion*, p.8.

27. *Ibid*, p. 8-9.

28. *Ibid*

29. *Ibid*

30. *Ibid*

31. *Ibid*

32. Willke, *Handbook on Abortion*, p. 159.

33. D. James Kennedy, *What If America Were A Christian Nation Again?* (Nashville, TN: Thomas Nelson Publishers; 2003), p. 105.

34. McDowell, *Ethix*, p. 94.

35. *Ibid*, p. 95.

36. Kennedy, *What If America Were A Christian Nation Again?*, p. 105.

37. *Ibid*

38. *Ibid*, p. 107.

39. *Ibid*, p. 108.

40. Motion filed in the Supreme Court of the United States, October 15, 1971 (Re: No. 70-18 and No. 70-40), titled *Motion and Brief Amicus Curiae of Certain Physicians, Professionals and Fellows of the American College of Obstetrics and Gynecology in Support of Appellees*; Dennis J. Horan et al. (United States District Court 1971), pp. 19, 29-30.

41. *Ibid*, p. 13-14.

42. Moore, *Five Lies of the Century*, p. 206.

43. White, *Two Million Silent Killings*, p. 43.

44. *Ibid*, p. 50.

45. Moore, *Five Lies of the Century*, p. 215.

46. McDowell, *Ethix*, p. 101.

47. Willke, *Handbook on Abortion*, p. 40.

48. *Ibid*, p. 40.

49. Ankerberg and Weldon, *The Facts on Abortion*, p. 18.

50. *Ibid*, p. 19.

51. *Ibid*, p. 20.

52. Powell, *abortion: the SILENT HOLOCAUST*, p. 52 – 54.

53. Willke, *Handbook on Abortion*, p. 32.

54. White, *Two Million Silent Killings*, p. 64-65

55. Ankerberg and Weldon, *The Facts on Abortion*, p. 21.

56. Mother Theresa, "Whatsoever You Do..." speech to the National Prayer Breakfast; (Washington, DC: February 3, 1994). Found at website: www.priestsforlife.org/brochures/mtspeech.html.

57. *Ibid*, p. 20.

58. White, *Two Million Silent Killings*, p. 123.

59. *Ibid*. p. 145.

60. Kenyn Cureton, "Standing For Life", SBC Life, January 2001, Executive Committee of the Southern Baptist Convention, Nashville, TN., p. 2-4.

61. *Ibid*

62. Citizen, n.d., p. 6.

63. Kennedy, *Character and Destiny: A Nation in Search of Its Soul*, p. 94.

Chapter 8
ALCOHOL: AMERICA'S BEVERAGE OF CHOICE

1. "Drug Strategies: Millennium Hangover: Keeping Score on Alcohol", 2002. www.vpcla.org/factAlcohol.htm.

2. *Ibid*

3. www.puberty101.com/d_alcohol.shtml

4. www.focusas.com/Alcohol.html; 7/20/2006.

5. Dr. Johnny Hunt, "Should Christians Drink? A Biblical Commitment to Total Abstinence" as preached at First Baptist Church, Woodstock, GA; September 1997.

6. www.teendrugabuse.net/stats.

7. www.marininstitute.org/youth/alcohol_youth.htm.

8. www.teendrugabuse.net/stats.

9. Katherine Ketcham and Nicholas A. Pace, *Teens Under the Influence* (New York, NY: Random House Publishing Group, 2003), p. 72.

10. Jay Strack, *Drugs and Drinking* (Nashville, TN: Thomas Nelson Publishers, 1985), p. 41.

11. www.drugwarfacts.org/alcohol.htm.

12. www.teendrugabuse.net/stats.

13. Dorothy P. Rice, "Economic Costs of Substance Abuse", 1995. (Proceedings of the Association of American Physcians 111(2), 1999), p. 119-125.

14. www.teendrugabuse.net/stats.

15. Fran Neumann, "Why are Pasadena Teenagers Drinking So Much?" (Pasadena Star News; May 4, 1993).

16. www.gangsandkids.com/gstates.html.

17. Michael Gartner, "Bring Back Prohibition" (USA Today, May 4, 1994).

18. www.teendrugabuse.net/stats.

19. www.alcoholalert.com/drunk-driving-statistics.html; 8/4/06.

20. *Ibid*

21. www.students.resa.net/ruhs/extracurricular/sadd/statistics.htlm

22. *Ibid*

23. www.drunkdrivinglawyers.com/alcohol-related-crashes.cfm.

24. www.students.resa.net/ruhs/extracurricular/sadd/statistics.htlm.

25. Hunt; "Should Christians Drink? A Biblical Commitment to Total Abstinence", 1997.

26. *Ibid*

27. *Ibid*

28. *Ibid*

29. *Ibid*

30. *Ibid*

31. *Ibid*

32. *Ibid*

33. Sharon Hersh, *Mom, Everyone Else Does!* (Colorado Springs, CO: Waterbrook Press, 2005), p. 127.

34. *Ibid*

35. *Ibid*

36. *Ibid*

37. *Ibid*

38. *Ibid*

39. *Ibid*, p. 128.

40. Hunt, "Should Christians Drink?", 1997.

Chapter 9
RANDOM CHANCE OR INTELLIGENT DESIGN?

1. Richard A. Swenson, *More Than Meets the Eye: Fascinating Glimpses of God's Power and Design* (Colorado Springs, CO: NavPress, 2000), p. 32-34.

2. *Ibid*, p. 33-34.

3. *Ibid*

4. Lorraine Peterson, *God's an Artist and You're a Masterpiece* (Grand Rapids, MI: Kregel Publications, 2004), p. 104.

5. *Ibid*

6. Swenson, *More Than Meets the Eye*, p. 29.

7. *Ibid*, p. 23.

8. Richard Swenson, More Than Meets The Eye: Fascinating Glimpse of God's Power and Design (Colorado Springs, CO: NavPress, 2000), p. 39-40.

9. *Ibid*, p. 40.

10. *Ibid*, p. 47.

11. *Ibid*, p. 51.

12. Kennedy, *Character and Destiny: A Nation in Search of Its Soul*, p. 181.

13. David Louis, 2201 *Fascinating Facts* (New York, NY: Greenwich House, 1983), p. 221.

14. Swenson, *More Than Meets the Eye*, p. 85-87.

15. Bill Gothard, *Character Sketches: From the Pages of Scripture Illustrated in the World of Nature* (Oak Brook, IL: Institutes in Basic Life Principles, 1985), 3:173.

16. Rita Thievon Mullin, *Animalogy: Weird and Wacky Animal Facts* (Bethesda, MD: Discovery Channel Publishing; New York, NY: Crown Publishers, 1998), p. 14.

17. Louis, 2201 *Fascinating Facts*, p. 10.

18. Mullin, *Animalogy*, p. 8.

19. Louis, 2201 *Fascinating Facts*, p. 74.

20. Geoff Chapman, "Weird and Wonderful Seals", Creation Ex Nihilo 17, no. 1 (December 1994 – February 1995), p. 36.

21. Bernie Smith, *The Joy of Trivia* (Los Angeles, CA: Brooke House, 1976), p. 100.

22. Jeffress, *Hell? Yes!*, p. 144-145.

23. *Ibid*, p. 143.

24. *Ibid*

25. Maxine Singer, "Believing Is Not Understanding" (Washington Post; August 18, 1999).

26. Jeffress, *Hell? Yes!*, p. 143.

27. Moore, *Five Lies of the Century*, p. 114.

28. Ron Carlson and Ed Decker, *Fast Facts on False Teachings* (Wheaton, IL: Harvest House Publishers, 1994).

29. *Ibid*, p. 9.

30. *Ibid*

31. Gary Parker, *Creation: Facts of Life* (Colorado Springs, CO: Master Books, 1994), p. 33-34.

32. National Geographic, n.d.

33. *Ibid*

34. *Ibid*

35. Newsweek, n.d.

36. Jeffress, *Hell? Yes!*, p. 148.

37. Dr. Gary Parker, "Evolution?". www.atschool.eduweb.co.uk/sbs777/vital/evolutio.html.

38. J. Madeleine Nash, "When Life Exploded" (Time magazine 146, no. 23; December 4, 1995, cover). Quoted in Ray Bohlin, *Evolution's Big Bang* (Richardson, TX: Probe Ministries, 1996).

39. Peterson, *God's an Artist and You're a Masterpiece*, p. 169.

40. *Ibid*, p. 170.

41. *Ibid*

42. Charles Darwin, *The Origin of Species*. www.atschool.eduweb.co.uk/sbs777/vital/evolution.html.

43. Mark Hartwig, Focus on the Family magazine (Colorado Springs, CO: June 2002), p. 2.

44. Swenson, *More Than Meets the Eye*, p. 70.

45. Peter Stower, *Science Speaks* (Wheaton, IL: Van Kampen, 1952), p. 167.

46. Charis Conn and Ilena Silverman, eds., *What Counts: The Complete Harper's Index* (New York, NY: Holt, 1991), p. 138.

47. Hugh Ross, *The Creator and The Cosmos: How The Latest Scientific Discoveries Reveal God* (Colorado Springs, CO: NavPress, 2001), p. 153.

48. Jeffress, *Hell? Yes!*, p. 160.

49. James Coppedge, *Evolution: Possible or Impossible?* (Northridge, CA: Probability Research in Molecular Biology, 1993), p. 110, 114. www.equip.org/free/DC745.htm.

50. Moore, *Five Lies of the Century*, p. 110.

51. Michael J. Behe, "Experimental Support For Regarding Functional Classes of Proteins To Be Highly Isolated From Each Other" (The Weekly Standard; June 7, 1999). www.arn.org/docs/behe/mb_smu1992.htm.

52. Jeffress, *Hell? Yes!*, p. 158

53. *Ibid*

54. *Ibid*, p. 159.

55. Peterson, p. 118.

56. *Ibid*

57. *Ibid*, p. 198

58. Robert Jastrow, *God and the Astronomers* (New York, NY: W.W. Norton, revised edition, 1992), p. 11.

59. American National Association of Biology Teachers 1995 position statement. Quoted in Phillip E. Johnson, *Defeating Darwinism by Opening Minds* (Downers Grove, IL: InterVarsity, 1997), p. 15.

60. Moore, *Five Lies of the Century*, p. 114-115.

61. Scientific American, July 2000.

62. Lee Strobel, *The Case for a Creator* (Grand Rapids, MI: Zondervan, 2004), p. 31.

63. *Ibid*, p. 31.

64. Discovery Institute, *Getting the Facts Straight* (Seattle, WA: Discovery Institute Press, 2001), p. 11.

65. Jastrow, *God and the Astronomers*, p. 14.

66. D. James Kennedy, *Why I Believe* (Nashville, TN: W. Publishing Group, 1980), p. 30.

67. Pierre Simon de La Place, *Evidences of Revelation*, p. 7.

68. Kennedy, *Why I Believe*, p. 31.

69. *Ibid*, p. 32.

70. Moore, *Five Lies of the Century*, p. 112-113.

71. H.S. Lipson, "A Physicist Looks At Evolution" (Physics Bulletin 31; 1980), p. 138. www.apologeticspress.org/inthenews/2003/itn-03-03.htm.

72. Norman Geisler & Ron Brooks, *When Skeptics Ask: A Handbook on Christian Sciences* Grand Rapids, MI: Baker Books, 1990), p. 214.

73. Moore, *Five Lies of the Century*, p. 117.

74. Paul Davies, *The Mind of God* (New York, NY: Touchstone, 1992), p. 16, 232.

75. Edward Harrison, *Masks of the Universe* (New York, NY: Collier, 1985), p. 263.

76. Owen Gingerich, "Dare a Scientist Believe in Design?" (In John M. Templeton, editor, *Evidence of Purpose*, New York, NY: Continuum, 1994), p. 25.

77. Kennedy, *Why I Believe*, p. 40.

Chapter 10
THE GLUT OF SMUT

1. Richard Land, *Imagine! A God-Blessed America* (Nashville, TN: Broadman & Holman Publishers, Nashville, TN. 2005), p. 55-56.

2. *Ibid*

3. *Ibid*

4. Phillip Yancey, *Finding God in Unexpected Places* (Nashville, TN: Moorings, 1995), p. 16.

5. Family Safe Media, *Pornography Statistics 2003*. www.familysafemedia.com/pornography_statistics.html.

6. *Ibid*

7. Ralph H. Earle, Jr. and Mark R. Laaser, *The Pornography Trap* (Kansas City, MO: Beacon Hill Press, 2002), p. 99.

8. Judith Reisman, *Soft Porn Plays Hard Ball: Its Tragic Effects on Women, Children and the Family* (Lafayette, LA: Huntington House, 1991).

9. www.familysafemedia.com/pornography_statistics.html.

10. *Ibid*

11. Luce, *Battle Cry For A Generation*, p. 87.

12. *Ibid*

13. Michael S. Kimmel, "'Insult' or 'Injury': Sex, Pornography and Sexism" in *Men Confront Pornography*, p. 317.

14. Michael Barron and Michael S. Kimmel, "Sexual Violence in Three Pornographic Media: Toward a Sociological Explanation" (Journal of Sex Research 37, May 2000), p. 2.

15. Dennis McAlpine interview, "American Porn" on "Frontline" (PBS, August 2001).

16. Pamela Paul, *Pornified* (New York, NY: Henry Holt and Company, 2005), p. 54.

17. "Porn in the U.S.A." www.CBSnews.com; November 21, 2003.

18. McAlpine, "American Porn", August 2001.

19. *Ibid*

20. Frank Coggrave, "Bugwatch: The Perils of Peer-to-Peer" (VNU Business Publications; March 31, 2004).

21. "Porn More Popular than Search" (Found at www.InternetWeek.com; June 4, 2004.)

22. Paul, *Pornified*, p. 16.

23. "NBC Evening News"; December 14, 1998.

24. Richard Johnson, "Page Six" (New York Post; May 4, 2004).

25. Ben Flanagan, "Porn Debate Garners Huge Turnout at U. Alabama" (The Crimson White; March 18, 2004).

26. Paul, *Pornified*, p. 113.

27. *Ibid*, p.112

28. Ebovie D. Hale, "Committee Approves Porn Magazine" (Harvard Crimson; February 11, 2004).

29. Jenna Russell, "BU to Get Own Sex Magazine" (Boston Globe; October 6, 2004).

30. Paul, *Pornified*, p. 114.

31. Paul, *Pornified*, p. 116.

32. *Ibid*, p. 9

33. *Ibid*, p. 116.

34. John Schwartz, "Leisure Pursuits of Today's Young Man" (New York Times, March 29, 2004).

35. Heard on Focus on the Family radio broadcast by Dr. James Dobson on the topic of pornography, n.d.

36. Speech by Judith Reisman given at a Science, Technology, and Space Hearing: "The Science Behind Pornography Addiction" (November 18, 2004). www.commerce.senate.gov/hearings/testimony.cfm?id=1343&wit_id=3910).

37. *Ibid*

38. National Institute of Mental Health, Office of Communications and Public Liaison, www.nimh.nih.gov. Child and adolescent mental health information: www.nimh.nih.gov/publicat/childmenu.cfm. (Barlow, Sakheim and Beck; The Journal of Abnormal Psychology)

39. Patrick Carnes, *Out Of The Shadows: Understanding Sexual Addiction* (Minneapolis, MN: CompCare, 1983).

40. Paul, *Pornified*, p. 151.

41. "Cerberian and SonicWALL Web Usage Survey Reveals 75% Accidentally See Porn at Work" (Business Wire; June 23, 2004).

42. Julie Forster, "X-Rated Surfing Common at Work" (Saint Paul Pioneer Press; February 14, 2004).

43. "State Ousts 23 Employees for Using Computers to Look at Porn" (Associated Press, Frankfort, KY; May 22, 2004).

44. Peter Bacque, "VDOT Computer Abuse Reported" (Richmond Times Dispatch, February 4, 2004).

45. J. Michael Parker, "Sexual Healing: Ministries Help Men with Purity Struggle" (San Antonio Express-News; January 31, 2004), p. 7B.

46. Ted Roberts, *Pure Desire* (Ventura, CA: Regal Books, 1999), p. 70.

47. J. Michael Parker, "Sexual Healing: Ministries Help Men with Purity Struggle" (San Antonio Express-News; January 31, 2004), p. 7B.

48. Bobby Ross, Jr., "Dallas Billboards Target Christians Addicted to Porn" (Associated Press; February 21, 2004).

49. Beau Black, "Evangelical Churches Target Porn Addiction" (Orlando Sentinel, February 21, 2004).

50. www.familysafemedia.com/pornography_statistics.html.

51. Robert T. Machael, John H. Gagnon, Edward O. Laumann and Gina Kolata, *Sex in America: A Definitive Survey* (Boston, MA: Little, Brown, 1994), p. 103.

52. Ted Roberts, *Pure Desire* (Ventura, CA: Regal Books, 1999), p. 27.

53. Paul, *Pornified*, p. 181-182.

54. *Ibid*

55. J.S. Lyons, R.L. Anderson, and D. Larsen, "A Systematic Review of the Effects of Aggressive and Non-aggressive Pornography," in *Media, Children and the Family: Social Scientific, Psychodynamic, and Clinical Perspectives*, ed. Dr. Zillmann, J. Bryant, and A.C. Huston (Hillsdale, NJ: Erlbaum Associates, 1993), p. 305.

56. Paul, *Pornified*, p. 80.

57. *Ibid*, p. 82.

58. Edward Donnerstein, Daniel Linz, and Steen Penrod, *The Question of Pornography: Research Findings and Policy Implications* (New York, NY: Free Press, 1987), p. 29.

59. Jennifer Schneider, "Effects of Cybersex Addiction on the Family" (Sexual Addiction and Compulsivity 7 2000: 31-58).

60. Paul, *Pornified*, p. 155.

61. *Ibid*, p. 163.

62. *Ibid*, p. 166.

63. *Ibid*, p. 167.

64. David B. Caruso, "Internet Fuels Child Porn Trafficking," (Associated Press, January 15, 2005).

65. "Global Campaign Against Child Pornography Is Launched," Found at: PRNewswire.com; April 22, 2004).

66. Richard Oakley and Jan Battles, "Cork to Research Teen Porn Addicts," (London Sunday Times; January 25, 2004).

67. www.familysafemedia.com/pornography_statistics.html.

68. Alan Guttmacher Institute; "Patterns of Contraception Use Within Teenager's First Sexual Relationships" (CPYU's Youth Cuture e-updates #51; January 14, 2004).

69. "Study Finds Strong Correlation Between Pornography and Rape," in Pornography: A Report, p. 72). (Author?? Editor? Publisher?)

70. Ibid

71. E.K. Sommers and Check, J.V. Violence and Victims, 1987, pp 2: 189-209. (Quoted by Peter Stock in his article "The Harmful Effects on Children of Exposure to Pornography," Canadian Institute for Education on the Family, November 2004).

72. Edward Donnerstein, "Aggressive Erotica and Violence Against Women" (Journal of Personality and Social Psychology, Vol. 39, No. 2, 1980) , pp. 269-277.

73. "Teen Pregnancy" on Women's Health Channel.

74. Child Trends Data Bank, "Teen Abortion" (June 8, 2004).

75. "$5 Million Taxpayer's Dollars Paying Morgenthaler's Rent," by Judi McLeod with files from Frank Kennedy.

76. From Dr. Neal R. Chamberlain lecture entitled "Sexually Transmitted Diseases".

77. "Hugh Hefner's Playboy Magazine Turns 50," (Knight Rider/Tribune Business News, December 14, 2003).

78. Robert R. McMillan, "Fewer Marriages and More Unwed Mothers" (Floral Park Dispatch - online edition; October 15, 1999).

79. "Ex-'Playboy' Publicist Helps Jumpstart Larry Flynt and Hustler" (Media Industry Newsletter; February 24, 2003).

80. Amara Bachu, Fertility of American Women: June 1994 (Washington DC: Bureau of the Census, 1995), xix, Table K. Cited in Maggie Gallagher, The Abolition of Marriage (Washington, DC: Regnery, 1996), p. 5.

81. "Hugh Hefner's Playboy Magazine Turns 50," (Knight Rider/Tribune Business News, December 14, 2003).

82. Richard Roehl and Hal R. Varian, "Circulating Libraries and Video Rental Stores" (First Monday, Volume 6,

Number 5 (May 2001). www.firstmonday.org/issues/issue6_5/roehl/index.html.

83. www.avert.org/about.htm and www.schoolnet.na/projects/Katutura_AIDS/schoolsaidsproject/oshakati/firstcase.html

84. "Ex-'Playboy' Publicist Helps Jumpstart Larry Flynt and Hustler" (Media Industry Newsletter; February 24, 2003).

85. G. Beato, "Xtreme Measures: Washington's New Crackdown on Pornography", n.d.

86. "Hugh Hefner's Playboy Magazine Turns 50," (Knight Rider/Tribune Business News, December 14, 2003).

87. "Genital Herpes Takes Center Stage in National Public Service Announcement Contest" (PR Newswire; June 5, 1996).

88. Cheryl Wetzstein, "Porn on the Web Exploding, Foes Fear Greater Risk to Children" (The Washington Times, October 9, 2003).

89. McMillian, "Fewer Marriages and More Unwed Mothers", online.

90. Beato, "Xtreme Measures: Washington's New Crackdown on Pornography".

91. Wetzstein, "Porn on the Web Exploding, Foes Fear Greater Risk to Children", 2003.

92. James Harder, "Porn 500: Blue Chip Connections to Porn Industry", n.d.

93. Hilliard Weinstein, Stuart Berman, and Willard Cates, Jr., "Sexually Transmitted Diseases Among American Youth: Incidence and Prevalence Estimates, 2000" (Perspectives on Sexual and Reproductive Health; January 1, 2004).

94. Frank Rich, "Naked Capitalists" (New York Times, May 20, 2001).

95. "N2H2 Foils 'Website Hijacker' Pornography Sites; N2H2's Filtering Software Addresses Growing Problem of Expired Domain Names Being Re-used By Pornographers" (PR Newswire; December 5, 2001.)

96. www.cdc.gov/std.

97. "Upscale Vendors Cash in on Pornography" (Knight-Rider/Tribune Business News; August 17, 2003).

98.Mark Pothier, "Some Boston-Area Small Video Stores Distinguish Themselves with Adult Fare" (Knight Rider/Tribune Business News; February 9, 2003).

99.Wetzstein, "Porn on the Web Exploding. Foes Fear Greater Risk to Children", 2003.

100.U.S. Representative Mark Souder (R-IN) Holds Hearing on "Cervical Cancer and HPV" (Washington Transcript Service; March 11, 2004).

101.American Family Council, "Tony Perkins' Washington Update"; February 23, 2004.

102."Global Campaign Against Child Pornography Is Launched" (Found on: PRNewswire.com; April 22, 2004).

103.CTV News; June 15, 2004.

104.Frank Curreri, "Man's Arrest Surprises Neighbors" (Las Vegas Review-Journal; February 18, 2004).

105. Mike Robinson, "Chicago School Principal Charge With Kiddie Porn" (Associated Press; March 29, 2004).

106.Peter Franceschina, "Ex-Youth Leader Receives 17_ Years for Child Porn" (Sun Sentinel - Fort Lauderdale; January 22, 2004).

107."Former Christian Radio Employee Pleads Guilty in Child Porn Case" (Associated Press; February 13, 2004).

108.Paul, Pornified, p. 196.

109.Ibid, p. 213.

Chapter 11
THE ABNORMALITY OF HOMOSEXUALITY

1.USA Today; March 2, 2006; p. 3B.

2.Ibid

3.Louis P. Sheldon, The Agenda (Lake Mary, FL: Frontline Publishers, 2005), p. 110.

4.Ibid, p. 256.

5.Ibid

6.Ibid

7.Joe Dallas, A Strong Delusion (Eugene, OR: Harvest House Publishers, 1996), p. 77.

8.Sheldon, The Agenda, p. 25.

9.Ibid

10.Marshall Kirk and Hunter Madsen, After the Ball; How America Will Conquer Its

Fear and Hatred of Gays in the 1990's (New York, NY: Penguin, 1989).

11.Marshall K. Kirk and Erastus Pill, "The Overhauling of Straight America: Waging Peace, Part II" (Guide Magazine, November 1987).

12.Ibid

13.Ibid

14.Sheldon, The Agenda, p. 222.

15.Kerby Anderson, "The Decline of a Nation" (Probe Ministries, www.probe.org/docs/decline.html)

16.Charles Colson, excerpt from "The Body" in Christianity Today; November 23, 1992), p. 29.

17.Stephen Lang, "Is Ignorance Bliss?" (Moody magazine, January/February 1996, vol. 96, no. 5), p. 13.

18.Michael Slackman, "Same-Sex Marriage's: Is There a Republican-Democratic Split?" (Baptist Press News, April 8, 2004).

19.Goldman, "Psychological Factors Generate HIV Resurgence in Young Gay Men", n.d.

20.Paul Cameron, PhD, William L. Playfair, MD, and Stephen Wellum, "The Longevity of Homosexuals: Before and After the AIDS Epidemic," Omega: The Journal of Death and Dying 29 (1994): 3. Quoted in Dr. D. James Kennedy, "Homosexuality" (Today's Conflict, Tomorrow's Crisis, 2001). www.frc.org/insight/is 3g2hs.html.

21.Ibid

22.David Island and Patrick Letellier, Men Who Beat the Men Who Love Them (New York, NY: Haworth Press, 1991), p. 14.

23.N.E. Murphy, "Queer Justice: Equal Protection for Victims of Same Sex Domestic Violence" (Valparaiso University Law Review 30, 1995), p. 335.

24.Gwat Yong Lie and Sabrina Gentlewarrier, "Intimate Violence in Lesbian Relationships: Discussion of Survey Findings and Practice Implications" (Journal of Social Service Research 15, 1991), pp. 41-59.

25. Alan P. Bell and Martin S. Weinberg, Homosexualities: *A Study of Diversity Among Men and Women* (New York, NY: Simon and Schuster, 1979).

26. Paul Cameron and Kirk Cameron, "What Is 'A Homosexual?" (Journal of the Family Research Institute 15, June-July 2000).

27. Tori DeAngelis, "New Data on Lesbian, Gay and Bisexual Mental Health" (American Psychological Association Monitor on Psychology 33; February 2002). www.apa.org/monitor/Feb02/newdata.html.

28. Judith A. Reisman, *Crimes & Consequences: The Red Queen and the Grand Scheme* (Arlington, VA: Institute for Media Education, 1998).

29. www.avi.org/men/node/view/70. Statistic from R.A. Royce and W. Winkelstein, "HIV Infection, Cigarette Smoking and CD4 + T-lymphocyte Counts: Preliminary Results from the San Francisco Men's Health Study" (*AIDS 1990*; 4), pp. 327-33.

30. Karen Paige Erickson and Karen F. Trocki, "Sex, Alcohol and Sexually Transmitted Diseases: A National Survey" (Family Planning Perspectives 26, December 1994), p. 261.

31. Peter Freiberg, "Study: Alcohol Use More Prevalent for Lesbians" (The Washington Blade; January 12, 2001), p. 21.

32. David McWhirter and Andrew Mattison, The Male Couple (Englewood Cliffs, NJ: Prentice-Hall, Inc., 1984), p. 207.

33. Maria Xiridou, Ronald Geskus, John De Wit, Roel Coutinho, and Mirjam Kretzschamar, "The Contribution of Steady and Casual Partnerships to the Incidence of HIV Infection Among Homosexual Men in Amsterdam," (*AIDS 17*; 2003), p. 1032.

34. *Ibid*

35. "When It Comes to Raising Kids, Same-Sex Marriage Isn't the Same" (Boston Globe; January 23, 2004).

36. Centers for Disease Control and Prevention, "Cases of HIV Infection and Aids in the United States, 2002" (HIV/AIDS Surveillance Report 14 (2002). http://www.niaid.nih.gov/factsheets/aidsstat.htm

37. Family Research Council, "Sexual Disorientation: Faulty Research in the Homosexual Debate" (June 1992). www.exodusinternational.org/library_06.shtml.

38. Paul Cameron, "The High Cost of Sodomy: Part I" in *Journal of the Family Research Institute 19* (March 2004), http:www.familyresearchinst.org/FRR_04_03.html.

39. Sheldon, *The Agenda*, p. 62.

40. Glenn T. Stanton, "Will Same-Sex Marriage Hurt Your Family" (Focus on the Family magazine, Single-Parent Family Edition, February/March 2004), p. 18.

41. Paper given by A.P. Bell, "Homosexualities: Their Range and Character" at Nebraska Symposium on Motivation; J.K. Cole and R. Dienstbier, editor (Lincoln, NE: University of Nebraska Press, 1973). Quoted by Paul Cameron, *What Causes Homosexuality?* (Lincoln, NE: Institute for the Scientific Study of Sexuality (ISIS), 1984).

42. A. Dean Byrd, Shirley E. Cox, and Jeffrey W. Robinson, "Homosexuality: The Innate-Immutability Argument Finds No Basis in Science" (Salt Lake Tribune; May 27, 2001).

43. *Ibid*

44. Camille Paglia, *Vamps and Tramps* (New York: Vintage Books, 1994), p. 226.

45. "Woman Corners Kerry on Issue of Civil Rights, 'Gay Rights,'" (Baptist Press News, March 7, 2004).

46. Sheldon, *The Agenda*, p. 30

47. Unwin, *Sex and Culture*, p. 37.

48. Sheldon, *The Agenda*, p. 30.

49. *Ibid*, p. 30-31.

50. *Ibid*

51. Anderson, "The Decline of a Nation", Probe Ministries.

52. "Non-Traditional Churches Welcoming Gays to Flock", p. 12. (Publication Unknown)

53. D. James Kennedy, *What If America Were A Christian Nation Again?* (Nashville, TN: Thomas Nelson Publishers, 2003), p. 151.

54. Sheldon, *The Agenda*, p. 180.

55. *Ibid*

56. Michael Medved, "Power, Maturity Steer Christian Movement" (USA Today; February 27, 2006), p. 15A.

57. Dr. Ira Gallaway, "Tears of Grief and Sorrow" (We Confess, March/April 2004).

Chapter 12
BRING BACK THE GLORY

1. Limbaugh, *Persecution*, p. 321.

2. *Spirit of Revival*, (Volume 1, Number 1, September 2004), p. 18.

3. *Ibid*, p. 18.

4. *Ibid*

5. *Ibid*

6. *Ibid*, p. 19.

7. *Ibid*, p. 20.

8. *Ibid*

9. *Ibid*, p. 21.

10. *Ibid*, p. 23.

11. *Ibid*, p. 26.

12. *Ibid*, p. 2.

13. *Ibid*, p. 44.

14. http://cc.msnscache.com/cache.aspx?q=4390412190331, p. 1.

15. *Ibid*, p. 2.

16. *Ibid*, p. 6.

17. http://www.lifeway.com/tlw/leaders/news.trends.asp

18. Limbaugh, *Persecution*, p. 321.

19. *Ibid*

20. "We Are The Body", music and lyrics by Mark Hall. (Camp Zoo Publishing, 2003).

21. Dr. D. James Kennedy, Character and Destiny: *A Nation In Search Of Its Soul*, (Grand Rapids, MI: Zondervan Publishing House, 1994) , p. 258.

22. *Ibid*, p. 275.

23. Printed in the Prayer Notebook of West Colonial Hills Baptist Church, Kingsport, TN; (Week 2, Day 11).

24. David Jeremiah, *Patriotic Turning Points*, (San Diego, CA: Turning Point for God, 2002), p. 45.

25. *Ibid*

26. *Ibid*